BE A BETTER READER

READER

EIGHTH EDITION

NILA BANTON SMITH

PEARSON

Pronunciation Key

Symbol	Key Word	Respelling	Symbol	Key Word	Respelling
a	act	(akt)	u	book	(buk)
ah	star	(stahr)		put	(put)
ai	dare	(dair)	uh	cup	(kuhp)
aw	also	(AWL soh)	ə	a *as in*	
ay	flavor	(FLAY vər)		along	(ə LAWNG)
e	end	(end)		e *as in*	
ee	eat	(eet)		moment	(MOH mənt)
er	learn	(lern)		i *as in*	
	sir	(ser)		modify	(MAHD ə fy)
	fur	(fer)		o *as in*	
i	hit	(hit)		protect	(prə TEKT)
eye	idea	(eye DEE ə)		u *as in*	
y	like	(lyk)		circus	(SER kəs)
ir	deer	(dir)	ch	chill	(chil)
	fear	(fir)	g	go	(goh)
oh	open	(OH pen)	j	joke	(johk)
oi	foil	(foil)		bridge	(brij)
	boy	(boi)	k	kite	(kyt)
or	horn	(horn)		cart	(kahrt)
ou	out	(out)	ng	bring	(bring)
	flower	(FLOU ər)	s	sum	(suhm)
oo	hoot	(hoot)		cent	(sent)
	rule	(rool)	sh	sharp	(shahrp)
yoo	few	(fyoo)	th	thin	(thin)
	use	(yooz)	*th*	then	(*then*)
			z	zebra	(ZEE brə)
				pose	(pohz)
			zh	treasure	(TREZH ər)

Acknowledgments: Grateful acknowledgment is made to the following for copyrighted material: **Pearson Education:** "Computer Software," "The ENIAC," "The First Computer Spreadsheet," "The First Mouse," "The First Web Software," "Making Formulas (retitled "Calculating with a Spreadsheet")" and "Types of Computers" adapted from *Pacemaker Computer Literacy: Teacher's Answer Edition.* Copyright © by Pearson Education, Inc. or its affiliate(s). Used by permission. All rights reserved. **John Wiley & Sons, Inc.:** "Name" from *Webster's New World Dictionary, Basic School Edition.* Copyright © 1989 by John Wiley & Sons, Inc. Reprinted by permission of John Wiley & Sons, Inc. **World Book, Inc.:** Excerpt from article "Gibbon" from *The World Book Encyclopedia (Volume 8, page 185.).* Copyright © 2007 by World Book, Inc. Reprinted by permission of the publisher. Note: Every effort had been made to locate the copyright owner of the material reproduced in this component. Omissions brought to our attention will be corrected in subsequent editions.

Photo Credits: Cover images, clockwise from top left: © Brand X Pictures, © Corbis, © iDesign/Shutterstock, Charmaine Whitman/Pearson, Cadalpe/Age Fotostock, © Vivid Pixels/Shutterstock, © Arlene Jean Gee/Shutterstock, © JuiceDrops, Mana Photo/Shutterstock, © Getty Images; Cover background: © JuiceDrops; Lesson and unit opener: © Stockbyte; p. 12: Everett Historical/Shutterstock; p. 13: © Bettmann/CORBIS; p. 18 (left): © Gertjan Hooijer/Shutterstock; p. 18 (right): © FloridaStock/Shutterstock; p. 28: NG Images/Alamy; p. 32: © Adam Borkowski/Shutterstock; p. 40: © Jupiterimages/Photos.com/Jupiter Images; p. 41: © Kmitu/Shutterstock; p. 75: © Brandon Cole/Workbook Stock/Jupiter Images; p. 97: © Berto Paeli/Shutterstock; p. 119: © Alys Tomlinson/Creatas Images/Jupiter Images; p. 127: © Eugene Bochkarev/Shutterstock; p. 128: © Shawn Pecor/Shutterstock; p. 139 (right): © 0293285137/Shutterstock; p. 159 (left): © akva/Shutterstock; p. 159 (right): © Bettmann/CORBIS; p. 160: © Hulton Archive/Getty Images; p. 161 (left): U.S. Army; p. 161 (right): Courtesy of SRI International; p. 172 (left): © Jeffrey Van Daele/Shutterstock.

Staff Credits: Joshua Adams, Melania Benzinger, Karen Blonigen, Laura Chadwick, Andreea Cimoca, Katie Colón, Nancy Condon, Barbara Drewlo, Kerry Dunn, Marti Erding, Sara Freund, Daren Hastings, Ruby Hogen-Chin, Mariann Johanneck, Julie Johnston, Mary Kaye Kuzma, Mary Lukkonen, Carol Nelson, Carrie O'Connor, Marie Schaefle, Julie Theisen, Chris Tures, Mike Vineski, Charmaine Whitman, Sue Will

ISBN-13: 978-0-7854-6658-1

ISBN-10:   0-7854-6658-4

PEARSON

Contents

Contents
continued

How to Use *Be A Better Reader*

For more than thirty years, **Be A Better Reader** has helped students improve their reading skills. **Be A Better Reader** teaches the comprehension and study skills that you need to read and enjoy all types of materials—from library books to the different textbooks that you will encounter in school.

To get the most from **Be A Better Reader**, you should know how the lessons are organized. As you read the following explanations, it will be helpful to look at some of the lessons.

In each of the first four lessons of a unit, you will apply an important skill to a reading selection in literature, social studies, science, or mathematics. Each of these lessons includes the following nine sections.

▶ BACKGROUND INFORMATION

This section gives you interesting information about the selection you are about to read. It will help you understand the ideas that you need in order to learn new skills.

▶ SKILL FOCUS

This section teaches you a specific skill. You should read the Skill Focus carefully, paying special attention to words that are printed in boldface type. The Skill Focus tells you about a skill that you will use when you read the selection.

▶ CONTEXT CLUES OR WORD CLUES

This section teaches you how to recognize and use different types of context and word clues. These clues will help you with the meanings of the underlined words in the selection.

▶ STRATEGY TIP

This section gives you suggestions about what to look for as you read. The suggestions will help you understand the selection.

▶ SELECTIONS

There are four kinds of selections in **Be A Better Reader**. A selection in a literature lesson is similar to a selection in a literature anthology, library book, newspaper, or magazine. A social studies selection is like a chapter in a social studies textbook or an encyclopedia. It often includes maps or tables. A science selection, like a science textbook, includes special words and sometimes diagrams. A mathematics selection will help you acquire skill in reading mathematics textbooks.

▶ COMPREHENSION QUESTIONS

Answers to the questions in this section can be found in the selection itself. You will sometimes have to reread parts of the selection to complete this activity.

▶ CRITICAL THINKING ACTIVITY

The critical thinking activity includes questions whose answers are not directly stated in the selection. For these questions, you must combine the information in the selection with what you already know in order to infer the answers.

▶ SKILL FOCUS ACTIVITY

In this activity, you will use the skill that you learned in the Skill Focus section at the beginning of the lesson to answer questions about the selection. If you have difficulty completing this activity, reread the Skill Focus section.

▶ READING-WRITING CONNECTION

In this writing activity, you will have a chance to use the information in the selection you read about, by writing about it. Here is your chance to share your ideas about the selection.

Additional Lessons

The remaining lessons in each unit give you practice with such skills as using a dictionary, an encyclopedia, and other reference materials; using phonics and syllabication in recognizing new words; locating and organizing information; and adjusting your reading rate. Other reading skills that are necessary in everyday life, such as reading a bus schedule, are also covered.

Each time you learn a new skill in **Be A Better Reader**, look for opportunities to use the skill in your other reading at school and at home. Your reading ability will improve the more you practice reading!

Adventures in Flight

LESSON 1

Skill: Plot

BACKGROUND INFORMATION

"The Flight of Daedalus" is a Greek myth that is more than 5,000 years old. Like most myths, it was handed down by word of mouth for many generations before it was written down. Myths focus on important conflicts in human life. "The Flight of Daedalus" focuses on people's desire to fly and on the effect of pride on human life.

SKILL FOCUS: Plot

A story's **plot** is the series of events that happen in the story. Most plots have five parts, which are shown in the following diagram.

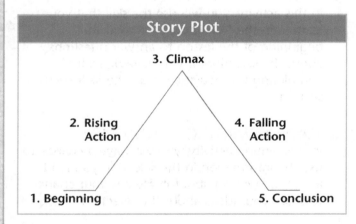

Story Plot

3. Climax

2. Rising Action

4. Falling Action

1. Beginning

5. Conclusion

1. **Beginning** The beginning of the plot introduces the main characters and the setting.
2. **Rising Action** The plot begins to build as a conflict develops. The main character struggles to achieve a goal or to solve a problem.
3. **Climax** The plot events build to a climax, or high point. This is the most exciting part of the story and often marks a turning point.
4. **Falling Action** The events after the climax show how the characters resolve, or deal with, the conflict in the story.
5. **Conclusion** A final event ends the story.

▶ Choose an exciting short story or novel you have read recently. Think about the parts of its plot. Make a large copy of the Story Plot Diagram on a separate sheet of paper. Then fill in events from the story under the correct labels.

CONTEXT CLUES: Footnotes

Footnotes are explanations of names and other special words that appear in a selection. When you read an unfamiliar name of a person, place, or thing, look for a footnote to help you figure it out. Words with footnotes have a small raised number next to them. The footnotes themselves appear at the bottom of a page. Notice the footnote in the sentence below.

With a fist of iron, he ruled the kingdom of Crete.[1]

Notice the raised number after the word *Crete.* The number is a signal to look at the bottom of the page for a footnote with the same number. The footnote will give a definition or an explanation of the term. Here is the footnote that explains *Crete.*

[1] *Crete (KREET): an island southeast of Greece.*

▶ Read the following sentence and the footnote. Then underline the details in the footnote that tell you the meaning of *Labyrinth.*

The most famous structure that Daedalus built for Minos was the Labyrinth.[2]

[2] *Labyrinth (LAB ə rinth): a building on ancient Crete with many winding passages and blind alleys; a maze.*

As you read the myth, use footnote clues to find the meanings of *Minotaur, Sicily,* and *Apollo.*

Strategy Tip

As you read "The Flight of Daedalus," use the diagram and the explanations on this page to help you understand the story's plot.

THE FLIGHT OF DAEDALUS

Long, long ago lived a proud and terrible king. His name was Minos (MEYE nohs). With a fist of iron, he ruled the kingdom of Crete.[1]

Daedalus (DED ə ləs), another proud man, also lived on the island of Crete. He was a sculptor and a builder. He may have been the finest builder of his time. Daedalus built many fine buildings for King Minos.

The most famous structure that Daedalus built for Minos was the Labyrinth.[2] It was designed as a prison and a trap. No one could find a way out of its passageways without knowing the design. Minos was very pleased with the Labyrinth. He imprisoned his enemies there. The Labyrinth was also home to the dreaded Minotaur.[3]

One day Minos became very angry with Daedalus. The builder had given away the secret of the Labyrinth. In anger, Minos imprisoned Daedalus in the Labyrinth. Within a short time, however, Daedalus managed to escape.

The sculptor found his son, Icarus (IK ə rəs), and planned to flee from Crete. However, Minos was determined to recapture Daedalus. The king's soldiers searched all the ships before they left the island.

Minos knew that Daedalus and Icarus were hiding in the countryside, but he didn't care. He was sure that Daedalus and Icarus could not escape from Crete. So Minos decided to let Daedalus wander free for a while. "Soon the master builder will realize that he is trapped here. He will have to admit that he is in my power and will give himself up. Then I will give him many difficult tasks to perform."

Daedalus tried many times to find a way to escape from the island. He stood on the rocky hills of Crete and stared out to sea. Above him, the sea gulls and other sea birds wheeled and dipped in the sky. Below, the sun glistened on the water in the harbor and on the helmets of Minos's soldiers. Daedalus could see the trap that Minos had set.

"I cannot let Minos defeat me," he thought. "I harbor and on the helmets of Minos's soldiers. Daedalus could see the trap that Minos had set.

"I cannot let Minos defeat me," he thought. "I must escape with my son. There must be a way off the island."

At times, Daedalus feared that he and his son would be captives on Crete forever. However, his quick mind kept searching for a way out. As he pondered, he watched the many birds that soared high in the blue sky. Suddenly, Daedalus was struck by a thought. "Minos may rule the land and sea, but he cannot control the air!" Daedalus said, as he watched feathers drop from the wings of the sea gulls.

He quickly sent his son in search of stray sea gull feathers. Icarus found tiny, soft feathers. He picked up long, strong feathers. He gathered black plumes and white ones. He found blue feathers and brown feathers. Soon Icarus had made a great mound of feathers of all kinds.

Then Daedalus set to work. He built a large wooden frame shaped like a bird's wing. He fastened feathers to it. Some he sewed on; others he stuck on with wax. Finally he used wax to mold all the feathers

[1] Crete (KREET): an island southeast of Greece.
[2] Labyrinth (LAB ə rinth): a building on ancient Crete with many winding passages and blind alleys; a maze.
[3] Minotaur (MIN ə tor): a monster with a bull's head and a man's body; the monster ate human victims.

into shape. Once he had finished this frame, he made another one and covered it with feathers, too. Now he had two huge wings, like those of a giant bird.

Daedalus fastened the wings to his shoulders. Would they work? He flapped the wings and tried to fly. After some minutes, the wings lifted him from the ground.

He could fly! However, Daedalus soon learned that there was more to flying than flapping his wings. He had to learn to swoop, to soar on the winds, to turn, and to gather speed.

Working as fast as he could, Daedalus then made wings for Icarus. Icarus watched gleefully as his father sewed and glued the feathers in place. Icarus could scarcely wait to put on the wonderful wings.

At last, the wings were finished. Daedalus fastened them to his son's shoulders. Icarus looked very handsome. The beautiful wings covered his entire body. His golden hair shone in the sunlight, and his eyes sparkled with excitement.

Icarus quickly learned to fly. He seemed to have been born to it. His father, knowing how daring Icarus could be, warned him often to be careful. "Don't fly too close to the water," he would say. "The fog will weigh you down. Also don't fly close to the sun. Its warmth will melt the wax on your wings."

Icarus listened impatiently to his father's warnings. He thought, "I can take care of myself!"

One fair morning, Daedalus said, "The wind is just right today. We shall fly to Sicily."[4]

Strapping on their wings, Daedalus and Icarus walked to the top of a rocky hill. Daedalus flapped his huge wings, rose in the air, and flew out over the sea. Icarus lifted himself with his wings and followed. Minos could never catch them now!

Daedalus headed out over the ocean, beating the air strongly and surely. Icarus swooped and turned as he followed his father. Flying free in the air, Icarus knew the joy of being a bird. He looked down at the white-capped waves. How wonderful to be soaring above them! Then he looked at the clouds above. How exciting it would be to fly above them!

Icarus forgot his father's warnings. Beating his wings faster and faster, he rose up and up. As he flew higher, the sun flickered and gleamed on his feathers. On and on he flew, higher and higher. The sun grew brighter.

The air became very warm, but Icarus flew on. As he flew, it became more and more difficult to climb higher. His wings drooped. Feathers began to fall like snowflakes. The sun's heat was melting the wax! Furiously, Icarus beat his wings, but they could no longer support him. As he fell toward the glittering ocean far below, Icarus cried out to his father.

[4] Sicily (SIS əl ee): an island in southern Italy.

Daedalus heard the cry and turned. He caught only a glimpse of his son as Icarus plunged into the white-capped waves. Nothing remained except a few feathers floating on the surface.

In deep grief, Daedalus flew on to Sicily. He went to the temple of the sun god <u>Apollo</u>.[5] There he hung up his wings as an offering to the god.

Daedalus had beaten his enemy, Minos, but at the terrible cost of the life of his son. Perhaps the gods were punishing Daedalus for daring to do something that humans were not meant to do: fly with the wings of a bird.

[5] Apollo (ə POL oh): a Greek god; the son of Zeus, king of the gods.

COMPREHENSION

1. Identify the three characters of the story.

   a. _____, king of Crete

   b. _____, a master builder

   c. _____, his son

2. What did the builder make for the king that pleased the king very much?

   _____

3. Explain why Daedalus was imprisoned?

   _____

   _____

4. Explain how Daedalus attached feathers to the wings he made.

   _____

   _____

5. What caused the feathers to drop from Icarus's wings?

   _____

   _____

6. Complete each statement with the correct word.

   Minotaur   Sicily   Apollo

   a. In Greek mythology, _____ is the god of light and the sun.

   b. The Strait of Messina separates

      _____ from the mainland of Italy.

   c. In Greek mythology, the _____ is a terrible monster that ate people.

CRITICAL THINKING

1. Discuss why it was a foolish idea for Minos to try to imprison Daedalus in the Labyrinth.

   _____

2. Tell why Icarus ignored his father's warnings about flying too close to the sun.

   _____

3. Why didn't Daedalus, like Icarus, forget himself and fly too close to the sun?

   _____

4. Explain how each character's pride leads to his downfall, or defeat, in the story.

_____

_____

5. Do you think that Daedalus will ever fly again? Use an event from the story to support your answer.

_____

_____

SKILL FOCUS: PLOT

The following list describes some of the events in the myth of Daedalus. On the diagram below, write the letter of each event next to the correct part of the plot. It may help if you first decide which event is the climax.

a. Daedalus escapes from the Labyrinth.

b. Daedalus sees Icarus fall into the sea.

c. Daedalus builds two pairs of wings so that he and Icarus can escape from Crete.

d. Daedalus hangs up his wings as an offering to the sun god Apollo.

e. Using their wings, Daedalus and Icarus head for Sicily.

f. Icarus, ignoring Daedalus's warnings, flies too close to the sun.

g. Alone, Daedalus flies to Sicily.

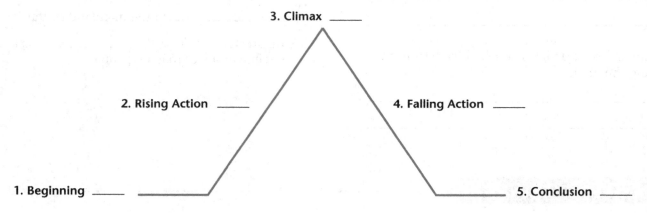

3. Climax _____

2. Rising Action _____

4. Falling Action _____

1. Beginning _____

5. Conclusion _____

Reading-Writing Connection

On a separate sheet of paper, write one paragraph describing pride as a good quality and another paragraph describing pride as dangerous. Use examples from everyday life to support your main ideas.

Skill: Comparing and Contrasting

BACKGROUND INFORMATION

In "Flying to Fame," you will read about two women pioneers in the history of flight. Many men and women have contributed to the amazing progress in flight. One woman was Amelia Earhart, a record-setting pilot of the 1930s. Another is Sally Ride, the first American woman in space.

SKILL FOCUS: Comparing and Contrasting

Comparing and contrasting are important ways to understand information. **Comparing** is finding out how two or more things are alike. **Contrasting** is noticing how they are different.

Writers can show comparison and contrast in different ways. One way is to first tell all about one person or thing and then tell all about the other one.

Read the following two paragraphs. Think about how you might compare and contrast the pilots.

Cal Rodgers, a little-known pioneer of flight, was the first person to fly across the United States. Taking off from New York in 1911, he landed 69 times before finally reaching California. In all, the 3,220-mile flight took 50 days.

Another little-known pioneer was Harriet Quimby. In 1912, Quimby flew across the English Channel. The first American woman pilot, she crossed the 22-mile stretch of water between England and France in about 30 minutes.

Compare the two paragraphs. Notice the similarities between the two pilots. Both were pioneers, and neither one was famous. Notice the differences. Rodgers was a man; Quimby was a woman. Rodgers flew a long flight over land in the United States. Quimby flew a short flight over water in Europe.

Use details from the two paragraphs to complete the Contrast Chart below.

CONTEXT CLUES: Details

When you read a word that you do not know, look for context clues to help you understand it. Context clues are words near the new word that make its meaning clearer. Often these clues are **details**, or small pieces of information that help you understand what the word means.

Read the sentence below.

*Sally Ride **donned** her space suit and her helmet with the ease that you slip on a coat and hat.*

If you don't know the meaning of *donned*, the phrase *with the ease that you slip on a coat and hat* can help you. The details in the phrase help you see that *donned* means "put on."

Circle the details that help you figure out the meaning of the word *gender*.

*These two women were also pioneers for their **gender**. They have proven that women, as well as men, have the courage and determination to make history.*

As you read the selection, use details to help you understand the meanings of the underlined words *spectator*, *endeavor*, and *vastness*.

> ### Strategy Tip
>
> As you read "Flying to Fame," look for ways in which Amelia Earhart and Sally Ride are alike and different.

Contrast Chart		
Cal Rodgers	**Topic**	**Harriet Quimby**
	Achievement	
	Date	
	Length of Flight	

Flying to Fame

Amelia Earhart and Sally Ride are **pioneers** (PEYE ə NIRZ) in the history of flight. They are two of the brave people who dared to venture into the unknown and prepare the way for later accomplishments in flight. These two women are also pioneers for their **gender** (JEN dər). They have proven that women, as well as men, have the courage and determination to make history.

✗ In 1932, a young woman named Amelia Earhart set off on a dangerous flight. She pulled on her leather flying gear, adjusted her goggles, and climbed into her propeller plane. Alone, she took off from Newfoundland, Canada, to cross the Atlantic Ocean. The world cheered when Earhart landed safely in Ireland. Amelia Earhart had become the first woman to fly solo across the Atlantic.

✗ Half a century later, on June 18, 1983, another woman set out to make history. Sally Ride donned her space suit and her helmet with the ease that you slip on a coat and hat. She climbed aboard the *Challenger* space shuttle with three other astronauts and blasted off into outer space. Sally Ride became the first American woman in space.

Amelia Earhart

Amelia Earhart was born on July 24, 1897, in Atchison, Kansas. While growing up, she liked to experiment with daring stunts. Once, Earhart jumped off her father's barn, using an umbrella for a parachute. Another time, she built a roller coaster on the roof of her father's tool shed. Even as a child, she was daring and full of ideas.

At the age of 19, Amelia Earhart discovered flying. She was working as a nurse's aide in a Canadian military hospital. One of her friends was a pilot in the Royal Flying Corps. She spent her free time at a nearby airfield, watching him fly. However, being only a <u>spectator</u> made her feel like a young athlete left on the bench to watch.

In her early twenties, Earhart began her thrilling and dangerous career as a pilot. The engines of early airplanes were not much bigger than a modern

In 1932, Amelia Earhart became the first woman to fly solo across the Atlantic.

motorcycle engine. In her first two months of flying, Earhart made two crash landings. She was a natural pilot, however. She worked hard to save enough money to buy her own plane in 1922.

When Amelia Earhart took to the air, flying was still a risky new <u>endeavor</u>. It was a difficult task that required skill, courage, and the determination to keep trying to succeed. Earhart pushed herself and the world's flying records to the limit. She set her first record by flying at 14,000 feet (4,200 meters), breaking the women's **altitude** (AL tə tood) record.

✔ In 1927, Charles Lindbergh made the first solo flight across the Atlantic Ocean. In 1932, Amelia Earhart became the first woman to fly solo across the Atlantic. Her flight brought her international fame. It also inspired her to set one new record after another.

✔✔ In 1935, Earhart became the first person to fly nonstop alone from Honolulu, Hawaii, to the U.S. mainland. Later she became the first person to fly nonstop from Los Angeles to Mexico City and from Mexico City to Newark, New Jersey.

Amelia Earhart's daring flights made her a hero to Americans. She was admired and cheered wherever she went. Her accomplishments seemed especially remarkable at the time because of her gender. Earhart, herself, deeply believed in gender equality. She believed that women "must earn true respect and equal rights from men by accepting responsibility."

Amelia Earhart's greatest challenge came on May 17, 1937. She had decided to attempt another record-breaking flight. She was ready to make a 27,000-mile (43,200-kilometer) trip around the world. She asked Fred Noonan, an experienced **navigator** (NAV ə GAY tər), to fly with her and plan the route they should take. Taking off from Oakland, California, they flew to Florida. Then they went on to South America, across the Atlantic to Africa, and on to Asia. Finally they arrived on the island of New Guinea (GIN ee). From there, they faced the most dangerous part of their journey. They would have to fly 2,556 miles (4,090 kilometers) across the Pacific Ocean and then land on tiny Howland Island. On July 2, Earhart and Noonan took off across the Pacific. Somewhere between New Guinea and Howland Island, the plane disappeared. Amelia Earhart and Fred Noonan were never heard from again.

Sally Ride

Even as a young girl, Sally Ride enjoyed challenges. She competed successfully with neighborhood boys in baseball and football. Once she threw a ball so hard that it broke a friend's nose. At the age of 12, Ride began to play tennis. She was soon winning tournaments. Sally Ride learned early to work hard at everything she did.

✚ As a young woman, Ride never planned a career in flying. In college, she continued to play tennis. She also studied hard. She spent nine years earning degrees in English, science, and physics.

"Then one day in 1977," Ride said, "I read an announcement in the paper that NASA was accepting applications. And all of a sudden, I realized that I wanted to do it. There was no question in my mind." Ride wrote to the National Aeronautics and Space Administration (NASA). She expressed her interest in becoming an astronaut. They accepted her immediately, along with five other women.

By the time Sally Ride joined NASA in 1978, astronauts had already walked on the moon. Training and scientific know-how were most important for space-age pilots. Ride joined a team of astronauts training for space flights. She worked closely with NASA scientists and other crew members.

After her training, Sally Ride was chosen by NASA to be the first woman to go up in the *Challenger* space shuttle. Ride was one of two mission specialists aboard the shuttle. Her job was to test a robot arm that put satellites into orbit. Ride's training for the mission was demanding. She had to practice many new skills. Ride and the other astronauts spent hours every day in conditions like those they would face in outer space. There they would have no weight because gravity would not exist.

As one of the first women astronauts, Sally Ride broke barriers for her gender. Treated with respect by fellow crew members, Ride was simply another good astronaut. She had confidence in NASA and in her own abilities and training.

Amelia Earhart took off across the huge, lonely Pacific Ocean to achieve a dream. Sally Ride faced an even greater vastness as she blasted off into the endless stretch of emptiness known as outer space. Amelia Earhart and Sally Ride will both be remembered as brave women and as pioneers in the history of flight.

Sally Ride was the first American woman in space.

1. Identify the first flight record that Amelia Earhart set.

   _____

   _____

2. How did Sally Ride break barriers for women?

   _____

   _____

3. On page 12, reread the two paragraphs that have an ✘ next to them. Underline the sentence that states the main idea in each paragraph.

4. Decide if each statement is true or false. Write *T* or *F* on the lines provided.

   _____ **a.** A <u>spectator</u> plays in a football game.

   _____ **b.** Learning to ride a bicycle can be a difficult <u>endeavor</u> for some children.

   _____ **c.** A lot of furniture is needed to fill the <u>vastness</u> of a large living room.

CRITICAL THINKING

1. Explain why Earhart asked Noonan to accompany her on her flight around the world.

   _____

   _____

2. What effect did Ride's space flight have on future astronaut teams?

   _____

   _____

3. On page 13, reread the paragraph with a ✚ next to it. Which of the following statements can you infer from the paragraph?

   a. Sally Ride hated to fly.

   b. Sally Ride is very intelligent.

   c. Sally Ride was a bad student.

   d. Sally Ride was often timid about facing new experiences.

4. On page 12, reread the paragraph with a ✔ next to it. Write a sentence that describes its main idea.

   _____

   _____

5. On page 12, reread the paragraph with ✔ ✔ next to it. Write a sentence that describes its main idea.

   _____

   _____

SKILL FOCUS: COMPARING AND CONTRASTING

A. Use the following chart to outline similarities between Amelia Earhart and Sally Ride. In the middle of the chart are general topics. Reread the selection for information on how the women's lives are similar. For each topic, write one sentence about each woman. The first one is done for you.

Comparison Chart		
Amelia Earhart	**Topic**	**Sally Ride**
Earhart was active and daring as a child.	Childhood	Ride was active and competitive as a child.
	Breaking barriers for women	
	Record setting	
	Taking risks	

B. Use the following chart to outline differences between Amelia Earhart and Sally Ride. In the middle of the chart are general topics. Reread the selection to find out how the women's lives are different on these topics. Then write one sentence about each.

Contrast Chart		
Amelia Earhart	**Topic**	**Sally Ride**
	Beginning of flying career	
	Destination and type of aircraft	
	Teamwork	

Reading-Writing Connection

Which of the two women do you admire more: Amelia Earhart or Sally Ride? On a separate sheet of paper, write a paragraph explaining your reasons.

Skill: Classifying

BACKGROUND INFORMATION

"On the Wings of a Bird" describes how birds fly. Some birds can cruise at speeds of 20 to 50 miles (32 to 80 kilometers) per hour, and some can go twice that fast. When they migrate, some birds fly for 1,000 miles (1,600 kilometers) without stopping. The design of a bird's body makes it a perfect flying machine. Scientists classify birds according to the size and shape of their wings and where they live.

SKILL FOCUS: Classifying

Classifying is a way to organize information by grouping similar things together. You may not realize it, but you classify people and things every day.

When scientists classify plants and animals, they break large groups into smaller ones. The members of each smaller group are similar in some way. Sea gulls and terns, for example, are two kinds of sea birds that are similar in many ways. Both have long wings, and both are powerful fliers. Both are found in beach areas. Scientists classify these two kinds of birds in the same group.

Flamingos and ibises are two other kinds of birds that live along the shore. However, they are not classified in the same group as sea gulls and terns. Scientists have classified flamingos and ibises in their own group. Can you figure out why?

When reading about different groups of animals, ask yourself these questions.

- How are the animals in the same group similar?

- How are the animals in one group different from the animals in another group?

▶ Complete the chart below. Use what you already know or look up information about sea gulls and flamingos to list ways they are different.

CONTEXT CLUES: Synonyms

Sometimes a context clue will be a **synonym** in the same or next sentence. Synonyms are words with similar meanings.

What synonym in the sentences below can help you figure out the meaning of the word *fused*?

> The finger bones are **fused**, so the bird cannot move them. Yet the bird's thumb is not joined to the fingers—the bird can open and close it.

If you don't know the meaning of *fused*, the synonym *joined* can help you. *Fused* and *joined* are synonyms. A bird's finger bones are joined together.

▶ Read the following sentences from the selection. Circle a synonym for the underlined word.

> The longest flight feathers, called primaries, are attached to the bird's hand section.... Another group of flight feathers, called secondaries, are **affixed** to the bird's lower-arm bones.

In the next selection, use synonym context clues to figure out the meanings of the underlined words *analogous*, *pliant*, and *vulnerable*.

> ### Strategy Tip
>
> When reading "On the Wings of a Bird," notice how the birds classified in one group are alike and how they are different from the birds in the other groups.

Sea Gulls and Flamingos		
Bird	**Where It Lives**	**What It Looks Like**
Sea gull		
Flamingo		

On the Wings of a Bird

People have always dreamed of flying through the air like birds. In the past, people believed that birds used their wings like oars to "row" through the air. Today we know that birds actually fly in a way that is similar to how airplanes with propellers fly.

How Birds and Airplanes Fly

An airplane wing has a special shape, called an **airfoil**. This shape keeps the plane up in the air. The bottom of an airfoil is flat, while the top is curved. Air flowing past an airfoil breaks up and then meets again behind the wing. The air on top of the curved wing has to go faster to get over the curve. This fast-moving air pulls away from the wing. At the same time, the slow-moving air on the bottom of the wing pushes up. This pulling on top and pushing on the bottom is called lift, which is what keeps an airplane in the air. Meanwhile, propellers give the airplane a forward movement, called **thrust**.

If you look carefully at a bird, you will see that its inner wing, close to its body, also has an airfoil shape. This is the part of the wing that keeps the bird in the air during flight.

To move forward, the bird uses the feathers at the end of its wing like propellers. Of course, a bird's feathers do not rotate like propellers. However, they do change position each time a bird flaps its wings. On the downstroke, the wing moves down and forward until the feathers are even with the bird's beak. Then the feathers quickly twist around and face front. Air flows over them, giving the bird the same forward pull that a propeller gives a plane.

To steer, a bird tips its wings from side to side. For balance, the bird raises or lowers its tail feathers, or moves them sideways.

How Wings Compare With Arms

Although you could not fly by flapping your arms, your arm bones are <u>analogous</u> (ə NAL ə gəs) to the bones in a bird's wing. How are the two structures similar? A bird's wing is made up of three sections, just as our arms are made up of an upper arm, a lower arm, and a hand. (See Figure 1.)

A bird's "hand" section is longer and narrower, compared with the rest of its arm, than a human hand is, compared to the rest of the arm. A bird's hand also has fewer bones—just two fingers and a thumb. These finger bones are fused, so the bird cannot move them. Yet the bird's thumb is not joined to the fingers—the bird can open and close it.

Many of the bones in a bird's wings are hollow. Hollow bones are an **adaptation** (ad ap TAY shən), a change that has occurred in the bird's body over time to help it survive. These hollow bones help birds fly more easily. Although they are hollow, the bones are strong and <u>pliant</u>, making the wings flexible in flight.

Long flight feathers are anchored to the bones of a bird's wing. The longest flight feathers, called

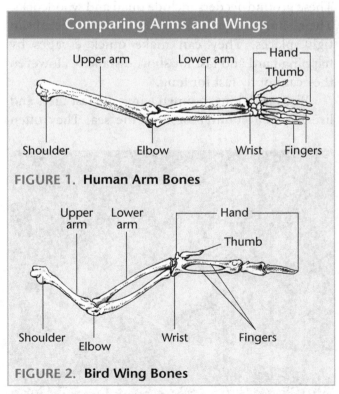

Comparing Arms and Wings

FIGURE 1. **Human Arm Bones**

FIGURE 2. **Bird Wing Bones**

A bird's "hand" is long and narrow, with two fused finger bones and a flexible thumb.

SCIENCE

primaries, are attached to the bird's hand section. Birds usually have ten primaries on each wing, which twist around and face front to give the bird its forward movement.

Another group of flight feathers, called *secondaries*, are shorter and affixed to the bird's lower-arm bones. There are usually more secondaries than primaries. A third group of flight feathers, the *tertiaries* (TER shee AIR eez), are located on the upper-arm section of the wing.

Classifying the Wings of Birds

Scientists classify birds according to the size and shape of the birds' wings and where the birds live. By studying the shape and size of a bird's wing, you can tell a great deal about how it lives.

Short, rounded wings are clues that a bird lives in woods, shrubs, or underbrush. Songbirds that perch on branches have short, rounded wings. These birds include sparrows, cardinals, and robins. With short, rounded wings, they can dart through trees and bushes without hurting themselves.

Ground-feeding birds have short, stubby wings. These ground-feeders include quail and woodcocks. Their short wings allow them to turn sharply in tight places. They can make quick escapes by flapping hard and fast for short distances. However, they cannot fly fast for long.

Birds with long, pointed wings are fast fliers and live in open country or near the sea. They often sweep through the sky, snatching insects in midair. Land birds in this group include swallows, swifts, and falcons. Shore birds in this group include sandpipers and plovers.

Birds that glide and soar belong to a group with big wings. This group, which includes eagles, hawks, and vultures, soar over land areas. They all have very wide wings, with deep slots in the wing tips. These slots prevent the birds from stalling as they circle slowly overhead. Other birds in this group, such as gulls and albatrosses, soar over the sea. They have very long, narrow wings with sharp tips.

Wing Size and Rate of Flapping

The size of a bird's wings determines how fast the bird must flap, or beat, them. Large wings have more lifting power than small ones, so large birds can flap their wings more slowly and still stay in the air. A vulture, for example, beats its wings only about once per second. Each stroke of its huge wings drives the vulture forward with great force.

Medium-sized birds, such as ducks and crows, must flap their wings two or three times per second to stay in the air. Small birds with stubby wings have to work even harder. A sparrow beats its wings 14 times per second, and a chickadee flaps about 25 times per second. The smallest bird, a hummingbird, beats its tiny wings about 70 times per second. The wings move so fast that they make a humming sound, which gives the bird its name.

Birds that live in woods, shrubs, and underbrush have short, rounded wings.

Birds that glide and soar have long, wide wings.

Wing Shape and Flight Speed

Different factors can affect a bird's speed while in the air. A sparrow heading home to its nest may cruise along at about 15 to 20 miles (24 to 32 kilometers) per hour. If an enemy suddenly starts to chase the sparrow, though, it may speed up to 35 miles (56 kilometers) per hour. Wind is a factor, too. If a bird is flying with the wind, it gets an extra push from behind. Flying against the wind slows it down.

The most important factor that determines flight speed, however, is the shape of a bird's wings. Songbirds with short, rounded wings cannot fly very fast. Their average speeds are about 15 to 25 miles (24 to 40 kilometers) per hour. Birds with long, pointed wings can usually fly about 40 to 50 miles (64 to 80 kilometers) per hour. Birds with big wings can fly 60 miles (96 kilometers) per hour or faster.

The fastest birds of all are falcons and swifts. Although their wings are not as big as those of eagles, the wings of falcons sweep back like those on a jet. With this arrangement of wings, a peregrine falcon can approach speeds of 100 miles (160 kilometers) per hour.

Taking Off and Landing

Take-offs and landings are the most difficult parts of a bird's flight. If a bird does not get off to a fast start, its wings will not lift it into the air. That is why birds flap their wings harder than usual when they are taking off. If the wind is blowing, birds always take off into the wind to get some help.

✔ Birds with long legs, such as herons and cranes, push off from the ground to get themselves into the air. The webbed feet of ducks and geese help them to run across the surface of the water until they gain enough flight speed. Many shore birds reach take-off speed by running across the sand while flapping their wings hard. Large birds, such as eagles, perch atop cliffs and high trees. To take off from these high places, they can simply leap into the air.

During landing, a bird is most <u>vulnerable</u>. Coming in too slowly is unsafe, because a bird might suddenly lose its lift and crash to the ground. Coming in too rapidly is also dangerous because a bird can easily damage its delicate wings and body by hitting a branch or other landing site too hard.

When a bird closes in on a landing target, it slows down in stages. First it spreads and lowers its tail. Then it lowers its legs and pushes them forward. Finally it "puts on the brakes" by cupping each wing like a parachute and fanning it back and forth.

Small songbirds usually land on branches. When they do, their legs bend at the joints, acting like shock absorbers. Larger birds that land on open ground slow down by running to a stop. Ducks and geese, which land on water, have the easiest of landings. They simply push their webbed feet forward and skid to a splashing stop.

Every creature on Earth adapts to fit a specific environment and a specific way of life. The adaptations of different kinds of birds have allowed them to make themselves at home in many different environments. Since ancient times, the beauty and grace of birds in flight have provided inspiration to people all over the world.

SCIENCE

COMPREHENSION

1. Describe the shape of an airfoil.

   _____

2. How does the size of a bird's wings affect the rate at which it beats its wings?

   _____

   _____

3. Where do birds with short, rounded wings often live?

   _____

4. Draw a line to match each word with its synonym.

   similar   **a.** vulnerable

   flexible   **b.** analogous

   unsafe   **c.** pliant

CRITICAL THINKING

1. Explain why having hollow bones helps a bird to fly.

   _____

2. Scientists studying a bird noted that it usually beat its wings 2.5 times per second. Draw a conclusion about this bird's size.

   _____

3. A thrush is a songbird about 8 inches long. About how fast might it normally fly?

   _____

4. Look at the paragraph with a ✔ next to it. Write a sentence that states the main idea of the paragraph.

   _____

5. A loon usually runs across the surface of a lake to gain enough speed to take off. Describe what type of feet a loon probably has.

   _____

SKILL FOCUS: CLASSIFYING

Complete the chart below, using details from the selection about each type of wings.

Types of Wings				
Wing Shape	Names of Birds	Habitat	Type of Flight	Speed
Short, rounded				
Long, pointed				
Big, wide				

Reading-Writing Connection

On a separate sheet of paper, write a paragraph about a bird that you often see in your neighborhood. Describe the bird in as much detail as you can. Write about the bird's wings, its habitat, and how it flies. If you wish, draw an illustration of the bird.

Skill: Reading Mathematical Terms

BACKGROUND INFORMATION

"Reading Mathematical Terms and Symbols" explains some math terms that will help you when you study geometry. In geometry, you will learn about familiar shapes, such as squares, triangles, and circles. The most basic concepts in geometry, however, are the point, the line, and the plane. This selection will help you understand these basic mathematical terms.

SKILL FOCUS: Reading Mathematical Terms

Some words have a familiar meaning in everyday life and a special meaning in math. Knowing mathematical terms is important for success in math. In ordinary speech, for example, the word *point* can mean "the main idea" or "a certain time." A *line* is a group of people waiting to buy or do something. A *plane* is a flying mode of transportation.

In mathematics, the words *point*, *line*, and *plane* have special meanings.

- A **point** is a position that has no dimensions. It cannot be seen.
- A **line** is many points placed next to each other. It goes on forever in one dimension.
- A **plane** has length and width but no height. It goes on forever in two dimensions.

Other words such as *intersect, perpendicular,* and *parallel* have special math meanings, too.

- When two lines or planes cross, they **intersect**. Two streets, for example, can cross each other, or intersect.
- When lines or planes intersect and form square corners, they are **perpendicular**. The walls of most rooms, for example, are perpendicular to the floor.
- Lines or planes that do not intersect are **parallel** when they travel in the same direction forever and are always the same distance apart. For example, two airplanes can fly parallel to each other at the same distance apart.

▶ Think about the meanings of the words *point*, *line*, and *plane*. Then fill in the chart below with their everyday meaning and math meaning.

Meanings of Words		
Word	Everyday Meaning	Math Meaning
point		
line		
plane		

WORD CLUES

As you read the next selection, look for these important words: *point, line, plane, intersect, perpendicular,* and *parallel*. The diagrams in the selection will help you understand their mathematical meanings. Also pay close attention to the symbols that stand for mathematical terms. These symbols are shortened ways of writing math words.

Strategy Tip

When reading, "Reading Mathematical Terms and Symbols," be sure that you understand each idea before you go on to the next one. In math, it is very important to fully understand every idea in order to understand the one that follows it.

Reading Mathematical Terms and Symbols

To study geometry, you must understand three important terms. They are *point*, *line*, and *plane*. A **point** has no dimensions. It cannot be seen. It has no size. A point is shown by a dot and named with a capital letter. This is the symbol for point *A*.

•A

A **line** is many, many points placed next to each other. It is endless in length but has no width. When a line is drawn, it looks as if it has a beginning and an end. However, the arrows on the line show that it goes on forever. A line can be named with a small letter. This is line *s*.

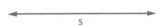

A line can also be named using two points. A capital letter is used to name each of the two points on the line. The two points can be placed anywhere on the line. This is line *AB*. The symbol for line *AB* is $\overleftrightarrow{AB}$.

Like a line, a **plane** goes on and on. It never ends. A plane has length and width but no height. A plane is named with a capital letter. Following this paragraph is plane *M*. The four-sided figure shows that it is a plane. Each side of a plane goes on forever. When you see this figure, you should remember that the sides do not mean that the plane

ends. The capital letter that names the plane is in the lower-right corner of the figure.

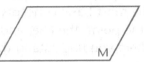

✔ When two lines cross, they **intersect**. Two lines intersect at a point. This is line *x* and line *y* intersecting at point *O*.

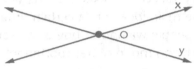

Two lines can intersect and form square corners. The lines are **perpendicular** to each other. Line *l* is perpendicular to line *m*. The symbol for showing that line *l* is perpendicular to line *m* is *l*⊥*m*.

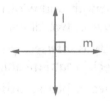

Sometimes two lines never intersect. The distance between them is always the same. When two lines never intersect, they are said to be **parallel** to each other. Line *a* is parallel to line *b*. The symbol to show that line *a* is parallel to line *b* is *a*∥*b*.

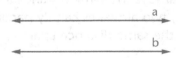

A line can also intersect a plane. A line and a plane intersect at a point. This diagram shows line *RS* intersecting plane *P* at point *L*. The dotted line shows the part of the line that is behind the plane.

Two planes can also intersect. When planes intersect, they always intersect in a line. This diagram shows plane *S* and plane *T* intersecting along line *CD*.

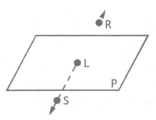

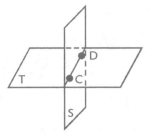

COMPREHENSION

1. Which mathematical term describes something with no dimensions? _____

2. Which mathematical term describes something with length but no width? _____

3. Which mathematical term describes something with length and width but no height? _____

4. When two lines cross, they _____.

5. Two lines that never intersect are _____ to each other.

6. Two lines that intersect and form square corners are _____ to each other.

7. Reread the paragraph with a check mark next to it. Draw a line under the sentence that states the main idea.

CRITICAL THINKING

1. Could two lines intersect each other at two points? Why or why not?

_____

_____

2. Could two planes intersect in a point? Why or why not?

_____

_____

3. Write the words *plane*, *point*, and *line* in order from the one that takes the least space to the one that takes the most space.

_____   _____   _____

MATHEMATICS

A. Write the name or symbol for each figure.

1.

‾‾‾‾‾‾‾‾‾‾

2. •C

‾‾‾‾‾‾‾‾‾‾

3.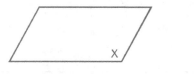

‾‾‾‾‾‾‾‾‾‾

4. d

‾‾‾‾‾‾‾‾‾‾

5. g

h

‾‾‾‾‾‾‾‾‾‾

6.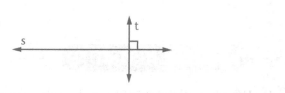

‾‾‾‾‾‾‾‾‾‾

B. Draw a diagram for each name or symbol.

1. point X

2. $\overleftrightarrow{CD}$

3. line m

4. plane D

5. $f \| g$

6. $g \perp h$

7. line CD and line ST intersecting at point H

8. line XY intersecting plane M at point C

Reading-Writing Connection

On a separate sheet of paper, write a paragraph describing something around you that includes perpendicular lines. Give as many details as possible.

Skill: Vowel Diphthongs

Say the words *oil* and *boy* to yourself. Listen to their vowel sound. The letters *oi* and *oy* stand for the same vowel sound. When this vowel sound appears at the beginning or in the middle of a word, it is usually spelled *oi*. When this same sound is at the end of a word, it is spelled *oy*. This sound is called a **vowel diphthong.**

A. Read the sentences below. Choose a word from the list to complete each sentence. Write the word on the line. Then circle the letters in each word that stand for the vowel diphthong.

coin	annoy	broil
enjoy	coil	noise

1. Some children _____ their parents by breaking their toys.

2. This vine will _____ around the tree.

3. Cars in heavy traffic often make _____ by honking their horns.

4. Mr. Larsen is planning to _____ the hamburgers over charcoal.

5. Joe and Ann _____ going to hockey games.

6. Numismatics, or _____ collecting, is a popular hobby.

Say the words *out* and *cow* to yourself. Listen to their vowel sound. The letters *ou* and *ow* stand for the same vowel sound. This sound is also called a vowel diphthong.

B. Read the sentences below. Choose a word from the list to complete each sentence. Write the word on the line. Then circle the letters in each word that stand for the diphthong.

town	cloud	crowd	shout
pouch	blouse	plow	brow

1. The cowhands rode off in a _____ of dust.

2. Heather wore her blue _____ with her gray skirt.

3. A _____ is larger than a village but smaller than a city.

4. In earlier times, an ox was used to pull a _____.

5. The female kangaroo carries her young in her _____.

6. A large _____ gathered at the scene of the fire.

7. Neil wiped the sweat from his _____.

8. Kerry tried to _____ to the other players on her team.

Skill: Vowel-Consonant Combinations

The **vowel-consonant combinations** *aw* and *al* and the vowels *au* stand for the same sound you hear in the words *claw*, *bald*, and *auto*. The vowel sound in all three words is the same, but the letters that stand for the sound are different.

Read the sentences below. Choose a word from the list to complete each sentence. Write the word on the line. Then circle the letters in each word that stand for the same sound you hear in the words *claw*, *bald*, and *auto*.

hawk	thaw	because	caught	fault	salt	ball
yawn	crawl	sauce	dawn	false	paw	gnaw
taught	pause	bald	haul	straw	halt	law

1. Tired people often _____.

2. Last year Ms. White _____ geometry.

3. It is not healthy for people to put too much _____ on their food.

4. Carol _____ four fish within a short time.

5. An answer that is not true is _____.

6. The sun rises at _____.

7. Mr. Barlaz poured _____ over the spaghetti.

8. Most babies _____ before they learn to walk.

9. It is Robert's _____ that we are late for dinner.

10. Althea left the party early _____ she was tired.

11. The hot sun made the ice start to _____.

12. My cat hurt its _____ while running on the gravel driveway.

13. Ruth was told to _____ before reading the story.

14. My grandfather is _____.

15. This _____ has a very sharp beak.

16. Ming's new truck can _____ our glass to the recycling plant.

17. My large _____ hat will protect my face from sunburn.

18. The horse will _____ if you pull on the reins.

19. The players kicked the _____.

20. After dinner, our dog would _____ on the bones that we gave him.

21. To drive when you are too young is against the _____.

Skill: Syllables

One way to help you pronounce long words is to divide the words into **syllables**. Then pronounce each syllable until you can say the whole word. There are several different rules for deciding how a word should be divided into syllables.

RULE 1: Compound Words

One of the easiest rules to use in dividing words is the one that is used with a compound word. Because a compound word is made up of two words, it must have at least two syllables. Always divide a compound word into syllables by separating it between the two smaller words first. If one or even both of the smaller words in a compound word have more than one syllable, it may be necessary to use another rule. However, you can pronounce most compound words if you divide them into two words.

sailboat   sail boat

A. Read the following compound words. Divide each word into two syllables by writing each of the two smaller words separately on the line next to the compound word.

1. weekday _____
2. seaweed _____
3. flashlight _____
4. driftwood _____
5. grassland _____
6. withdraw _____

7. bathtub _____
8. baseball _____
9. windshield _____
10. drumstick _____
11. highchair _____
12. background _____

RULE 2: Words With Double Consonants

Another rule is for words with double consonants. Divide the word into two syllables between the two same consonants and read each syllable.

tennis   ten nis

B. Divide the following two-syllable words into syllables. Write each syllable separately on the line next to the word.

1. raccoon _____
2. penny _____
3. lesson _____
4. slipper _____
5. lettuce _____
6. kitten _____
7. sudden _____

8. rabbit _____
9. tunnel _____
10. splatter _____
11. muffin _____
12. gossip _____
13. hammer _____
14. traffic _____

Skill: Main Idea—Stated or Unstated

When you read a textbook or reference book, the **main idea** of each paragraph will often be stated in a sentence. The rest of the paragraph will contain the supporting details that give additional information about the main idea.

Sometimes the main idea of a paragraph is not stated in one of the sentences. The information given in the paragraph will help you to **infer**, or figure out, the main idea yourself. To do this, you need to ask yourself what the paragraph is about. Then think of a sentence that summarizes this idea.

Read the following selection from beginning to end to become familiar with the content. Then reread each paragraph. Think about whether the main idea in each paragraph is stated or unstated.

Shooting for the Moon

1. Dr. Mae Jemison leads an adventure-filled life, but one of her most exciting days was September 12, 1992. "I had this big smile on my face," said Jemison. "I was so excited. This is what I had wanted to do for a very long time." Jemison was aboard shuttle mission STS-47 Spacelab, a cooperative mission to outer space between the United States and Japan.

2. Space travel is exciting, but in some ways it only emphasizes what a small planet Earth is. "The first thing I saw was Chicago. I looked out the window and there it was," she said about seeing her hometown from the shuttle. "I looked over at one point, and there was Somalia."

3. Dr. Jemison believes that space technology benefits everyone, especially people in the so-called developing nations. *Developing nations* is a term that means all the countries without major industries. In the space age, she says, old-fashioned telephone lines and electrical generators are no longer necessary. She thinks that the space age will enable the developing nations to skip over the industrial age.

4. When she was in medical school, Jemison studied social medicine in Cuba. Later she practiced medicine with rural Kenyan villagers and Cambodians who had escaped Communist rule in Thailand. She also worked as a Peace Corps medical officer in Sierra Leone and Liberia.

5. Jemison insists, however, that she does not do what she does just for the good of other people. "I don't believe in [doing good just to be unselfish]," she said. "I've gotten much more out of what I have done than the people I was supposed to be helping." Jemison was in a camp in Thailand for refugees, people who had left their countries to escape war and find freedom. "I learned more about medicine there than I could have in a lifetime somewhere else," she said.

6. Only a handful of women have gone up in space, and Jemison was the first African American

Dr. Mae Jemison aboard Spacelab, where astronauts perform experiments in a weightless environment.

woman to do so. "When I'm asked about the relevance to black people of what I do, I take that as an [insult]. It presupposes that black people have never been involved in exploring the heavens, but this is not so. Ancient African empires—Mali, Songhay, Egypt—had scientists and astronomers.

7. "The fact is that space and its resources belong to all of us, not to any one group," Jemison emphasizes. "We need more African Americans and Latinos in the field. If we're not there from the beginning, helping to determine what happens to these resources, we'll have no say in how they are to be used."

8. Jemison chose some very special objects to take with her in the shuttle: "an Alvin Ailey American Dance Theater poster, an Alpha Kappa Alpha banner, a flag that had flown over the Organization of African Unity, and [important writings] from Chicago's DuSable Museum of African American History and the Chicago public school system." She explained, "I wanted everyone to know that space belongs to all of us. There is science in dance and art in science."

9. When poet Nikki Giovanni interviewed Jemison in 1993 after her shuttle mission, she asked Jemison what her ideal space trip would be. Jemison replied, "Me in a clear bubble floating through the galaxy . . . shooting for the moon." When asked whom she would take with her, she said, "Sneeze, my cat. I think I'd like to have Sneeze. He came with me from Africa, so he's used to flying. Then if some aliens came by and invited me to another galaxy—well, look for me on a television mystery. I'm gone."

A. For each paragraph in the selection, if the main idea is stated, write *stated* on the line. If the main idea is unstated, choose a main idea from the sentences below and write the letter on the line. You will not use all the listed main ideas.

a. Jemison's cat, Sneeze, came with her from Africa, so he's used to flying.

b. Dr. Jemison has done much to help people all over the world.

c. Black people have always been involved in studying the mysteries of the universe.

d. Jemison worked as a Peace Corps officer in Sierra Leone and Liberia.

e. Old-fashioned telephone lines and electrical generators are no longer necessary in the developing world.

f. On September 12, 1992, Jemison reached her goal of going up in a space shuttle.

g. Jemison has a clear picture of her ideal space trip.

Paragraph 1:	_____	**Paragraph 6:**	_____
Paragraph 2:	_____	**Paragraph 7:**	_____
Paragraph 3:	_____	**Paragraph 8:**	_____
Paragraph 4:	_____	**Paragraph 9:**	_____
Paragraph 5:	_____		

B. Now go back to each paragraph that has a stated main idea. Underline the sentence that states the main idea.

Skill: Using a Dictionary

In a dictionary, you may find pages of words that all begin with the same first three letters. To find a word on these pages, you will need to look at the fourth letter of the word. When words begin with the same three letters, they are arranged in **alphabetical order** according to the fourth letter of the words. For example, the word *collar* is listed before the word *color* because *l* comes before *o* in the alphabet.

A. On the numbered lines, write each set of words below in alphabetical order according to the first four letters in each word. Cross out each word in the list after you write it.

beam	1. _____		stole	1. _____
beagle	2. _____		stove	2. _____
bear	3. _____		stomach	3. _____
beauty	4. _____		stoop	4. _____
beat	5. _____		store	5. _____
beach	6. _____		stodgy	6. _____
beaver	7. _____		stop	7. _____
bean	8. _____		stoke	8. _____
bead	9. _____		stone	9. _____
beak	10. _____		stock	10. _____

At the top of each dictionary page are two words in boldface type. These words are called **guide words**. Guide words help you quickly and easily find the entry words, the words for which the dictionary gives definitions. They tell you the first and the last entry word on the page. All the other entry words on the page come between these two words in alphabetical order.

B. Below is a pair of guide words that might appear on a dictionary page. Following them is a list of entry words. If the entry word would be on the same page as the guide words, write *yes* next to the word. If the entry word would appear on an earlier page, write *before*. If the entry word would appear on a later page, write *after*.

parboil / parson

1. parrot _____		7. pastry _____
2. part _____		8. pardon _____
3. parcel _____		9. paragraph _____
4. pass _____		10. parlor _____
5. parasol _____		11. Paris _____
6. parent _____		12. parade _____

In a dictionary, an entry word, plus all the information about it, is called an **entry**. The entry word always appears in boldface type. If the entry word has more than one syllable, it is divided into syllables to show where the word can be divided at the end of a line of writing. The entry word is followed by a **respelling** of the word in parentheses. The respelling shows you how to say the word. The **part-of-speech label** follows the respelling. The labels are usually abbreviated as follows: *adj.* for adjective, *adv.* for adverb, *conj.* for conjunction, *interj.* for interjection, *n.* for noun, *prep.* for preposition, *pron.* for pronoun, and *v.* for verb.

The **meanings** of an entry word are arranged according to parts of speech. For example, if an entry has noun meanings, all the noun meanings are grouped together and numbered following the *n.* label. Any meanings the word may have for any other part of speech are numbered and placed after the abbreviated part-of-speech label. Many words that appear in dictionary entries are synonyms for the entry word.

At the end of some entries are idioms. An **idiom** is a group of words that has a meaning different from the meaning that the individual words have by themselves.

C. Use the following dictionary entry to answer the questions below.

name (nām) *n.* **1** a word or words by which a person, animal, thing, or place is known: title [Grace, Lopez, Wyoming, and poodle are *names.*] **2** a word or words used instead of the real name, sometimes in order to insult [They were mean and called him *names*, such as "liar" and "cheat."] **3** reputation [Guard your good *name.*] ◆*v.* **named, nam′ing 1** to give a name to [He *named* the child after her mother.] **2** to tell the name or names of [Can you *name* all the presidents?] **3** to refer to; mention [to *name* an example]. **4** to choose for a certain position; appoint [She was *named* president of the company.] **5** to fix or set, as a date for a meeting, a price, etc. —**in the name of, 1** for the sake of [in the *name* of good sense]. **2** by the authority of [Open in the *name* of the law!] —**to one's name,** belonging to one.

1. What is the entry word? _____

2. Write the respelling. _____

3. How many noun meanings follow the part-of-speech label *n*? _____

4. How many verb meanings follow the part-of-speech label *v*? _____

5. Write the first verb meaning. _____

6. Write the second idiom. _____

7. Write the two synonyms given for the entry word as a noun. _____

8. Write the idiom that has the same meaning as the underlined words in the following sentence.

   I ordered the equipment <u>by the authority of</u> my supervisor. _____

Help-wanted ads are found in the classified section of the newspaper. The classified section lists advertisements for all kinds of things arranged by subject. In the help-wanted listings, ads for the same kinds of jobs are listed together. Each ad begins with a job title or a descriptive heading that identifies the job. Ads are listed in alphabetical order by job title or key word. Sometimes a job agency places ads. A job agency provides the service of hiring employees for companies.

Most help-wanted ads give the job seeker a variety of information. In addition to the job title, a help-wanted ad may describe the skills needed for the job. It may also state that previous experience, or former work in the same type of job, is required. An ad tells how to apply for the job. Other information, such as salary, or pay, may be included.

Because help-wanted ads must give a lot of information in a small amount of space, abbreviations, or shortened forms of words, are used. For example, *exp.* is the abbreviation for the word *experience.* Sometimes the abbreviations contain the first few letters of the word; sometimes the abbreviations use only consonants. If you use context clues, you can usually figure out the abbreviations.

Sometimes an ad may state that the company requires a résumé. A résumé is a sheet of written information about yourself and your work experience that you make available to a company. If the company wants to meet you after reading your résumé, someone at the company will contact you for an interview.

Examine the help-wanted ads below.

BANKING

ASST MANAGER
San Jose-based bank seeks exp. asst manager for new branch location. Responsible for developing and managing relationships with clients. Spanish-speaking prefd. We offer a competitive benefits pkg. Fax résumé with cover letter and sal. rqrmnts to Union Bank, 555-7938.

BANKING

Head Teller. Prestigious bank looking for head teller. Must have 5 yrs bank exp. Must be good with numbers and people. Responsible for staff training and development. Competitive salary. Great oppty for the right person. Apply online at www.Hartbank.com.

BANKING

Lending officer. Financial company has immed. opening for individual with lending exp. Needs strong oral and written communication skills. Call Mr. Temprano at 555-0901, Wkdys, 10–4.

BANKING

Secy—Executive Offices
Must type 60 wpm and have computer and spreadsheet skills; P/T Mon–Thurs 8 A.M.–11 A.M. For appt., call Jonathan Chong at 555-8188.

BANKING

TELLER TRAINEE
Entry-level positions at major area bank. Must be H.S. grad. No exp. necessary. Responsible for handling cash and general office duties. Interviews 9–5, Sept 7, 8, 9 at 736 N. Bayview Ave., Rm. 400. Ask for Don Sullivan.

BANKING

Teller. Local credit union seeks F/T teller for dwntwn branch. Recent grad OK. Must work Sats. $12/hr. $250 hiring bonus. Fax résumé to Travis Price, 555-3231.

BANKING

Jobs! Jobs! Jobs!
Tellers	to $20,000
College Grad Trainees	to $30,000
Loan Officers	to $40,000
Branch Managers	to $60,000
Accountants	to $80,000

Banking Unlimited Agency will find the right job for you. 30 E. Orange Street, Suite 1000; 555-7690

A. Read the abbreviations from the help-wanted ads on page 32. On the lines, write the words the abbreviations stand for. If necessary, use context clues from the ads.

1. grad _____   6. yrs _____

2. P/T _____   7. secy _____

3. immed. _____   8. sal _____

4. prefd _____   9. oppty _____

5. Sats _____   10. rqrmnts _____

B. Use the information in the ads to answer the questions.

1. Where would you go to apply for a job as a teller trainee? _____

2. For which position could you apply online? _____

3. Which job might be appropriate for someone who wants to work just a few hours a day? _____

4. According to the Banking Unlimited Agency, how much might a trainee earn? _____

5. Which job ad asks for someone with good skills at speaking and writing? _____

6. Which bank wants a Spanish-speaking assistant manager for one of its branches? _____

7. How much experience would you need to apply for the job as head teller at Hart Bank? _____

8. Which two ads suggest faxing a résumé to show interest in a job? _____

_____

9. How would you learn more about the jobs that the Banking Unlimited Agency offers?

_____

10. What is the highest-paying job that the Banking Unlimited Agency lists? _____

11. How is the local credit union trying to attract applicants? _____

_____

12. Jonelle just graduated from high school and has no job experience. She needs a job,

but doesn't want to work on weekends. What job might be best for her? _____

13. Why do you think the Hart Bank wants a head teller who is "good with numbers and people"?

_____

_____

14. The head teller position offers a "competitive salary." What is a competitive salary?

_____

A Look at the Past and Present

LESSON 11

Skill: Theme

BACKGROUND INFORMATION

When a young Japanese-American girl in "A Simple Arrangement" spends a year with her grandparents in Japan, she struggles to adapt to Japanese customs. Before 1945, Japanese families were bound by strict customs. Now these rules have relaxed somewhat. However, family relationships and customs are still much more formal in Japan than in the United States.

SKILL FOCUS: Theme

Theme is the meaning or message of a story. It is an important idea about life that the author wants to share with readers.

Sometimes an author states the theme of a story directly. Usually, however, you will have to figure out the theme for yourself. To do that, pay attention to what the characters do and say. In addition, a story's title can be a clue to its theme.

The following questions will help you infer the theme of a story.

- What does the story's title mean?
- What do the main characters discover about themselves in the story?
- What do the characters learn about life?
- What message is the author giving to readers?

▶ Many stories and movies have similar themes, or messages about life. In the next column is a chart with two common themes. Next to each one, write the name of a story you know that conveys that message.

Common Themes	
Theme	**Story or Movie**
People must often over-come many difficulties to achieve an important goal.	
People often do not realize how valuable life is until a tragedy strikes.	

CONTEXT CLUES: Antonyms

Some context clues are **antonyms**, or words with opposite meanings.

In the sentence below, look for the antonym that helps you figure out the meaning of *outspoken*.

*Keiko was shy, not **outspoken** like Tomi.*

If you don't know the meaning of *outspoken*, the word *shy* can help. *Shy* and *outspoken* are antonyms, so *outspoken* means "not shy."

▶ Read the following sentences. Circle the antonym that helps you figure out the meaning of the underlined word.

*Manners are much more casual in America, Tomi thought. In Japan, everyone's behavior seems so **formal**.*

Use antonym context clues to find the meanings of the underlined words *adept*, *proportion*, and *serene* in the following selection.

(Strategy Tip)

As you read, use the questions on this page to help you figure out the story's theme.

A Simple Arrangement

"I give up!" Tomi cried. She threw the spray of yellow flowers to the floor.

Her cousin Keiko blinked her eyes in amazement. Keiko was shy, not outspoken like Tomi. Tomi had never learned to keep her feelings to herself as Japanese girls are taught to do. Keiko did not know what to say.

"I'm sorry that I shouted," Tomi said. She bent down to pick up the flowers. "It's just that I'll never learn to arrange flowers."

"Yes, you will," Keiko said gently. "It is the Japanese way."

"That's just it!" Tomi burst out again. "I'm not Japanese. I'm American. I was born in California, and I lived there all my life until now. My parents may be Japanese, and I may look Japanese, but that just makes it harder. Everyone expects me to do things the Japanese way, but I can't!"

All the anger Tomi had felt these last few months came rushing out. She hadn't wanted to come to Japan in the first place. When her grandparents had invited her to spend a year in Japan, however, Tomi's father said that it was a fine idea. Once Father made up his mind, it was no use arguing. The word of a Japanese father is not questioned—even in America!

Once she was in Japan, Tomi had honestly tried to be the sort of girl her grandparents wanted her to be. She had worked very hard at doing well in school and at becoming <u>adept</u> in flower arranging. However, her hands seemed clumsy working with flowers. She felt that she did everything wrong.

"I think you are very lucky to be both Japanese and American," Keiko said. "You have two homes and two languages. That is something special."

"You're the one who's lucky," said Tomi. "You belong here. I don't."

Tomi cut three flowers from the spray and put them in the bowl as she had seen Mr. Tanaka, her teacher, do many times. She had cut the stems in the Japanese way so that they were three different lengths. The flower with the short stem represented Earth. The tall flower stood for heaven. The medium length flower stood for human beings, who link heaven and Earth.

Once heaven, human beings, and Earth were in harmony, the flower arrangement succeeded. An arrangement was supposed to have <u>proportion</u>. However, Tomi's flowers looked unbalanced. The design was all wrong. It was supposed to be so simple to achieve a pleasing arrangement of flowers. Why couldn't she learn how to do it? Would Tomi ever be able to please her grandparents?

Tomi sighed. "I hoped I could make a pretty flower arrangement for the party tonight," she said sadly. "It would make Grandmother so happy."

Keiko's eyes danced at the thought of the celebration. "Are you going to wear the kimono that Grandmother and Grandfather gave you when you arrived here?" she asked. "It is so beautiful."

"I know it is," Tomi said, "but I wouldn't feel right wearing it." The long, flowing kimonos that many Japanese women wear on special occasions looked lovely on them. Kimonos were really much prettier than Western clothes, Tomi thought. Yet she would make a fool of herself in a kimono. Kimonos are narrow, so you have to take short steps with your knees close together. Otherwise the kimono will flap open. Tomi was sure she would forget about walking properly. She would look clumsy and silly. It was better not to even try.

"It's time for me to go home and help my family get ready for tonight," Keiko said. She got to her feet and crossed the room in quick, graceful steps.

Tomi felt a stab of envy as she watched her cousin. Keiko would wear a kimono to the family gathering tonight. Keiko would know the right things to do and say, too. Manners are much more casual in America, Tomi thought. In Japan, everyone's behavior seems so formal. It is so important to do everything just right. Tomi always seemed to do everything wrong.

After Keiko had gone, Tomi felt tears in her eyes. She thought about her family back in California. More than anything, she wanted to feel like part of a family again. She would never be accepted here, not when she couldn't even arrange a few flowers!

Tomi picked up the flowers again. The words of Mr. Tanaka came back to her: "Arranging flowers is a simple thing, but it cannot be done unless your heart is <u>serene</u>."

"That must be my problem," Tomi said to herself. "My heart is anything but serene. I feel tense and anxious. My heart is not at peace."

Just then, Grandmother came into the room. Her arms were filled with packages of food for the party.

"I smell rice burning!" Grandmother said.

Oh, dear! Tomi suddenly remembered that she had put rice on the stove to cook. She had hoped to please Grandmother by making the evening rice, but she had forgotten it. The water must have boiled away. The rice would be black and burned. Couldn't she do anything right?

Tomi fled from the house. Once she was in the garden, she let the tears fall. She sank into the soft moss and put her face in her hands. She had never felt so lost and alone.

It was very quiet. Her sobbing slowed, and she wiped her eyes. She looked around the garden. How beautiful it was! A pine branch was reflected in the little pond. The cherry tree was a huge ball of white blossoms.

It was a tiny garden, yet every inch of it was a delight. Her grandfather had planned it that way, she knew. It was very Japanese to draw from each thing its special beauty. The Japanese found joy in the smallest things. Things as simple as the moon rising or a bird singing were treated as treasures.

Tomi had been in the garden many times, but she had always been too busy to notice how carefully planned yet simple it was. Few other Americans would have noticed it either, she thought. Americans moved too fast. They didn't have time to watch a flower bud.

Perhaps she had been trying to move too fast, Tomi thought. She had been in such a great hurry to learn everything right away. If she moved a bit more slowly, perhaps she would find the beauty in simple things. The Japanese knew there was comfort in beauty. I'm lucky to be Japanese, Tomi thought. Lucky to be here. Lucky just to be alive!

Tomi hugged that warm feeling to her as she went back inside. Her heart was full of joy as she slipped off her shoes at the door.

"Where is the pot I burned, Grandmother?" she asked. "I want to scrub it clean."

"I've done it for you," said Grandmother.

Tomi waited for her to say more about the burned rice. Tomi had acted like an American again, wasting food! However, her grandmother just went on with the preparations for dinner. She knows I can't help being what I am, Tomi thought. I am American, too.

Relieved, she picked up the yellow flowers again. This time her hands moved easily as she placed the stems in the bowl. She arranged the flowers slowly and with love for their beauty.

She stepped back to see the results. It was a very simple arrangement. There were just three stems. Yet it looked natural, almost as if the spray grew right out of the bowl. It was beautiful and right and Japanese.

That night, Tomi put on the silk kimono that her grandparents had given her. It was as blue as the

sky and had peach blossoms scattered across it. The long, flowing sleeves fell almost to the floor.

That evening, Tomi's steps were not always as tiny as they should have been. Most of the time, though, she remembered how to walk, and she knew she looked fine. Like Keiko, Tomi helped make the passing moments of the evening beautiful.

Grandmother said nothing about the flowers, and Grandfather didn't mention the kimono, but Tomi saw the glow of pride in their eyes. She felt their love reach out and wrap her like a cloak.

In the garden, the wind blew among the cherry trees, scattering the white flowers like confetti against the moon. Tomi watched each petal fall through the air of the peaceful Japanese evening.

COMPREHENSION

1. Why does Tomi go to Japan?

_____

_____

2. Explain why Keiko says Tomi is lucky.

_____

_____

3. Why does Tomi think that Keiko is lucky?

_____

_____

4. What do the shortest, tallest, and medium-sized flowers in a Japanese arrangement represent?

_____

_____

5. Why does Tomi run to the garden and cry?

_____

_____

_____

6. Explain why Tomi doesn't want to wear a kimono.

_____

_____

7. Draw a line to match each word with its meaning.

proportion   a. skilled

    adept   b. calm and peaceful

    serene   c. balance of parts

CRITICAL THINKING

1. If Keiko visited the United States, what customs and traits might she have to get used to?

_____

_____

2. Describe how Tomi is changing as a result of her time in Japan.

_____

_____

_____

3. Describe the grandparents' attitude toward Tomi at the end of the story.

_____

_____

4. Mr. Tanaka told Tomi that flower arranging is done with different lengths of stems and a serene heart. Part of this statement is a fact, and part is opinion. Which is which?

_____

_____

5. Do you think Tomi is likely to keep some Japanese customs when she is back in the United States?

_____

_____

SKILL FOCUS: THEME

1. Think about the title of the story. To what kind of arrangement does it refer?

_____

_____

2. Explain why Tomi has difficulty with the simple arrangement.

_____

_____

3. What other Japanese customs are difficult for Tomi?

_____

_____

4. Why is Tomi's visit to her grandparents' garden a turning point for her?

_____

_____

5. Discuss the author's message or theme.

_____

_____

_____

Reading-Writing Connection

On a separate sheet of paper, write a paragraph describing a time when you felt that you could not find a way to fit in or adapt to a new situation.

Skill: Cause and Effect

BACKGROUND INFORMATION

"Worlds Under Our Feet" tells about archaeologists (ARK ee AHL ə jəsts) working in cities. Archaeologists are scientists who study the people, customs, and life of the past. To learn more, they excavate (EKS kə vayt), or dig, at sites where people once lived. As they carefully dig through layers of soil, they find clues about how people lived in the past. These clues might include pieces of broken pottery, tools, statues, walls, temples, and even entire cities.

SKILL FOCUS: Cause and Effect

When one event causes another event to happen, the process is called cause and effect. A **cause** is an event that makes something happen. An **effect** is what happens as a result of the cause.

One effect can be the cause of another effect. That effect can then cause something else to happen. In this way, a chain of causes and effects occurs.

The following paragraph explains a chain of causes and effects.

> Archaeological digs in cities have another benefit, too. When archaeologists go to work in cities, local newspapers and TV stations cover the stories. As a result, people in the area come out to see the sites. This causes people to become more interested in archaeology and history. The end result is that the general public acquires a higher level of knowledge about the city and its past.

The first cause is archaeologists digging in cities. The effect is that newspaper and TV reporters cover the event. The effect of the media coverage is to encourage people to come out and see the site. This causes people to learn more about their city's history.

▶ Complete the cause-and-effect chain at the bottom of the page. Use details from the paragraph. The first parts of the chain have been done for you.

CONTEXT CLUES: Details

The **details** in sentences are often context clues. Such details can help you figure out the meaning of a new word. In the sentences below, look for details that explain the meaning of the underlined word.

> Inside the temple, archaeologists found more than 600 <u>artifacts</u>. These included life-sized statues, as well as hundreds of smaller Aztec objects.

If you don't know the meaning of *artifacts*, the details *life-sized statues* and *smaller Aztec objects* will help. These details suggest that artifacts are objects preserved from the past.

▶ Read the following sentence. Circle the details that help you figure out the meaning of the underlined word.

> They <u>surveyed</u> the site, making maps showing where they would dig.

In the following selection, use details to figure out the meanings of the underlined words *demolished*, *integral*, and *inhabitants*.

Strategy Tip

As you read "Worlds Under Our Feet," look for cause-and-effect relationships. Recognizing causes and effects will help you understand the ideas in the selection. Keep in mind that the effect can cause something else to happen.

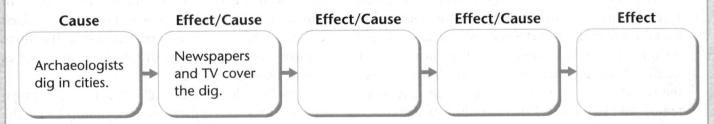

Cause	Effect/Cause	Effect/Cause	Effect/Cause	Effect
Archaeologists dig in cities.	Newspapers and TV cover the dig.			

WORLDS UNDER OUR FEET

The Lost Temple of the Aztecs

In early 1978, workers laying cables in the center of Mexico City had a big surprise. Suddenly their equipment struck a huge stone. This was no ordinary stone. It was perfectly round and covered with ancient carvings!

Work at the site stopped. **Archaeologists** came to investigate. They soon realized that the stone stood for the legendary Aztec moon goddess. According to historical records, this fabulous stone had been kept at the Great Temple of the Aztecs. This temple was once the most sacred place in the Aztec world. Would an excavation of the site reveal the temple?

Mexican archaeologists planned carefully before digging. They surveyed the site, making maps showing where they would dig. They also determined the techniques they would use.

We often think of archaeologists digging in deserts and jungles. Yet today more archaeological sites are in crowded cities. Construction workers often find these sites by accident.

Excavating a site in a busy, modern city is expensive and difficult. In Mexico City, for example, archaeologists had to make sure their digging would not damage surrounding buildings. People who lived and worked in the area had to be protected. The site itself had to be secure. Water was another problem. Mexico City was built on the site of a lake. Ground water was close to the surface and could flood the site.

The Great Temple of the Aztecs was gradually unearthed. The topmost level had been <u>demolished</u> by the Spanish conquerors. Although that part of the building had been destroyed, five lower levels remained intact.

First built in 1325, the temple had been rebuilt several times. Inside the temple, archaeologists found more than 600 **artifacts** (ART ə fakts). These included life-sized statues, as well as hundreds of smaller Aztec objects. Today visitors from all over the world can see and marvel at the ancient Aztec temple and the artifacts that were buried with it.

In 1978, electrical workers in Mexico City accidentally discovered the site of this ancient temple.

Other Archeological Discoveries

The Aztec temple in Mexico City was an extraordinary discovery. Yet less dramatic sites are found every year. In recent years, workers burying cables in Barcelona, Spain, found a stone wall and tower that had surrounded the city in the 1400s. Construction workers in New York City uncovered an African American graveyard from the 1700s. In Athens, Greece, work on a new subway line yielded ancient statues and buildings. Discoveries like these present archaeologists with special opportunities and difficult decisions.

Just how do temples, walls, cemeteries, and even entire cities get buried underground? Over the years, the ground level gradually rises, burying the past beneath it. Layers of decaying plants pile up. Soil, eroded from rocks and hills, is deposited. Pieces of demolished buildings and even garbage raise the ground level.

Century after century, this material piles up in horizontal layers, covering entire buildings. This process is called **stratification** (STRAT ə fə KAY shən). Studying the layers deposited over the centuries is one way that archaeologists date artifacts from the past.

Uncovering Colonial America

For archaeologists, every new site is a chance to learn about the past. In cities, construction sites often present the best digging opportunities. In 2000, for example, a four-block park behind Independence Hall in Philadelphia was dug up to build a new museum.

Dozens of houses built in the 1700s and 1800s had once stood on the site. They had been bulldozed years ago to build the park, called Independence Mall. Now while digging up the mall, workers exposed the foundations, yards, and wells of houses that were hundreds of years old.

Archaeologists were excited. A bit of colonial America had suddenly been unsealed. They were eager to learn as much as they could. Over the next few months, they uncovered nearly a million artifacts from the 1600s and 1700s.

Most of the artifacts were of little material value—scraps of newspaper, kitchen tools, bottles, lamps, and shoes. However, the artifacts were of great historical value because they revealed the **diversity** (də VER sə tee) of the colonial population.

Among the artifacts were American Indian beads and tools, as well as the remains of a log cabin where free African Americans or American Indians had lived. Americans from many different ethnic backgrounds and income levels had apparently been living peacefully in the same small neighborhood at the same time that the Constitution was being written just a few blocks away.

Archaeological digs in cities have another benefit, too. When archaeologists go to work in cities, local newspapers and TV stations cover the stories. As a result, people in the area come out to see the sites. This causes people to become more interested in archaeology and history. The end result is that the general public acquires a higher level of knowledge about the city and its past.

Archaeology or Development?

In the United States, government officials support the work of archaeologists. Because construction work can destroy valuable artifacts, Congress passed a law that requires builders to allow archaeologists to study construction sites before the work begins.

Inspired by the success of this federal law, many states and cities passed similar laws to protect their local heritage. As a result of these new laws, an increasing number of artifacts from our nation's past are being preserved.

At a new construction site, archaeologists first take samples from a few small sections of the ground. Usually they find nothing at all. In some cases, however, the laws protecting these sites have proven their value.

At one site in Ohio, for example, a company planned to build a new industrial park. When

New laws require builders to allow archaeologists to study a construction site before building begins.

archaeologists took samples at the site, they found artifacts from an American Indian community that may have existed there more than 10,000 years ago.

Sometimes discoveries are made after construction gets underway. In these cases, conflicts can develop between archaeologists and builders. Archaeologists work slowly and carefully. They see the earth as a gold mine of clues about the past. Often they want to preserve their discoveries.

Builders, however, have different goals. For them, time is money, and they have tight schedules to meet. If an archaeological site is preserved, builders may have to give up their plans to develop the site. For them, preserving the past may mean a loss of money and opportunity.

Usually the archaeologists and the builders compromise. Each side benefits, but each must make sacrifices. Because most sites cannot be preserved, archaeologists may study them intensely for a short period of time. In order to have a permanent record of their work, they take photographs and measurements of everything they find. The site itself will soon disappear beneath a building. However, archaeologists have preserved evidence that can be studied for clues to the past.

Cooperation in Athens

A good example of cooperation between archaeologists and builders occurred in Greece in 1994. The city of Athens was about to extend its subway system. Athens, the birthplace of democracy, was the center of culture in ancient Greece. The digging of new subway tunnels was bound to uncover archaeological sites.

The construction companies in charge of the new subway made an important decision: Archaeology would be an <u>integral</u> part of the project. They would allow archaeologists to have full access to the sites. Construction companies even provided money for these studies.

By studying ancient writings, archaeologists identified the sites where ruins might be found. Ancient shrines, gardens, and schools were all discovered at the sites of some of the new subway stations. The construction companies planned the construction so that archaeologists would have more time at these sites. One of the most important

sites was a school where **Aristotle** (AR is tot əl), a Greek philosopher, once taught.

Once they were fully studied, the excavations at Athens were covered up. However, the new Athens subway became a mini-museum. Displays of artifacts appear in several stations. One of the stations was designed around the remains of ancient buildings found there.

Saving the Sites

Archaeologists, citizens, and politicians often work together to save important sites. In 1991, for example, construction workers digging near City Hall in New York City found a cemetery. In the 1700s, this ground had become the final resting place of thousands of African Americans.

When the graveyard was unearthed, many African Americans regarded it as an important part of their cultural heritage. As a result, they wanted the site to be preserved. Archaeologists wanted to preserve the site, too, because it was the earliest and largest colonial cemetery ever found.

These two groups pressured local and national government officials to give the burial site the care and recognition it deserved. As a result, bones and artifacts from the site were sent to a university for study. The site was declared a landmark by both New York City and the U.S. government.

There will be a memorial to mark the place where the bones will be reburied. There will also be a museum at the site to interpret the historic and scientific importance of the findings.

Another controversial site was uncovered in Miami in 1999. In the heart of Miami's business district, a high-rise building was under construction. While digging the foundation, workers found a perfectly round, 40-foot-wide circle of carved stones and post holes.

Archaeologists agreed that the long-vanished Tequesta Indians had built the circle about 2,000 years ago. The Indians had probably used the circle as a calendar. Almost nothing is known about Miami's earliest <u>inhabitants</u>. For this reason, archaeologists saw the site as a rare opportunity to find out how people in the area lived thousands of years ago. The builder, however, was determined to finish the construction project.

In order to save the site, archaeologists and American Indians wrote letters and made speeches. As a result, many schoolchildren and other citizens became involved in the crusade to save the site. Thanks to the efforts of concerned citizens, county officials seized the site and stopped construction.

Virtual Archaeology

In many cities, the cost of preserving ancient sites is too high. Also modern buildings may be blocking part of the site. Yet these problems disappear with a technique called "time slicing."

Two thousand years ago, the Romans invaded Great Britain. One of the large cities they built there was called Viroconium. It now lies buried under a town called Wroxeter. Today archaeologists are uncovering the ancient Roman city. They are doing so, however, without moving a shovelful of soil!

Using a portable radar machine, archaeologists send electrical pulses into the ground. When these pulses hit something in the ground, they bounce back to a receiver. The receiver registers the "echoes" and sends them to a computer. These "echoes" reveal the size and shape of buried structures. Using this data, the computer makes a three-dimensional image of the underground site.

At Viroconium, archaeologists are time-slicing a 140-acre site. One of the computer's first images shows a stone church. Nearly 100-feet long, it may be the oldest-known church in England. The computer has also mapped ancient Roman buildings. When the project is complete, you will be able to tour the entire underground site by popping a CD-ROM into your computer.

For many people, virtual archaeology may not seem as satisfying as real dirt and stone. Still it is a practical, money-saving tool. Archaeologists can use this new tool to "uncover" sites that would otherwise remain a mystery.

Past and Future

Today many archaeological sites and objects are threatened as never before. Why should we protect and preserve them? Why should we study the past?

For most people, the past is a source of interest and wonder. The past can teach us many practical lessons we can apply to our lives today. We can take pride in what the people before us have accomplished. The past is something that belongs to everyone. In that way, the past unites us all.

COMPREHENSION

1. What clue led archaeologists to discover the Great Temple of the Aztecs in Mexico City?

   _____

   _____

   _____

2. Explain how federal and state laws help archaeologists.

   _____

   _____

3. Explain why the 40-foot stone circle found in Miami was an important discovery.

   _____

   _____

   _____

4. How do the views of builders and archaeologists usually differ regarding archaeological sites in cities?

   _____

   _____

   _____

5. Answer each question. Write *yes* or *no* on the line.

   _____ a. Does material from demolished buildings add to stratification?

   _____ b. Is studying historical texts an integral part of archaeology?

   _____ c. Do the earliest inhabitants of an area always leave behind written records?

1. Discuss how stratification helps archaeologists to date artifacts from the past.

   _____

   _____

2. Explain why it is important for builders and archaeologists to cooperate closely.

   _____

   _____

3. What can average citizens do to help preserve archaeological finds in their towns?

   _____

   _____

SKILL FOCUS: CAUSE AND EFFECT

Read the following paragraph. Then fill in the cause-and-effect chain to show the series of events that lead to the final effect. The first cause is provided for you.

In the United States, government officials support the work of archaeologists. Because construction work can destroy many valuable artifacts, Congress passed a law that requires builders to allow archaeologists to study construction sites before the work begins. The success of this law inspired many states and cities, and they passed similar laws to protect their local heritage. As a result of all these new laws, an increasing number of artifacts from the nation's past are being preserved.

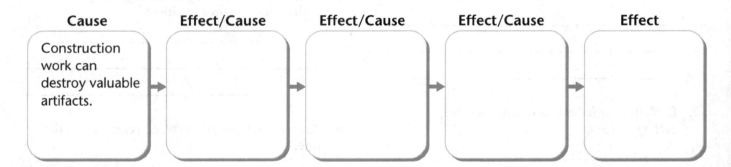

Cause	Effect/Cause	Effect/Cause	Effect/Cause	Effect
Construction work can destroy valuable artifacts.				

Reading-Writing Connection

Suppose that you were on one of the archaeological digs described in the selection. On a separate sheet of paper, write a diary entry that tells what you might have seen and done on a typical day. Explain why you think your work is important.

Skill: Reading a Diagram

BACKGROUND INFORMATION

In "The Nervous System," you will read about the human nervous system. Made up of billions of nerve cells, the nervous system carries messages that allow the body to function and to respond to the outside world. Our thoughts, emotions, and movements are all products of our nervous system. The selection begins with the smallest unit of the nervous system, the neuron, and progresses to the largest unit, the central nervous system.

SKILL FOCUS: Reading a Diagram

Diagrams can help you understand the words and ideas in a science selection. A diagram is a drawing that shows the structure of something or the relationships between different parts of a system. When interpreting a diagram, read the paragraphs near the diagram first. Then study the diagram.

Sometimes a paragraph in the text will refer you to a diagram. It might say, for example, "See Figure 2." Usually that is the best time to pause in your reading and study the diagram.

To understand a diagram, read its title, caption, and labels. The title tells you what the diagram shows. The caption explains the diagram in more detail. Labels name the parts of the diagram.

Often you will want to go back and reread the paragraphs that refer to a diagram. Using the text and the diagram together is the best way to get a full understanding of a science topic.

The following steps will help you understand the diagrams in your reading.

1. Read the paragraphs that come just before and just after the diagram. Then study the diagram.

2. Look back at the diagram from time to time as you continue to read.

3. Use the diagram and the text together to sum up what you have read.

▶ Study the diagram of a neuron, or nerve cell at the top of the next column. Then answer the questions that follow.

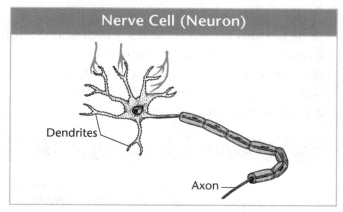

Nerve Cell (Neuron)

Dendrites

Axon

How many axons lead away from the cell body?

_____

How many dendrites are shown as part of this

neuron? _____

CONTEXT CLUES: Appositive Phrases

An **appositive phrase** is a group of words that explains the meaning of a new word. Usually the appositive phrase appears right after the new word and is set off with commas or dashes. In the sentence below, find the appositive phrase that helps you figure out the meaning of *conscious*.

The cerebrum controls all __conscious__ activity, or those activities that you are aware of.

If you don't know the meaning of *conscious*, the appositive phrase *those activities that you are aware of* gives you the meaning.

▶ Read the following sentence. Circle the appositive phrase that shows the meaning of *spinal cord*.

This part of the brain connects directly to the __spinal cord__, a long bundle of nerves that extends down through the backbone.

Use appositive phrases to find the meanings of the underlined words *hemispheres*, *involuntary*, and *internal* in the following selection.

> ### Strategy Tip
>
> As you read, use the steps on this page to understand the diagrams.

The Nervous System

The nervous system is the body's communication system. It carries messages about the outside world and about the body itself. It carries messages that allow muscles to move. It also keeps the body's organs functioning.

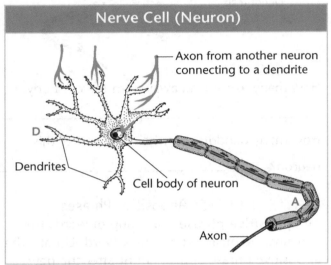

FIGURE 1. **The neuron is the basic unit of the nervous system.**

Neurons

The basic unit of the nervous system is the **neuron** (NUR ahn), or nerve cell. A neuron has three parts. It has a cell body and two kinds of threads that extend from it. The long thread is the **axon** (AK sahn), and the short threads are the **dendrites** (DEN drytz). See Figure 1.

Some neurons have more than one dendrite, but most neurons have only one axon. The dendrites carry messages to the cell body. The axon carries messages away from the cell body. The axon of one neuron connects to a dendrite of another neuron. When a message travels through the nervous system, it is sent by the axon of each neuron. The dendrite of the next neuron receives the message from the axon and passes it on.

Nerves are bundles of neuron fibers, or threads. Different kinds of nerves do different jobs in the nervous system. **Sensory** (SEN sər ee) **nerves** carry messages to the brain and the spinal cord. Motor nerves carry messages from the central nervous system to the body's muscles. Connecting nerves connect sensory and motor nerves. See Figure 2.

Parts of the Nervous System

The nervous system has two basic parts. The **central nervous system** is made up of the brain and the spinal cord. The **peripheral** (pə RIF ər əl) **nervous system** is made up of the nerves that branch

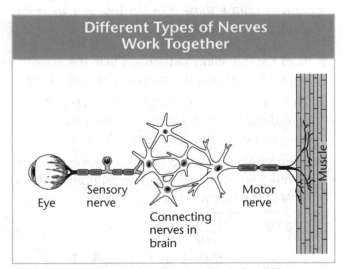

FIGURE 2. **Different kinds of nerves do different jobs in the body.**

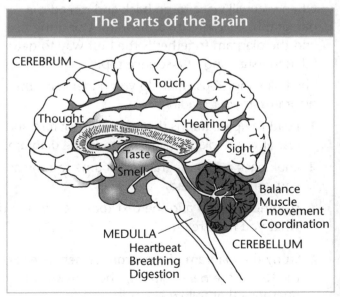

FIGURE 3. **The brain is the center of the nervous system. It has three main parts.**

out from the brain and the spinal cord. The **autonomic** (aw toh NOM ik) **nervous system** is a part of the peripheral nervous system. It is made up of the nerves that regulate the internal organs of the body.

Central Nervous System The brain is like the switchboard of a telephone system. Most of the "calls" from the outside world travel through the nerves to the brain. The brain takes in the information from the nerves and sends out orders through the nerves. Although the brain is the main control center, the spinal cord also plays a major role in receiving and sending messages to the sensory and motor nerves.

The brain itself is divided into three main parts: the **cerebrum** (sə REE brəm), the **cerebellum** (sair ə BEL əm), and the **medulla** (mi DUL ə). See Figure 3. The cerebrum is the largest part of the brain. It is divided into two hemispheres, or halves, by a deep groove. The left hemisphere controls the right side of the body. It is thought to affect the use of language, mathematics, and logical thinking. The right hemisphere controls the left side of the body. Scientists think it affects musical and artistic ability and emotions.

Information from the five senses comes to the cerebrum. It is the thinking part of the brain, where memory is stored. The cerebrum controls all conscious activity, or those activities that you are aware of.

The cerebellum is located underneath the cerebrum. It controls balance and movement of the muscles. The cerebellum also regulates how groups of muscles work together. For example, it coordinates the movements between the hands and the eyes that allow a person to catch a ball. That is, it makes the hands and eyes work well together. The cerebellum affects involuntary activity, the kind of activity that you are not conscious of.

The medulla is the part of the brain that regulates the body's internal organs—the organs inside the body. It controls such vital activities as breathing, the beating of the heart, and the digestion of food. It also controls sneezing, coughing, hiccupping, vomiting, and swallowing.

This part of the brain connects directly to the spinal cord, a long bundle of nerves that extends down through the backbone. All messages to and from the brain go through the spinal cord.

Peripheral Nervous System The peripheral nervous system is made up of the nerves that connect the central nervous system to the rest of the body. *Periphery* (pə RIF ər ee) means "outer edge." The peripheral nervous system reaches the outer parts of the body, including the hands and feet. See Figure 4.

Nerves of the peripheral nervous system work closely with the central nervous system. The optic nerve, for example, connects the back wall of the eye to the brain. When a person sees something, the eyes receive the image. The image is then sent to the brain by the optic nerve. The brain then "tells" the person what he or she is seeing.

Not all messages are carried to the brain. The nerves can bypass the brain for faster reactions. When a person touches something hot, for example, he or she doesn't first think "hot" before moving. The person moves almost instantly, without thinking. This is called a reflex action. In a reflex action, the command to move is sent from the spinal cord instead of the brain.

The autonomic nervous system controls the beating of the heart, the digestion of food, and

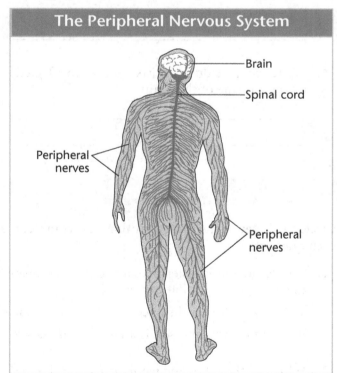

The Peripheral Nervous System

Brain

Spinal cord

Peripheral nerves

Peripheral nerves

FIGURE 4. **The peripheral nervous system branches out from the brain and the spinal cord and reaches the outer parts of the body.**

breathing. *Autonomous* (aw TAHN ə məs) means "independent." The autonomic nervous system works independently of a person's thoughts. The heart beats, food is digested, and breathing continues automatically. The medulla is the control center for the autonomic nervous system. Messages that begin in the medulla keep the body's internal organs functioning.

The **sympathetic** (sim pə THET ik) and the **parasympathetic** (pair ə sim pə THET ik) **systems** are the two parts of the autonomic nervous system. The sympathetic system works to speed up the heart and send more blood to the muscles during times of physical activity, anger, or stress. The parasympathetic system works to slow down the heartbeat and send blood back to the digestive system during times of rest. In these ways, the body always gets the power and the rest that it needs.

COMPREHENSION

1. Describe a neuron.
   _____
   _____

2. Explain the purpose of dendrites.
   _____
   _____

3. Tell how the axon is different from dendrites.
   _____
   _____

4. What activities do scientists believe are affected by the left side of the brain?
   _____
   _____

5. Explain the purpose of the autonomic nervous system.
   _____
   _____

6. Complete each sentence by filling in the correct word.

   hemispheres   involuntary   internal

   a. The engine and the transmission are among the _____ parts of a car.

   b. A globe can be divided into two halves, or _____.

   c. When the pupil of the eye enlarges in bright sunlight, it is a(n) _____ action.

CRITICAL THINKING

Circle the letter of the statement that best completes each sentence or answers each question.

1. A reflex action is faster than an action that involves thought because the nerve message that causes it
   a. travels a shorter distance.
   c. is hotter.
   b. occurs when a person is angry.
   d. is stronger.

2. Which of the following would cause a reflex action?
   a. solving a math problem
   c. deciding what to order in a restaurant
   b. seeing a good friend
   d. stepping on a sharp rock

3. If a person saw a charging lion, which part of the autonomic nervous system would react?

   a. peripheral system   c. parasympathetic system

   b. sympathetic system   d. central nervous system

4. When a person awakens from a nap feeling refreshed, it is because the parasympathetic nervous system has

   a. stopped the body's functions.   c. slowed down the body's functions.

   b. speeded up the body's functions.   d. reversed the body's functions.

5. If the heart did not have nerves,

   a. it would expand.   c. it would not be part of the central nervous system.

   b. it could not receive the message to beat.   d. it would beat too fast.

6. If a person is left-handed, which hemisphere of the cerebrum controls the activity of writing?

   a. left   b. right   c. both   d. neither

SKILL FOCUS: READING A DIAGRAM

1. Look at Figure 1. Put a ✔ on the cell body. Put a *D* next to a dendrite and an *A* next to the axon.

2. Look at Figure 2. In your own words, explain how the nervous system might work if a person sees danger and runs from it.

   _____

   _____

   _____

3. Look at Figure 3. Name the three parts of the brain and the function of each part.

   _____

   _____

   _____

4. In your own words, explain what is shown in Figure 4.

   _____

   _____

   _____

Reading-Writing Connection

On a separate sheet of paper, write a paragraph explaining which part of the human nervous system you would like to know more about. Give reasons for your choice.

Skill: Reading Decimals

BACKGROUND INFORMATION

"How to Read Decimals" explains decimals and how to read the names of the values shown to the right of a decimal point. You may not use the word *decimals* very often, but decimals are definitely part of your life. On any given day, for example, your family might buy 10.3 gallons of gas and then drive 3.4 miles to the store. There you might buy 3.5 pounds of apples and 1.87 pounds of hamburger. When you get to the cash register, the price of your purchases is shown in decimals, too—$12.74. Understanding decimals is a big help in everyday life.

SKILL FOCUS: Reading Decimals

Some numbers are written with periods called **decimal points**. A decimal point separates a number into two parts. The digits to the left of the decimal point are whole numbers. The digits to the right of the decimal point are parts of a whole. For example, the number 126.73 has a decimal point. The decimal point shows that 126 is a whole number. Since 73 is to the right of the decimal point, it represents only part of a whole number. The number 33.4 also has a decimal point. It shows you that 33 is a whole number and that 4 represents only part of a whole.

When reading a decimal, say the word *and* in place of the decimal point. The number 126.73, for example, is read as *one hundred twenty-six and seventy-three hundredths.* The number 33.4 is read as *thirty-three and four tenths.*

▶ Look at each decimal in the first column of the chart below. In the second column, write the words that show how to say each number.

WORD CLUES

A **suffix** is a word part added to the end of a base word to change its meaning. For number words, *-th* is a common suffix. When the suffix *-th* is added to a number word such as *ten, hundred,* or *thousand,* the value of the number word is decreased. A math word with the suffix *-th* has a value of less than a whole number. The suffix *-th* can be used with any place value to the right of the decimal point. The suffix *-th* makes a very big difference. A *hundred* kilometers, for example, is very different from a *hundredth* of a kilometer. If you run 100 kilometers, you have run 10,000 times farther than a hundredth of a kilometer!

▶ Add the suffix *-th* to each of these number words. Write the new words on the lines.

ten _____

hundred _____

thousand _____

Strategy Tip

When reading "How to Read Decimals," remember the names of the place values to the right of the decimal point. These numbers represent values of less than 1.

Saying Decimals	
Decimal	**How to Say It**
8.9	
33.65	
12.1	
147.98	

How to Read Decimals

A period that appears in a number is called a **decimal point**. The places to the left of a decimal point show whole numbers numbers with values of 1 or more.

```
ten thousands
  thousands
     hundreds
        tens
          ones
6   1  ,  2   8   4  .  3   9   5   7
```

The whole number in the example above is sixty-one thousand, two hundred eighty-four.

Places to the right of a decimal point are called **decimal places**. They show values of less than 1. The suffix -th is used in naming each decimal place. The places to the right of the decimal point are tenths, hundredths, thousandths, and ten-thousandths.

```
ten thousands
  thousands
     hundreds
        tens
          ones      tenths
                      hundredths
                        thousandths
                          ten-thousandths
6   1  ,  2   8   4  .  3   9   5   7
```

The tenths place is the first place to the right of the decimal point. A number in the tenths place is $\frac{1}{10}$ as large as the same number in the ones place. Think about a dollar bill. It takes 10 dimes to make a dollar. A dime is one-tenth of a dollar. One tenth can be written as the decimal 0.1 or as the fraction $\frac{1}{10}$. A dime is 0.1 or $\frac{1}{10}$ of a dollar.

The hundredths place is the second place to the right of the decimal point. A number in the hundredths place is $\frac{1}{100}$ as large as the same number in the ones place. It takes 100 pennies to make a dollar. A penny is one-hundredth of a dollar. One-hundredth can be written as the decimal 0.01 or as the fraction $\frac{1}{100}$. A penny is 0.01 or $\frac{1}{100}$ of a dollar.

The thousandths place is the third place to the right of the decimal point. A number in the thousandths place is $\frac{1}{1,000}$ as large as the same number in the ones place. This is a very small part of a dollar, and no coin is made for that value. One-thousandth of a dollar is called a *mil*. Mils are used in the financial world. It takes 1,000 mils to make a dollar. One-thousandth can be written as the decimal 0.001 or as the fraction $\frac{1}{1,000}$. A mil is 0.001 or $\frac{1}{1,000}$ of a dollar.

The ten-thousandths place is the fourth place to the right of the decimal point. A number in the ten-thousandths place is $\frac{1}{10,000}$ as large as the same number in the ones place. One ten-thousandth can be written as the decimal 0.0001 or as the fraction $\frac{1}{10,000}$.

A number with digits only in the decimal places can be written in two ways.

0.7 or .7

These two numbers have the same value. You read this number as though it were a whole number: *seven*. Then you add the name of the place value: *tenths*. The number is read like this: *seven tenths*.

ones	tenths	hundredths	thousandths	ten-thousandths	
0 .	7				seven tenths
0 .	0	4			four hundredths
0 .	6	1			sixty-one hundredths
0 .	0	0	2		two thousandths
0 .	8	3	5		eight hundred thirty-five thousandths
0 .	0	3	4	2	three hundred forty-two ten-thousandths
0 .	9	0	3	1	nine thousand thirty-one ten-thousandths

A number that includes digits on both sides of the decimal point is read in two groups.

9,295.17

First read the digits to the left of the decimal point as a whole number: *nine thousand two hundred ninety-five*. The decimal point stands for the word *and*. Then read the decimal value as though it were a whole number: *seventeen*. Then add the name of the place value of the last digit: *hundredths*. The number is read like this: *nine thousand two hundred ninety-five and seventeen hundredths.*

The number can also be written as a whole number and a fraction. The decimal number is written as a fraction. The whole number remains the same. Because 7, the last digit in the decimal, is in the hundredths place, the denominator of the fraction is 100. It is read the same as the decimal number.

$$9{,}295 \tfrac{17}{100}$$

Read the following number.

$$263.783$$

Read the digits to the left of the decimal point first. Say the word *and* when you reach the decimal point. Then read the digits to the right of the decimal point. Because the last digit is in the thousandths place, add the word *thousandths*. The number is read like this: *two hundred sixty-three and seven hundred eighty-three thousandths.* The number is written as a whole number and a fraction as below.

$$263 \tfrac{783}{1{,}000}$$

Look at the following number.

$$49.5036$$

It is read like this: *forty-nine and five thousand thirty-six ten-thousandths.*

Remember that a decimal point separates whole numbers from numbers that are less than one whole. The numbers to the right of a decimal point are always less than 1.

COMPREHENSION

1. Write the place values on the lines for each digit in this number.

1   2   ,   3   4   5   .   6   7   8   9

2. When you hear *and* in a number being read, it stands for a _____.

3. If a dollar bill is one, what part of a dollar is a dime? A penny? A mil? Write each amount as a fraction and as a decimal.

   one dime = _____ or _____ of a dollar.

   one penny = _____ or _____ of a dollar.

   one mil   = _____ or _____ of a dollar.

CRITICAL THINKING

1. Tell about the places in your daily life where you see decimals and fractions used.

   _____

   _____

2. These numbers all have the same digits. Explain why the numbers have different values.

   0.015   .0015   .0105

   _____

   _____

3. Circle the smallest value in each row.

a.	.7	.04	.71	.001
b.	.04	.102	.5	.05
c.	.317	.0146	.09	.4

4. Circle the largest value in each row.

a.	.08	.095	.2	.18
b.	.27	.41	.0896	.38
c.	.1	.09	.075	.275

A. Write each number in the correct columns. Add the decimal points where they belong.

	ten thousands	thousands	hundreds	tens	ones	tenths	hundredths	thousandths	ten-thousandths
54 and 9 tenths									
6,702 and 8 tenths									
7 hundredths									
1 and 38 hundredths									
7 thousandths									
91 thousandths									
643 thousandths									
56 and 2 thousandths									
312 and 54 thousandths									
6 ten-thousandths									
923 ten-thousandths									
1,246 ten-thousandths									
172 and 73 ten-thousandths									
4,317 and 6,431 ten-thousandths									
80,008 and 8 ten-thousandths									

B. Write the fraction for each decimal. Do not simplify the answers.

0.2 _____ 0.0091 _____ 884.18 _____

0.65 _____ 6.9 _____ 329.861 _____

0.634 _____ 45.05 _____ 25.0106 _____

0.4372 _____ 2,379.025 _____ 7,563.4007 _____

C. Draw lines to match the decimals, the fractions, and the correct way to read each number. The first one has been done for you.

.789 ——————— $\frac{789}{1,000}$ ——————— 789 thousandths

78.9 $78\frac{7,809}{10,000}$ 7 and 8,009 ten-thousandths

7.089 $78\frac{9}{10}$ 78 and 9 tenths

78.09 $7\frac{89}{1,000}$ 78 and 9 hundredths

78.7809 $7\frac{8,009}{10,000}$ 78 and 7,809 ten-thousandths

7.8009 $78\frac{9}{100}$ 7 and 89 thousandths

Reading-Writing Connection

On a separate sheet of paper, write two paragraphs describing a real-life situation in which knowing about decimals and fractions can help you.

Skill: Vowel-Consonant Combinations

The **vowel-consonant combinations** *air*, *ear*, and *are* can stand for the same sound. The words *hair*, *bear*, and *square* have the same vowel sound, but the letters that stand for the sound are different in each word.

A. Choose a word from the list to complete each sentence below. Then circle the letters in each word that stand for the same sound you hear in *hair*, *bear*, and *square*.

share	prepare	pears	stare
wear	stairs	chair	fair

1. Theo's favorite fruit is _____.

2. Clarkstown School is having a book _____ next week.

3. Jorge helped his father _____ dinner by making the salad.

4. If you _____ at the sun, you could damage your eyes.

5. My sister and I _____ clothes.

6. It is considered proper to push your _____ in before you leave the table.

7. Sarah likes to _____ heavy sweaters in the winter.

8. You have to walk up two flights of _____ to get to my apartment.

The vowel-consonant combination *ear* can stand for different sounds. The words *bear*, *earth*, and *beard* have the same vowel letters followed by *r*, but the vowel sound the letters stand for is different in each word.

B. Choose a word from the list to complete each sentence below.

clear	search	fear	early
heard	tear	learn	near

1. When Warren lost his key, we had to _____ to find it.

2. Have you _____ the news about Governor Harris?

3. We got up _____ every morning when we camped last summer.

4. Elena will _____ how to drive a car next year.

5. Please be careful not to _____ your dress.

6. Many people _____ certain kinds of animals.

7. The sky is always bright blue on a _____ day.

8. Jamal wanted to sit _____ his best friend, Mohammed.

Skill: Syllables

RULE 3: Words With a Prefix or Suffix

A prefix always has at least one sounded vowel. This means that a prefix always contains at least one syllable. You can divide a word that has a prefix between the prefix and the base word.

misspell   mis spell

Most suffixes have at least one sounded vowel. This means that a suffix usually contains at least one syllable. You can divide a word that has a suffix between the base word and the suffix.

quickly   quick ly

A. Divide each of the words below into two syllables between the prefix or suffix and the base word. Write each syllable separately on the line next to the word.

1. backward _____
2. worthless _____
3. mistrust _____
4. impure _____
5. fearful _____
6. biplane _____
7. rainy _____
8. midday _____

9. statement _____
10. preheat _____
11. painter _____
12. nonsense _____
13. nearness _____
14. redo _____
15. mistreat _____
16. yearly _____

RULE 4: Words With Two Consonants Between Two Sounded Vowels

A word that has two consonants between two sounded vowels is usually divided into syllables between the two consonants.

winter   win ter

B. Divide each of the words below into two syllables. Write each syllable separately on the line next to the word.

1. signal _____
2. blanket _____
3. master _____
4. admit _____
5. plastic _____
6. sandal _____
7. helmet _____

8. window _____
9. escape _____
10. dentist _____
11. walnut _____
12. napkin _____
13. magnet _____
14. perfume _____

LESSON 17

Skill: Prefixes

A **prefix** is a word part that is added to the beginning of a word to change its meaning. Nine prefixes and their meanings are given below.

Prefix	Meaning	Prefix	Meaning
bi-	having two, or happening every two	sub-	under or below
de-	away from or undo	tri-	having three, or happening every three
mid-	middle	uni-	having only one
non-	not	re-	again
semi-	half or partly		

A. Read each word below and the meaning that follows it. Write the correct prefix next to each word.

1. _____day — middle of the day
2. _____monthly — once every two months
3. _____frost — to become unfrozen
4. _____freezing — below freezing
5. _____sweet — partly sweet
6. _____rail — to go off the rails

7. _____angle — a shape with three angles
8. _____circle — half a circle
9. _____cycle — one-wheeled vehicle
10. _____sense — not making sense
11. _____play — play again

B. Use one of the words above to complete each sentence below.

1. It is so cold outside that it must be _____.

2. Another word for twelve o'clock noon is _____.

3. We sat in a _____ around the fire.

4. Mr. Barker had to _____ his freezer.

5. A _____ is difficult to ride because it has only one wheel.

6. I read the letter, but it sounded like _____.

7. A broken track caused the train to _____.

8. Our craft club meets _____.

9. Because they tied their last game, the two teams had to _____ it.

10. In geometry class, we learned how to calculate the angles of a _____.

Skill: Main Idea—Stated or Unstated

When you read a textbook or reference book for information, the main idea of each paragraph will often be stated in a sentence. The rest of the paragraph will contain the supporting details that give additional information about the main idea.

Sometimes the main idea of a paragraph is not stated in one of the sentences. The information in the paragraph will help you to infer, or figure out, the main idea. To do this, think of a sentence that summarizes the supporting details of the paragraph.

Read the selection below. Decide if the main idea in each paragraph is stated or unstated.

Nō and Kabuki Plays

1. Plays are an important form of entertainment in most countries. Two kinds of drama unique to Japan are Nō and Kabuki. Music is used in both types of drama. Originally, men performed both men's and women's parts in Nō and Kabuki plays. These are the only similarities between the two types of Japanese drama.

2. Kabuki costumes are fancy, bright, and heavy. On the other hand, Nō costumes are quite simple. Kabuki stages are huge and elaborate. Nō stages are only 18 feet (5.4 meters) square. The only scenery used on a Nō stage is a background wall with a tree painted on it. The audience must use a lot of imagination.

3. Nō plays started in the fourteenth century to entertain the upper classes. All parts of a Nō play must follow a certain set of rules. A Nō actor may look as if he is sleepwalking. The action of the play is slow. Certain actions stand for certain things. For example, a few steps forward mean the end of a journey. An important part of a Nō play is the chorus that chants much of the story.

4. Kabuki plays were developed in the seventeenth century for the common people. Theater was the main amusement of the merchants of that time. Kabuki plays reflect the merchants' happy moods. The players wear thick makeup and exaggerate their movements and facial expressions to communicate feelings.

5. Music is important to Kabuki plays. Kabuki actors sing, dance, and speak their lines to music in the background. Musicians play instruments, such as flutes, drums, and gongs. They also use the samisen, a three-stringed instrument shaped somewhat like a banjo. Another common instrument has two small blocks of wood that are banged on the floor.

A. For each paragraph of the selection, if the main idea is stated, write the word *stated* on the line. If the main idea is unstated, choose a main idea from the sentences given below and write the letter on the line.

  a. Because Kabuki plays are more exciting, they are more popular than Nō plays.

  b. A Nō play is noted for its rules and for the controlled movements of the players.

  c. Kabuki plays reflect the fun and showiness preferred by seventeenth-century Japanese merchants.

  d. One difference between Nō and Kabuki plays is that Nō is simpler.

  e. Kabuki actors exaggerate their movements to show emotions.

  Paragraph 1: _____   **Paragraph 3:** _____   **Paragraph 5:** _____

  Paragraph 2: _____   **Paragraph 4:** _____

B. Go back to each paragraph that has a stated main idea. Underline the sentence that states the main idea.

Skill: Following First-Aid Directions

Choking occurs when food or another foreign body completely blocks a person's air passage, making it impossible for the person to breathe or speak. A person choking on food could die in as little as four minutes. A **first-aid technique** called **abdominal thrusts** can be used to rescue a choking person. This procedure forces the object blocking the breathing passage out through the mouth.

If a choking victim can speak or cough, he or she should try to cough up the object. If the person cannot cough up the object, call an ambulance. If a victim cannot speak or cough, he or she is not getting air, and abdominal thrusts should be used. Choking victims who cannot speak should signal for help by clutching their throat.

First Aid for the Choking Victim
Abdominal Thrusts

Universal sign for choking

WHAT TO LOOK FOR IN THE VICTIM
1. Cannot speak or breathe
2. Skin turns blue
3. Collapses

WITH THE VICTIM STANDING OR SITTING

1. Stand behind the victim or behind the victim's chair if he or she is sitting. Wrap your arms around the victim's waist.

2. Place the thumb side of your fist against the victim's abdomen, above the navel and below the rib cage.

3. Grab your fist with the other hand and give quick inward and upward thrusts into the abdomen. Repeat these thrusts until the object is forced out or the victim becomes unconscious.

4. If the victim is sitting, stand behind the victim's chair and perform the procedure the same way.

5. After the object is dislodged, the victim should see a doctor for follow-up care.

WHEN THE VICTIM IS UNCONSCIOUS

1. Call 911.
2. Sweep two fingers inside the victim's mouth to try to remove the object. If this does not remove the object, follow steps 3–7.
3. Straddle both of the victim's legs.
4. Place the heel of one hand on the middle of the abdomen just above the navel. Place the other hand on top. Point the fingers of both hands toward the victim's head.
5. Give quick thrusts toward the head and into the abdomen.
6. After giving five thrusts, lift the victim's lower jaw and tongue with your fingers and thumb. Slide one finger down inside the victim's cheek and try to hook the object out. Repeat thrusts if object blocking the air passage has not been freed.
7. After the object is dislodged, the victim should see a doctor for follow-up care.

NOTE: If you are alone and start to choke, press your abdomen onto a firm object, such as a counter, desk, or table.

A. Look at the steps below and on the next page for performing abdominal thrusts when the victim is standing or sitting. They are not in the correct order. Write *1* in front of the step you would follow first, *2* in front of the next step, and so on.

_____ Place the thumb side of your fist against the victim's abdomen, above the navel and below the rib cage.

_____ Stand behind the victim or behind the victim's chair if he or she is sitting.

_____ Repeat these thrusts until the object is forced out or the victim becomes unconscious.

_____ Wrap your arms around the victim's waist.

_____ Grab your fist with the other hand and give quick inward and upward thrusts into the abdomen.

B. Read the statements about abdominal thrusts below. On the line, write _T_ if the statement is true or _F_ if the statement is false.

_____ **1.** A victim is a person who gives first aid.

_____ **2.** When food completely blocks the air passage, it is impossible for a person to breathe or speak.

_____ **3.** Abdominal thrusts require that the choking victim be slapped on the back four times.

_____ **4.** Abdominal thrusts can be done with the victim standing, sitting, or lying on his or her stomach.

_____ **5.** Someone choking can perform abdominal thrusts on himself or herself if no help is around.

_____ **6.** If a choking victim cannot speak or breathe, he or she is not getting any air.

_____ **7.** You could save a person's life using abdominal thrusts.

_____ **8.** Abdominal thrusts force food down a choking person's throat into the stomach.

_____ **9.** The rescuer faces the victim who is lying down.

_____ **10.** A rescuer may need to repeat abdominal thrusts several times to free the object blocking the air passage.

C. Write the answer to each question. Use complete sentences.

1. For what kind of emergency are abdominal thrusts used? _____

_____

2. Why do you think it is important for everybody to know how to perform

abdominal thrusts? _____

_____

3. Why are choking victims unable to speak or breathe? _____

_____

4. What do rescuers do with their hands for standing or sitting victims? _____

_____

5. What do rescuers do with their hands for victims lying down? _____

_____

6. How should you let someone know that you are choking? _____

_____

The Sea Around Us

LESSON 20

Skill: Mood

BACKGROUND INFORMATION

In "The Dolphin Disaster," you will read about a group of dolphins that become trapped and need to be rescued. Although dolphins live in the sea, they are air-breathing, warm-blooded mammals in the same family as whales. To find their way in the ocean, dolphins send out sound waves and listen for echoes. In this way, they find out about objects in their path without using their eyes.

SKILL FOCUS: Mood

Mood is the atmosphere, or feeling, an author creates in a story. Some moods might be happy, scary, sad, or suspenseful. A writer creates mood by using vivid details that appeal to readers' senses and other words that convey emotion. Often the story's setting also helps to create a mood.

Read the passage below. Notice the words and phrases that build a mood of suspense.

> *The abandoned beach house, isolated on the lonely dune, seemed too quiet as Chris entered. As he passed down a dark hallway, a door creaked open at the back of the house. A sudden chill ruffled the hair on the back of his neck.*

The setting above, an abandoned and isolated beach house, helps to create a suspenseful mood.

▶ Read the passage below. Then fill in the chart to identify the mood of the passage.

> *Sunlight danced on the warm, emerald waters of Pleasant Bay. Happy children stretched out on the golden sand or played in the gentle surf. Sea gulls soared overhead in a clear, blue sky.*

Identifying Mood	
Setting	
Details that convey emotion	
Overall mood	

CONTEXT CLUES: Comparisons

Comparisons in a sentence can help you figure out the meanings of new words. The words *like* and *as* usually signal a comparison.

In the following sentence, look for the comparison that explains the meaning of *winch*.

> *He ran the nylon rope over the **winch**, which looked like a spool with a crank at the side.*

The author compares the winch to a spool with a crank on the side. If you don't know what a *winch* is, the comparison helps you visualize its appearance.

▶ Read the following sentence. Circle the comparison that helps you figure out the meaning of the underlined word.

> *Beaching the boat, he **sprinted** up the low cliff like a runner racing for the finish line.*

As you read the selection, use comparison context clues to figure out the meanings of the underlined words *aspired*, *cove*, and *ebbing*.

Strategy Tip

As you read "The Dolphin Disaster," look for vivid details that convey emotion. Use these details to decide the story's overall mood.

The Dolphin Disaster

S*kreek!* A single sea gull wheeled across the low, gray sky. The fog was closing in on Port Hegen like a dirty cotton curtain. Most of the lobster boats were still outside the harbor. Ralph Hemming was busy setting his lobster traps when he spotted the first of the dolphins.

"Must be two hundred, maybe three hundred dolphins out there," he said, using the radio that linked his boat to shore. "Odd. Haven't seen them this close to shore in years."

Annie Sloan's voice came over the radio. "We had some up at the cape last year. A story in the newspaper said that over a dozen died. They got trapped in shallow water."

The radio crackled as another voice came in. "Hey, Ralph. Do you have Spooner with you?"

Hemming swung his rumbling boat toward a bright red float that marked one of his sunken traps. He pressed the microphone button. "He's on the wharf mending some of our traps."

"Too bad," said the other voice. "Spooner might have an idea why they're headed so close to the shallows. He knows all about these things."

Other voices on the radio agreed. Meanwhile Ralph Hemming was busy hooking up his trap line, a rope tied to the trap. He ran the nylon rope over the winch, which looked like a spool with a crank at the side. By turning the crank, the winch would pull the heavy, wooden trap up from the bottom, 100 feet below.

Ralph thought about his son, Spooner. For a 16-year-old, Spooner knew the sea well. He was always reading about the sea and its creatures. In some ways, he knew more about the ocean than some adults who had spent their lives on the water. One thing was sure, though. Spooner wouldn't fish for a living like his grandfather and father. Oh, he'd work with the sea all right, but he'd probably pursue his goal of studying ocean science. Spooner <u>aspired</u> to be an oceanographer just as much as many boys his age dreamed about becoming football players.

Dolphins! Hundreds of them arching out of the water in sleek, dark curves!

Spooner was so struck by the sight that he dropped the lobster trap that he was mending. He ran to the end of the wharf.

The dolphins were in the middle of the channel, moving toward Bald Point. Spooner strained his eyes, but the fog, edging nearer to shore, made it difficult to see the dolphins clearly.

Spooner scrambled down the worn, wooden steps to the pebbly beach. His shoes clattered on the smooth stones. The tide had already begun to go out. Pushing his family's rowboat to the water's edge, Spooner floated it and jumped in. He swung the small outboard motor into the water and yanked on the rope several times. This will be the day that the motor won't start, he thought. Finally the motor buzzed into life.

The fog was getting thicker. In a matter of moments, the dolphins would be swallowed up in the thick folds of the fog. Spooner headed the boat out into the narrow channel. He knew the waters of this rocky coast by heart. He knew that he could track down the dolphins.

Even so, Spooner nearly missed them in the fog. The narrow entrance to Bald Point Cove was only 50 feet wide, with low cliffs rising on both sides. Catching a movement in the water out of the corner of his eye, Spooner swung his boat toward land. Beaching the boat, he sprinted up the low cliff like a runner racing for the finish line.

The little cove was like a soup bowl 300 yards across. At high tide, the water in the cove was 20 feet at its deepest. At low tide, the cove was a stretch of mud.

Spooner stood looking down at the cove. Below he saw hundreds of dolphins swimming around the small pool. They darted this way and that, circling, confused. Something was very wrong.

Then Spooner remembered the story in the newspaper last year. More than 20 dolphins had died in shallow water off Cape Cod. Some scientists believed that the dolphins' ability to find their way by using echoes had failed for some reason. These dolphins must have lost their way and swum into the narrow channel by accident. Now they were trapped in the shallow water of the cove.

Spooner watched as the ebbing tide ran out of the cove like water out of a cracked bowl. The dolphins were swimming faster in crazier circles. He had to get help fast. He would head for home and get his sister Audrey. She wasn't very interested in the sea, but she was a terrific organizer. She would help!

Only half an hour later, Spooner and Audrey watched Mr. Shell push back his sleeves and lean against his counter. "Look, kids, I'll be glad to help, but I can't leave the store just now. After six, when I close…"

"Then it will be too late!" cried Audrey.

Mr. Shell was the third person in the village that Audrey and Spooner had approached. They had gotten lots of sympathy but no help. Spooner had the feeling that no one really believed how much danger the dolphins were in. Spooner and Audrey ran out of the store and down toward the town wharf.

"Spooner! Audrey! What's up?" They turned to see Paul Sequeira coming up from the docks. He was 72 years old, but he still worked his lobster traps every day, as he had for more than 50 years.

"It's dolphins, Mr. Sequeira. Hundreds of them. They're trapped in Bald Point Cove, and the tide will be out soon!" Spooner quickly told Mr. Sequeira what he had seen.

"I heard on the radio that they were close to shore," said Mr. Sequeira. "Fog's so thick, everyone's coming in now. We'll round up some help. Come on."

It seemed only minutes later that Spooner, Audrey, Mr. Sequeira, and nine others hurried to the cove. More help was on the way. Mr. Sequeira had radioed the police, too.

Water was running out of the cove like sand from an hourglass. The water was only 3 feet deep and getting lower every minute. Spooner couldn't help looking back and forth from his watch to the widening stretch of mud in the cove.

Already a few dolphins were stuck in the mud. The others swam frantically in the shallow water. In less than an hour, all the water in the cove would be gone.

How could they get the animals out of danger? Suddenly Spooner remembered something that he had read. "Form a line! We'll move toward them and herd them into the channel!"

The rescuers moved into the water and did as Spooner said. They forced the dolphins toward the narrow channel leading to the sea. Audrey cheered as some of the dolphins slipped through the opening.

More people came. They herded more and more animals out to the sea. Unfortunately the dense fog

was making it difficult to see. The dolphins still in the cove darted about desperately. They were frantic and frightened.

"Audrey!" called Mr. Sequeira. "Get out to my boat and radio for some nets. Hurry!"

Audrey splashed through the shallow water, climbed the cliff, and slid down the other side. She rowed quickly but cautiously. The fog had almost totally hidden Mr. Sequeira's lobster boat anchored in the channel. When she was finally on board, she made contact with Port Hegen. The nets were on their way, but would they reach the cove in time? Audrey hurried back.

There were about 70 dolphins still in the cove when the water ran out completely. The rescuers couldn't bear to watch the stranded animals die in the mud. They used their heavy nets to drag and tug and slide the heavy animals into the channel.

The workers were able to save about half of the remaining dolphins. The rest had been stuck in the mud too long. Already they were dying.

Later on the wharf, Ralph Hemming put his arms around his son and daughter. "You did your best, kids. That's all you can ever do."

"Aye," said Mr. Sequeira. "If it hadn't been for you kids, hundreds of dolphins would have died. Think of the hundreds that we saved."

Spooner blinked away tears. "I know we saved most of them. Yet I can't help thinking that if we knew why they swam into the cove, we could have saved all of them."

In spite of the tragedy, Spooner's dad smiled to himself. He could see that his son planned to spend even more time in the library learning about the ocean. Perhaps some good would come out of the situation after all.

COMPREHENSION

1. Identify the main character in the story.

_____

_____

2. Who is Paul Sequeira?

_____

_____

3. Explain how the dolphins become trapped.

_____

_____

4. List two methods that the rescuers use to save the dolphins.

_____

_____

5. Explain why some of the dolphins die in spite of the rescue efforts.

_____

_____

6. What is the climax, or the most exciting event, of the story?

_____

_____

7. Draw a line to match each word with its meaning.

aspired   a. small, sheltered body of water

cove   b. dreamed of doing something

ebbing   c. flowing back, as the tide does toward the sea

CRITICAL THINKING

1. Circle three character traits that Spooner shows during the rescue.

selfishness   carelessness   concern

determination   intelligence   laziness

2. Describe the effect the sighting of dolphins has on the people of Port Hegen.

_____

_____

3. Discuss why some of the people in Port Hegen are willing to work so hard to save the dolphins.

_____

_____

4. Why is Mr. Hemming proud of Spooner and Audrey at the end of the story?

_____

_____

5. Circle the letter next to the statement that best states the theme of the story.

a. Living near the sea is dangerous.

b. Dolphins often get stranded in coves when the tide goes out.

c. People working together can overcome almost any problem.

d. Most people do not care about dolphins.

1. Several incidents in "The Dolphin Disaster" have outcomes that are uncertain at first. For example, as you read the story, you may have asked yourself the following questions.

   • Will Spooner be able to find the dolphins?

   • Will Spooner get enough help?

   • Will the nets arrive in time?

   • Will the rescuers save the dolphins before the water runs out of the cove?

   As a result of these uncertainties, what kind of mood, or atmosphere, has the author created?

   _____

2. In the list below, circle the letter next to the phrases and details that do *not* develop the story's mood.

   a. *Skreek!* A single sea gull wheeled across the low, gray sky.

   b. so struck by the sight that he dropped the lobster trap that he was mending

   c. only minutes later

   d. motor buzzed into life

   e. fast-ebbing tide

   f. Dolphins! Hundreds of them

   g. darted this way and that, circling, confused

   h. water was running out of the cove like sand from an hourglass

   i. Audrey was a terrific organizer.

   j. looking back and forth from his watch to the widening stretch of mud in the cove

   k. in the library learning about the ocean

3. Setting often contributes to a story's mood. In this story, a fog "was closing in on Port Hegen like a dirty cotton curtain" and "in a matter of moments, the dolphins would be swallowed up in the thick folds of the fog." What effect does the fog have on the mood of the story?

   _____

   _____

Reading-Writing Connection

On a separate sheet of paper, write a paragraph describing a time when you worked on an important project with a team of family members, friends, or classmates. Create a mood in your paragraph.

Skill: Recognizing Propaganda

BACKGROUND INFORMATION

"Remember the *Maine*" tells about the 1898 sinking of the U.S. battleship *Maine* in Cuba, an event that led to the Spanish-American War. About 260 Americans died in the blast. At the time, Americans believed that the Spanish had sunk the ship. In 1976, Navy researchers again studied the incident. They concluded that heat from a coal fire might have caused ammunition aboard the ship to explode, sinking it. To this day, no one knows for sure exactly what happened.

SKILL FOCUS: Recognizing Propaganda

Propaganda is information that is designed to change or shape public opinion. It often twists or distorts the truth in order to convince people to believe or do something. Propaganda tells only one side of an issue. Only facts that support a group's point of view are given. To sway large numbers of people, these facts are often presented in an emotional way.

To recognize propaganda, follow these steps.

1. **Identify the facts.** Distinguish facts from opinions. Remember that a fact is a statement that can be proven or checked. An opinion is a judgment that cannot be proven.

2. **Identify errors of fact.** Look for ways that facts have been slanted to suit the writer's point of view.

3. **Analyze the emotional appeal.** Study the words used by the writer, and decide if they have been chosen to sway emotions.

4. **Reach conclusions.** Ask what the purpose of the propaganda is and whether this purpose has been achieved.

▶ The two headlines in the chart at the top of the next column appeared in different newspapers after a devastating forest fire at a national park. Read the headlines and put a check mark next to the one that uses propaganda. Then circle the words in the headline that helped you to decide that it is propaganda.

Headline	Uses Propaganda
Fire Claims 500 Acres of National Park	
Careless Campers Destroy our National Heritage	

CONTEXT CLUES: Footnotes

Sometimes unfamiliar names and words in a selection are explained in **footnotes**. Footnotes are numbered and appear at the bottom of a page. When you come across an unfamiliar word, check to see if there is a small, raised number after the word. Then find the same number at the bottom of the page. Following the number will be an explanation of the word's meaning.

Read the following sentence and footnote.

> At the same time, American **jingoists**[1] demanded that the United States show its strength by being more aggressive.
>
> [1] jingoists (JING goh ists): people who favor an aggressive foreign policy that might lead to war with other nations.

Notice the raised number 1, which is called a "superscript," after the term *jingoists*. This is a signal to look for a footnote. The footnote below it gives an explanation of the term.

▶ Read the sentence and the footnote below. Circle details in the footnote that tell you the meaning of the underlined phrase.

> These newspapers had a great influence on __public opinion__.[2]
>
> [2] public opinion: the expressed views of a group of people about issues of common interest or concern; views based not on what is certain but on what the people as a whole think to be true or likely.

As you read the selection, use footnote clues to find the meanings of the words *detention camps*, *man-of-war*, and *tenders*.

Strategy Tip

As you read "Remember the *Maine*," think about how propaganda was used to turn Americans against Spain.

Remember the *Maine*

On February 15, 1898, the United States' battleship *Maine* sat in the harbor of Havana, Cuba. Suddenly the *Maine* blew apart in a huge explosion killing 260 American sailors.

To this day, no one is sure what caused the explosion. The ship's captain gave no cause for the disaster in his report. A Navy investigation failed to uncover any clear evidence. Yet most Americans believed that Spain blew up the ship. Americans repeated, "Remember the *Maine*." Emotions ran high. Soon the American people demanded war with Spain.

Why did Americans think that Spain had sunk the *Maine*? Why were they so eager to go to war? The story of the *Maine* is an important lesson in American history.

Dangers to Peace

In the beginning of 1898, the United States was at peace. The United States had not fought in a major war since the Civil War. A generation had grown up without knowing the horrors of war. The nation took peace for granted.

✘ However, several events were occurring that were dangerous to peace. Some Americans wanted the United States to become a world power by controlling more land. These people were called **imperialists** (im PIR ee ə lists), or empire builders. They dreamed of an American empire. At the same time, American jingoists[1] demanded that the United States show its strength by being more aggressive. Another danger to peace came from several of the leading U.S. newspapers. These newspapers tried to sway their readers' emotions to support a war. They paid little attention to facts in their news stories. These newspapers had a great influence on public opinion.[2] They played an important role in the story of the *Maine*.

Cuba

The island of Cuba is 90 miles (145 kilometers) off the southeastern coast of the United States. In the 1890s, it became a focus of American interest. Businesses had invested money in Cuba's sugar fields. Politicians recognized Cuba's geographic and military importance to the United States. Americans, in general, were concerned about the political situation in Cuba.

For years, Cuba had been under Spanish rule. Many Cubans wanted independence. In 1895, some Cubans attempted a revolt against Spain. The revolt failed. Spain sent a new governor, General Weyler, to the island. He treated the rebels cruelly. He set up <u>detention camps</u>[3] in which many Cuban prisoners became sick and died.

Americans were shocked by the news from Cuba. They wanted to know more. Two New York newspapers saw a chance to sell more copies. They made Cuba a hot news topic.

Yellow Journalism

The two New York newspapers were Joseph Pulitzer's *The World* and William Randolph Hearst's *Journal*. These newspapers competed with each other for stories about Cuba. They printed shocking stories with screaming headlines. In these stories, Spain was always the villain. A group of Cubans in New York was giving information to the papers. The information was slanted, or **biased** (BY əst), in favor of the rebels. It told only one side of the story.

The stories in *The World* and the *Journal* had little to do with the facts. Instead they tried to catch the readers' attention and sway their emotions. This kind of journalism became known as yellow journalism. Yellow journalism is a kind of propaganda.

[1] jingoists (JING goh ists): people who favor an aggressive foreign policy that might lead to war with other nations.
[2] public opinion: the expressed views of a group of people about issues of common interest or concern; views based not on what is certain but on what the people as a whole think to be true or likely.

[3] detention camps (di TEN shən KAMPS): places where people are held temporarily as prisoners. In an attempt to cut off supplies to Cuban rebels, General Weyler ordered peasants to gather in detention camps.

✖✖ With great emotion, the newspapers reported about conditions in Cuba. One article read: "You would sicken at the sight of thousands of women and children starving to death in Cuba today… filthy skeletons dying on bare, foul boards." Another paper stated in an editorial: "If Spain will not put an end to murder in Cuba, the United States must."

✔ The two newspapers urged the United States to go to war with Spain. Hearst told one photographer who was going to Cuba, "You supply the pictures. I'll supply the war." The stories that the New York newspapers printed had a great effect. They were picked up by newspapers all over the country. Public opinion became set against Spain.

The Sinking of the *Maine*

Riots erupted in Havana, the capital of Cuba, in 1898. President McKinley ordered the battleship *Maine* into Havana Harbor. He wanted to protect American citizens in Cuba. Shortly after the *Maine* arrived in Havana, it exploded.

Captain Sigsbee was the officer in charge of the *Maine*. He immediately made the following report about the explosion.

> *Maine blown up in Havana Harbor at nine-forty tonight and destroyed. Many wounded and doubtless more killed or drowned. Wounded and others on board Spanish <u>man-of-war</u>[4] and Ward Line steamer. Send lighthouse <u>tenders</u>[5] from Key West for crew and the few pieces of equipment above water. No one has clothing other than that upon him. Public opinion should be suspended*

[4] man-of-war: a fighting ship.
[5] tenders: ships that take care of other ships, supplying food, rescuing crew members, and so on.

The *Maine* explosion was reported on the front page of *The World*.

until further report . . . . Many Spanish officers, including representatives of General Blanco, now with me to express sympathy.

The newspapers reported the explosion to the American people in a very different way. On page 68 is a copy of the front page of *The World* from February 17, 1898, two days after the explosion.

War Fever

No one was ever able to prove that Spain had sunk the *Maine*. The explosion may have been an accident. Cuban rebels may have secretly caused it to draw the United States into war with Spain.

Whatever the cause, American public opinion was against Spain.

President McKinley tried to keep war from breaking out. He offered a peace plan to Spain. The plan suggested that Cuba become independent. Spain turned down McKinley's plan.

War fever ran high in the United States. The newspapers continued printing stories against Spain. Finally President McKinley recognized Cuba as an independent country. As a result, Spain declared war on the United States. The next day, Congress declared war on Spain. The Spanish-American War had begun.

COMPREHENSION

1. Circle the letter next to the correct cause for the effect described in the sentence below.

   The New York newspapers reported shocking stories about Cuba because

   a. they cared about the Cuban people.

   b. they wanted to sell newspapers.

   c. they owned property in Cuba.

   d. the editors were Spanish.

2. Who gave the *Journal* and *The World* information about Cuba?

   _____

   _____

3. Reread the paragraph with an ✘ next to it. Then underline the sentence that best states the paragraph's main idea.

4. Reread the paragraph with ✘ ✘ next to it. Underline the sentence that best states the paragraph's main idea. Then circle two details that support the main idea of the paragraph.

5. Complete each sentence by writing the correct word or phrase on the line.

   detention camps   man-of-war   tenders

   a. A ship that fights or is ready to fight is

   a _____.

   b. Many Cubans died in _____ set up by General Weyler.

   c. Survivors of the *Maine* were rescued

   by _____.

CRITICAL THINKING

1. Match the words in the left column with their descriptions in the right column.

   _____ imperialists   **a.** wanted the United States to control more land

   _____ newspapers   **b.** wanted to use U.S. war power to show its strength

   _____ jingoists   **c.** wanted to sell papers by printing war stories

   _____ Americans   **d.** were convinced that Spain had sunk the *Maine*

2. In 1898, the Cuban people were fighting for independence from Spain. Compare this struggle to an event in American history.

_____

_____

3. Identify each of the following statements as a fact or an opinion. Circle the letter next to each statement that expresses an opinion.

    a. "If Spain will not put an end to the murder in Cuba, the United States must."

    b. The island of Cuba is 90 miles (145 kilometers) off the southeastern coast of the United States.

    c. The United States should show its strength by being warlike toward other nations.

4. Reread the paragraph with a ✔ next to it. Write a sentence stating its main idea.

_____

_____

SKILL FOCUS: RECOGNIZING PROPAGANDA

Use Sigsbee's message and *The World*'s front page on pages 68–69 to answer the following questions.

1. Identify the facts and opinions.

    a. List the facts in Captain Sigsbee's message.

        Facts include: _____

        _____

    b. What opinion can you identify in his message?

        _____

    c. List the facts in *The World* report.

        _____

        _____

    d. What information in *The World* report is based on opinions?

        _____

        _____

2. Identify errors of fact.

    a. What does Captain Sigsbee say in his message about the cause of the explosion?

        _____

    b. What does *The World* report that Sigsbee thinks is the cause?

        _____

c. What does Sigsbee report about the actions of the Spanish after the explosion?

_____

d. Does this information appear in _The World_?

_____

3. Analyze the emotional appeal.

   a. Does Captain Sigsbee seem interested in turning public opinion against Spain?

   _____

   b. What effect might the drawing of the explosion in _The World_ have on readers? Why?

   _____

   _____

   c. The third headline in _The World_ uses the word _enemy_. What emotional impact might this word have on readers?

   _____

   _____

4. Reach conclusions.

   a. What overall message does _The World_ report convey?

   _____

   _____

   b. What emotional effect does _The World_ report have on a reader?

   _____

   _____

   c. How might _The World_'s report have influenced the outbreak of the Spanish-American War?

   _____

   _____

Reading-Writing Connection

Look through recent newspapers and find a photograph that catches your attention. On a separate sheet of paper, write a headline about what the photograph shows. Use emotional words to sway people's opinions.

Skill: Cause and Effect

BACKGROUND INFORMATION

In "The Amazing Sea Journeys," you will read about animals that migrate through the sea. Fish and other ocean animals migrate for several reasons. Some move in search of food. Others move to reproduce. Escaping colder waters in winter is another cause of migration.

SKILL FOCUS: Cause and Effect

A **cause** is an event that makes something happen. An **effect** is what happens as a result of a cause. In a cause-and-effect relationship, one event causes another event to occur. To find an effect, ask, "What happened?" To find a cause, ask, "Why did it happen?"

Sometimes two or more causes produce a single effect. Think about the causes and the effect explained in the following paragraph. Then study the Cause-and-Effect Chart that follows.

Sadly, dams on many rivers prevent many salmon from reaching their spawning grounds. Water pollution and illegal fishing also kill many salmon on their way upstream. As a result, salmon populations are declining rapidly.

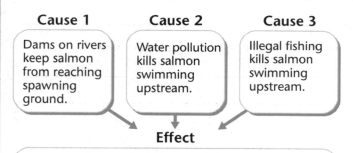

Cause 1	Cause 2	Cause 3
Dams on rivers keep salmon from reaching spawning ground.	Water pollution kills salmon swimming upstream.	Illegal fishing kills salmon swimming upstream.

Effect

Salmon populations are declining rapidly.

▶ Read the sentences below. Then fill in the Cause-and-Effect Chart in the next column.

After spawning, the salmon are exhausted. They are susceptible to infection and are also liable to become easy prey for birds and bears. Therefore, many of them do not make it back to the sea.

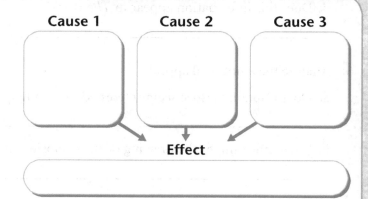

Cause 1	Cause 2	Cause 3

Effect

CONTEXT CLUES: Synonyms

Synonyms are words with similar meanings. You can use a synonym context clue to figure out the meaning of a new word.

Read the sentences below. Look for a synonym to help you understand the meaning of *metamorphose*.

Before heading back to sea, however, the eels change their shape. They __metamorphose__ into a more slender and streamlined form that is better suited for the long journey ahead.

If you don't know the meaning of *metamorphose*, the synonym *change* can help you. When animals metamorphose, they change their shape.

▶ Read the sentences below. Then circle the synonym that can help you figure out the meaning of the underlined word.

Some scientists __speculate__ that the whales find their way along the shore by trial and error. These scientists think that the whales simply swim close to shore and follow the outlines of the landscape.

As you read the selection, look for synonyms to help you understand the meanings of the underlined words *collectively*, *feat*, and *susceptible*.

Strategy Tip

As you read, look for causes and effects of animal migration in the ocean.

THE AMAZING SEA JOURNEYS

How do animals know when and where to migrate? How do they manage to travel thousands of miles to the same locations every year? Scientists are only now beginning to find the answers to these intriguing questions.

The Mysterious Journey of the Eels

Eels are long, thin fish that look like snakes. Freshwater eels are found in rivers, streams, and ponds all over the world. For some reason, however, eels migrate thousands of miles out to sea to lay their eggs. Amazingly, they always end up in the same location in the vast Atlantic Ocean. Almost all eels are born in the Sargasso Sea, a large area of the Atlantic Ocean southeast of Bermuda.

At birth, the eels are less than .25 inch (0.6 centimeter) long. They drift helplessly with the tides. Later the young eels, called elvers, begin to swim back toward the freshwater streams from which their parents came. For some of them, it is a 3,500-mile (5,600-kilometer) trip that can take several years.

When the eels reach the mouth of a river, the males tend to stay in the tidal area there. The female eels, however, may mass together into giant balls or join together to form long eel ropes. Swimming collectively against the current in this way is easier than it would be for each eel to swim upstream by itself. Gradually the eels separate, breaking off to swim up smaller streams.

✔ Eels seem determined to find the waters from which their parents came. To do so, some eels have climbed over walls. Others have wriggled through wet grass like snakes. Observers have even seen eels travel over land on the backs of frogs. Eventually they arrive at the stream or pond where they will spend most of their lives.

When female eels are between 8 and 9 years old, the time arrives for their return migration to the sea. Little is known about the biological instinct that tells eels when and where to migrate. Before heading back to sea, however, the eels change their shape.

They **metamorphose** (met ə MÔR fohz) into a more slender and streamlined form that is better suited for the long journey ahead.

Swimming downstream, the female eels join some of the males, who have remained in the tidal waters. Together they make the long trip back to the Sargasso Sea, where each female lays millions of eggs. This egg-laying process is called **spawning**. In time, another generation of elvers will migrate to a freshwater river. For the adults, however, the journey is over. After spawning, the adult eels die in the Sargasso Sea.

The Return of the Salmon

Eels heading out to sea might encounter salmon, whose migration takes them in the opposite direction. Between the ages of 2 and 6 years old, most adult Atlantic salmon live far out in the ocean. There many of them grow to be more than 5 feet (1.5 meters) long.

When the time comes to spawn, schools of salmon make their way from the ocean to their freshwater spawning grounds. The timing of the migration varies according to the river each group of salmon is bound for. The fish somehow know how to time their trips so that they can breed in winter.

Salmon always return to the streams in which they were hatched. The explanation for this remarkable ability to return home lies in the salmon's sense of taste. Even after four years at sea, a salmon remembers the taste of the stream where it was born. It follows its taste buds home.

Many salmon must travel hundreds of miles upstream to reach their breeding grounds. During the migration, they can swim up to 70 miles (115 kilometers) per day. This is a remarkable feat, considering that they do not eat while in fresh water. Their achievement is also remarkable because they must often leap up waterfalls and overcome other obstacles to reach their destination.

Sadly, dams on many rivers prevent many salmon from reaching their spawning grounds.

SCIENCE

Water pollution and illegal fishing also kill many salmon on their way upstream. As a result, salmon populations are declining rapidly.

After laying and fertilizing their eggs in the river, the male and female adults drift slowly back to sea. After spawning, the salmon are exhausted. They are susceptible to infection and are also liable to become easy prey for birds and bears. Therefore, many of them do not make it back to the sea. Those that do survive spend the rest of the year in the sea. They return to the spawning ground the following winter.

After hatching, the young salmon gradually make their way downstream. They spend some time in the river **estuary** (ES chə wair ee), the tidal area where the river meets the sea. This gives them time to get used to a saltwater diet. Finally they enter the sea, where they usually stay for four years before starting the cycle all over again.

The Long Voyage of the Gray Whales

The great migrations of whales span the ocean, from the tropics to the poles. The gray whale has one of the longest migrations of all. It spends the summers in special feeding grounds in the polar seas above Alaska. Then in autumn, it migrates back to its winter breeding and calving grounds off the coast of Mexico. That is a journey of about 5,000 miles (8,000 kilometers). Like other animal travelers, gray whales return to the same locations each season.

This amazing journey, however, may not even be necessary. People once thought that gray whales needed warm water to raise their young but were unable to find enough food to survive there for long periods. However, scientists now know that many similar species of whales live in polar waters year-round. They are able to breed and raise their young in cold water. Gray whales could probably do this, too.

Why, then, do gray whales make their long migration? Some scientists think that ancient climate changes may account for the migration pattern. Thousands of years ago, food may have been much more plentiful in tropical seas than it is today. At that time, gray whales may have lived in tropical waters year-round. Over the centuries, therefore, they established a pattern of breeding and calving in warm water.

At some point long ago, changing ocean temperatures may have caused food supplies in tropical seas to decline. At the same time, the amount of food in polar regions could have been increasing. In search of nourishment, the gray whales may have gradually moved farther and farther into arctic waters. Over time, the gray whales could have established this annual pattern of visiting cold water for summer food and then returning to their traditional breeding areas in the tropics.

Different scientists have different theories to explain how gray whales find their way through the open sea. Some scientists speculate that the whales find their way along the shore by trial and error. These scientists think that the whales simply swim close to shore and follow the outlines of the landscape.

Another theory claims that whales are able to detect Earth's magnetic fields. Whales appear to move parallel to these magnetic fields. This behavior leads scientists to believe that the whales may have a "biological travel clock" that they can set to the magnetic fields of the regions they pass through. Small magnetic particles have been found in the brains of whales. These particles may detect and interpret the magnetic fields the whales swim through.

Magnetic fields may also explain why whales sometimes get stranded on beaches. Whales tend to get stranded in areas where magnetic-field lines cross an irregular coastline, rather than running parallel to shore.

Loggerhead Homecoming

Studies of loggerhead sea turtles support the theory that some ocean animals use magnetic fields during migration. Full-grown loggerhead turtles are 3 feet (90 centimeters) long and weigh about 350 pounds (160 kilograms). Their heavy heads give them their distinctive name. Between May and September each year, about 10,000 female loggerhead turtles migrate across the Atlantic Ocean from Europe to bury their eggs on the beaches of Florida, Georgia, and South Carolina.

Once the eggs hatch, the tiny turtle hatchlings scurry into the ocean. Ocean currents carry them out to sea. Scientists know that most of Florida's loggerheads wind up in the Mediterranean Sea off the coast of Spain.

At age 20, a female loggerhead is ready to lay eggs. After swimming thousands of miles across the Atlantic, she crawls ashore at the same beach where she hatched 20 years before. How is she able to find this exact spot after so many years at sea?

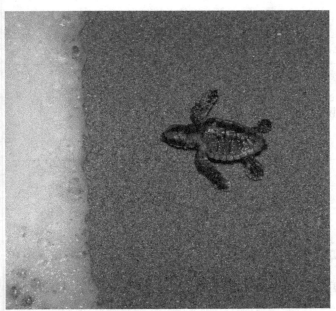

Loggerhead turtle hatchlings are born on beaches and scurry to the ocean.

Scientists suspect that loggerheads may be **imprinted** at birth with an awareness of Earth's magnetic field at their home beach. Imprinting refers to a rapid learning process that occurs in some animals soon after birth that determines the animals' behavior for the rest of their lives.

To test this theory, scientists placed loggerheads in harnesses and suspended them in tanks of water. A system of magnetic coils around the tank let the researchers change the magnetic field the turtles encountered. By flipping the magnetic field 180 degrees, the scientists tricked the turtles into turning around and swimming in the opposite direction.

Scientists learned that the first light the turtles see determines their initial direction. If that first light comes from the east, for example, the turtles will immediately begin swimming toward magnetic east. They then follow Earth's magnetic fields to find their way back home.

As scientists develop new techniques and experiments for studying animal migration, they may make more discoveries about this fascinating aspect of animal behavior. However, some facts about these amazing animal journeys may forever remain a mystery.

SCIENCE

COMPREHENSION

1. Find the paragraph with a ✔ next to it. Underline the sentence that tells its main idea.

2. Explain why eels metamorphose before migrating out to sea.

   _____

   _____

3. Describe how spawning salmon manage to return to the same stream in which they were born years earlier.

   _____

   _____

4. Identify where loggerhead turtles born in Florida spend most of their lives.

   _____

   _____

5. Write the letter of each word's synonym on the line next to the word.

   _____ collectively   **a.** liable

   _____ feat   **b.** together

   _____ susceptible   **c.** achievement

CRITICAL THINKING

1. In some ways, the eel's migration to spawn is the opposite of that of the salmon. Explain.

   _____

   _____

2. Describe how scientists might prove that gray whales or loggerhead turtles return to the same locations each time they migrate.

   _____

   _____

3. Suppose gray whales *do not* use Earth's magnetic field to navigate through the sea. Give other possible reasons that might explain why the whales sometimes get stranded on beaches.

   _____

   _____

SKILL FOCUS: CAUSE AND EFFECT

On the lines, write two causes for each effect the author presents in this selection. You may look back at the selection.

1. **Effect:** Female eels have little difficulty swimming upstream.

   a. **Cause:** _____

   b. **Cause:** _____

2. **Effect:** Thousands of years ago, gray whales began to roam farther and farther north.

   a. **Cause:** _____

   b. **Cause:** _____

3. **Effect:** Loggerhead turtles find their home beaches after 20 years at sea.

   a. **Cause:** _____

   b. **Cause:** _____

Reading-Writing Connection

Use a library or the Internet to find out about another ocean animal that migrates. On a separate sheet of paper, write a paragraph that describes the animal's migration. Include two cause-and-effect relationships in your paragraph.

Skill: Word Problems

BACKGROUND INFORMATION

"Word Problems That Have Unnecessary Information" will help you solve math word problems. A word problem is any practical problem that you can use math to solve. Knowing how to solve a math word problem can make life a lot easier.

SKILL FOCUS: Word Problems

The sentences in a **word problem** include all the information you need to solve it.

Use the following five steps to solve word problems.

1. **Read the problem.** Think about the question that is being asked. Be sure that you know what the labels used with each number mean.

2. **Decide how to find the answer.** Decide how to find the answer—by adding, subtracting, multiplying, or dividing. Decide whether you will need to do one operation or two operations to get the answer. Then write the one or two mathematical sentences that will give you the answer. Sometimes a word problem includes facts that you do not need to solve it. Do not be fooled by this **unnecessary information.** Cross it out so that you do not get confused.

3. **Estimate the answer.** Make an educated guess about the answer, based on the information given. Use rounded numbers to make your estimate. If two operations are needed, estimate the answers to both.

4. **Carry out the plan.** Solve the first sentence you have written. Then solve the second one.

5. **Reread the problem.** Does your answer make sense? How close is it to your estimate?

▶ Read the following word problem. Then answer the questions in the next column.

Mei earned $240 this week working as a guide on a whale-watch ship. That is $25 more than she earned last week. This week, Mei put $50 of her money into her savings account. She spent half of what she had left getting her mountain bike fixed. How much did this week's repair cost?

Does the question ask about this week or last week?

_____

How much money did Mei earn this week? _____

What information in the problem is not needed

to solve it? _____

Now go back to the problem and cross out the unnecessary information.

WORD CLUES

As you read word problems, look for key words that will help you solve them. If two operations are needed to solve the problem, you must look for key words for both operations.

Key words such as *and, total, all together, times,* and *twice as much* usually tell you that the answer will be larger than the numbers in the problem. To find the answer, you will need to add or multiply.

Key words such as *how much more, left, divide,* and *each* usually tell you that your answer will be less than at least one of the numbers in the problem. You will need to subtract or divide.

▶ Underline the key words in this problem that show that you have to add and then divide.

On their fishing trip, the three Crosley brothers spent a total of $125 for a boat rental, $95 for fishing equipment, and $65 for other expenses. They agreed to divide the total cost of the trip equally among themselves. How much did each brother pay?

Strategy Tip

While reading each problem in "Word Problems That Have Unnecessary Information," decide which information is needed to solve the problem and which information is unnecessary.

Word Problems That Have Unnecessary Information

Many facts have been collected about the sea. These facts can be put together to solve word problems about the sea.

Use the following five steps in solving word problems.

1. Read the problem.
2. Decide how to find the answer.
3. Estimate the answer.
4. Carry out the plan.
5. Reread the problem.

Read the Problem

The Bathysphere *dove to a depth of 914 meters in 1934. In 1948, the* Benthoscope *dove $1\frac{1}{2}$ times deeper. In 1960, the* Trieste *dove 8 times deeper than the* Benthoscope. *How many meters deep did the* Trieste *dive?*

Read the problem again. Be sure that you know the label that is used with each number fact. Are there any words that you do not know? If so, look them up to find their meanings. What question does the problem ask? Often the question is asked in the last sentence of a word problem. *How many meters deep did the* Trieste *dive?*

Decide How to Find the Answer

The problem gives you many number facts. Written as sentences, the facts are the following.

1. The *Bathysphere* dove 914 meters.
2. The *Bathysphere* dove in 1934.
3. The *Benthoscope* dove $1\frac{1}{2}$ times deeper.
4. The *Benthoscope* dove in 1948.
5. The *Trieste* dove 8 times deeper than the *Benthoscope.*
6. The *Trieste* dove in 1960.

Enough facts are given in the problem to solve it. However, some of the facts given are not needed to solve the problem. When extra information is given, decide which facts are not needed and cross

them out. In this problem, facts 2, 4, and 6 are not necessary to answer the question.

You will need to do two arithmetic operations to find the answer. First you need to figure out how deep the *Benthoscope* dove. When you know how deep the *Benthoscope* dove, you can then figure out how deep the *Trieste* dove. For the first operation, you must multiply. The key words are $1\frac{1}{2}$ *times deeper.* This is your mathematical sentence.

$$914 \times 1\frac{1}{2} = n$$

For the second operation, you must multiply again. The key words *8 times deeper* tell you to multiply. This is your mathematical sentence.

$$n \times 8 = m$$

In this mathematical sentence, the letter n stands for the answer to the first operation. The letter m stands for the number of meters the *Trieste* dove.

Estimate the Answer

Use rounded numbers to make an estimate. Round to the nearest 1 or 100.

First operation: $900 \times 2 = n$
                               $1,800 = n$

Second operation: $1,800 \times 8 = m$
                               $14,400 = m$

Your estimate is 14,400.

Carry Out the Plan
Do the arithmetic.

First operation: $914 \times 1\frac{1}{2} = n$
                               $1,371 = n$

Second operation: $1,371 \times 8 = m$
                               $10,968 = m$

Reread the Problem

After rereading the problem, write the complete answer. *The* Trieste *dove 10,968 meters.* How close is your answer to your estimate? If your answer is not close, you should start over.

Use the five steps to solve this problem.

Read: *In 1930, William Dow extracted 90 micrograms of gold from 12,000 liters of sea water. In 1965, Dr. Bayer extracted 1.4 micrograms of gold from 100 liters of sea water. Who extracted more gold per liter of sea water?*

Decide: The problem lists four number facts.

1. Dow extracted gold in 1930.

2. Dow extracted 90 micrograms of gold from 12,000 liters of water.

3. Bayer extracted gold in 1965.

4. Bayer extracted 1.4 micrograms of gold from 100 liters of water.

The question can be answered using facts 2 and 4. Facts 1 and 3 are not necessary.

You will need to do two arithmetic operations to find the answer. First you need to figure out how much gold per liter Dow extracted and then how much gold per liter Bayer extracted. For both operations, you must divide. The key word for both operations is *per*. These are your mathematical sentences.

$$90 \div 12{,}000 = d$$
$$1.4 \div 100 = b$$

Estimate: Round each number.

$$100 \div 12{,}000 = d$$
$$.008 = d$$
$$1 \div 100 = b$$
$$.01 = b$$

Carry Out:
$$90 \div 12{,}000 = d$$
$$.0075 = d$$
$$1.4 \div 100 = b$$
$$.014 = b$$

Reread: *Dow extracted .0075 microgram of gold per liter. Bayer extracted .014 microgram of gold per liter. Bayer extracted more gold per liter of water than Dow did.*

COMPREHENSION

1. In which step do you figure out which information is not needed?

   _____

2. Explain how you make an estimate.

   _____

   _____

3. What should you do if you have extra information in a problem?

   _____

4. Draw a line to match each operation to its key word.

   multiply   **a.** per

   divide   **b.** times

CRITICAL THINKING

1. Explain why a word problem might have extra information.

   _____

   _____

2. Why are labels important in word problems?

   _____

3. In the second problem in the selection, tell why the letters *b* and *d* are used.

_____

4. In the first problem, why was the letter *n* used in both operations?

_____

SKILL FOCUS: WORD PROBLEMS

To solve each word problem below, you will need to carry out two operations. Also, some problems contain unnecessary information. Cross out any facts that are not needed.

1. Read: In 1965, Americans used 310 billion gallons of water per day. By 1980, they were using 130 billion more gallons of water per day. Fifteen years later, however, Americans were using 38 billion gallons of water less per day. Americans were using 500 gallons per day per person. How much water per day were Americans using in 1995?

Decide: _____

_____

Estimate: _____

Carry Out: _____

Reread: _____

2. Read: A seaweed farm that covers 10 square kilometers produces 72,576 metric tons of seaweed. A dredging site that covers 21 square kilometers produces 272 metric tons of gold for a profit of $150 million. Is there more seaweed or more gold in a square kilometer of seawater?

Decide: _____

_____

Estimate: _____

Carry Out: _____

Reread: _____

Reading-Writing Connection
On a separate sheet of paper, describe an everyday problem or situation that you could solve by using two mathematical operations. Write the word problem and solve it.

Skill: Syllables

RULE 5: Words With One Consonant Between Two Sounded Vowels
Many words have only one consonant between two sounded vowels. This rule will help you in dividing such words. Such words are divided differently depending on whether the first vowel is long or short.

Rule 5a: A word that has one consonant between two sounded vowels with the first vowel long is usually divided into syllables before the consonant.

spider   spi der

A. Use Rule 5a to divide each word below into two syllables by writing each syllable separately on the line next to the word.

1.	pilot	_____	9.	bacon	_____
2.	robot	_____	10.	odor	_____
3.	music	_____	11.	flavor	_____
4.	private	_____	12.	major	_____
5.	even	_____	13.	locate	_____
6.	human	_____	14.	total	_____
7.	spiral	_____	15.	moment	_____
8.	minus	_____	16.	student	_____

Rule 5b: A word that has one consonant between two sounded vowels with the first vowel short is usually divided into syllables after the consonant.

rapid   rap id

B. Use Rule 5b to divide each word below into two syllables by writing each syllable separately on the line next to the word.

1.	shiver	_____	9.	pedal	_____
2.	robin	_____	10.	magic	_____
3.	closet	_____	11.	seven	_____
4.	dragon	_____	12.	planet	_____
5.	clever	_____	13.	second	_____
6.	medal	_____	14.	melon	_____
7.	travel	_____	15.	legend	_____
8.	river	_____	16.	shovel	_____

C. Say each of the words below to yourself. If the first vowel is long, use Rule 5a to divide the word into two syllables. If the first vowel is short, use Rule 5b.

1. cabin _____
2. paper _____
3. lilac _____
4. lemon _____
5. silent _____
6. lizard _____

7. model _____
8. wagon _____
9. clover _____
10. petal _____
11. spinal _____
12. satin _____

RULE 6: Words With Blends

The word *zebra* has two consonants between two sounded vowels. Because the consonant blend *br* makes one sound, it is treated in the same way that a single consonant is treated. The word is divided in this way: *ze bra*.

In a word that has three consonants between two vowels, it is possible that two of the consonants are a blend or a digraph. You treat the blend or digraph as one consonant. For example, *congress* has a *gr* blend. You divide the word between the consonant and the consonant blend: *con gress*.

D. Circle the blend or digraph in each of the words below. Then divide the word into two syllables by writing each syllable separately on the line next to the word.

1. explore _____
2. leather _____
3. athlete _____
4. other _____
5. pumpkin _____
6. detract _____

7. bushel _____
8. surprise _____
9. gather _____
10. central _____
11. compress _____
12. imply _____

When a word ends in *-le*, the *-le* and the consonant before it make up a syllable, as in *bun dle*.

E. Divide the words below into two syllables by writing each syllable separately on the line next to the word.

1. cradle _____
2. gentle _____
3. bugle _____
4. handle _____
5. dimple _____
6. noble _____

7. sample _____
8. stable _____
9. thimble _____
10. fable _____
11. title _____
12. maple _____

LESSON 25

Skill: Accented Syllables

When words contain two syllables, one of the syllables is stressed, or accented, more than the other. In dictionaries, the **accent mark** (') is placed at the end of the syllable that is said with more stress. For example, the first syllable in the word *picnic* is said with more stress than the second syllable.

pic'nic

Words that have three syllables usually are accented on one of the first two syllables. When you are trying to pronounce a word with three syllables, say the word with more stress on the first syllable. If the word does not sound right, say it again, giving the most stress to the second syllable.

com pu'ter

A. Say each of the following words to yourself. Write an accent mark after the syllable that should be stressed.

1.	peo ple	**8.**	di rec tion	**15.**	car na tion
2.	riv er	**9.**	hu man	**16.**	mo tel
3.	con tain	**10.**	im por tant	**17.**	buf fa lo
4.	chem i cal	**11.**	gar den	**18.**	ca noe
5.	pos si ble	**12.**	de vel op	**19.**	wag on
6.	fig ure	**13.**	or gan ize	**20.**	tor pe do
7.	con so nant	**14.**	por cu pine	**21.**	for get ting

Words of four or more syllables usually have two accented syllables. In the word *caterpillar*, the first syllable, *cat*, has the most stress. This syllable receives the **primary accent mark** ('). The third syllable, *pil*, has more stress than the remaining two syllables, but less stress than the first syllable. The **secondary accent mark** (') is placed after that syllable.

cat'er pil'lar

B. Say each of the following words to yourself. Write the primary accent mark (') after the syllable that has the most stress. Write the secondary accent mark (') after the syllable that has the second-most stress.

1.	sec re tar y	**6.**	e lec tro mag net
2.	bron to sau rus	**7.**	al li ga tor
3.	ar ma dil lo	**8.**	mar i o nette
4.	hip po pot a mus	**9.**	in vi ta tion
5.	cem e ter y	**10.**	en cy clo pe di a

LESSON 26

Skill: Schwa Sound

> The vowels *a, e, i, o,* and *u* can all have the same sound. This sound is a soft sound like a short *u* pronounced lightly, as in *uh.*

Pronounce *around.* Did the *a* sound like a soft, short *u*? _____

Pronounce *agent.* Did the *e* sound like a soft, short *u*? _____

Pronounce *animal.* Did the *i* sound like a soft, short *u*? _____

Pronounce *collect.* Did the *o* sound like a soft, short *u*? _____

Pronounce *circus.* Did the *u* sound like a soft, short *u*?_____

This short, soft *u* sound is called the **schwa** sound. In dictionary respellings, the symbol ə stands for the schwa sound. If you look up the word *lament* in a dictionary, you will find it respelled this way.

lə ment'

A. Say each of the words below to yourself. Write an accent mark after the syllable that is stressed. Then circle the letter that stands for the schwa sound.

1. wag on	6. gar ment	11. ap pear	16. stan za
2. a ware	7. pos si ble	12. mov a ble	17. choc o late
3. gal lop	8. sup ply	13. ash en	18. sug ar
4. eas i ly	9. ze bra	14. at tack	19. mir ror
5. ap ply	10. op po site	15. se rum	20. med i cine

Look at the words in the list above. Does the schwa sound come in the accented or unaccented syllable? Write the correct word in the sentence below.

The schwa sound always falls in an _____ syllable of a word.

B. Read the passage below. Circle the letter or letters in each underlined word that stand for the schwa sound.

Animals in Africa

Africa has many large animals. One of the largest of all beasts is the elephant. It lives in a family herd of blood relatives and travels around eating grass and leaves. The gorilla is another fairly big animal. It is the largest of the apes. It looks fierce, but it is really a peaceful animal.

The lion and the leopard are among the fiercest of the land beasts. The crocodile, which lives in lakes, rivers, and marshes, is much feared. The hyena is disliked because of its horrible shrieks.

Skill: Main Idea and Supporting Details

When you read a paragraph that is packed with information, first find the **main idea**. Second, find the **supporting details** that give more information about the main idea.

The following paragraph is about the American colonists. The main idea and supporting details are listed after the paragraph.

The American colonists were unhappy under the rule of England. In 1774, colonial leaders formed the First Continental Congress to decide on possible actions to take. They asked the King of England to abolish, or do away with, certain laws that the colonists thought were unfair. They also asked that British troops leave the colonies.

Main Idea:
The American colonists were unhappy under the rule of England.

Supporting Details:
a. They formed the First Continental Congress to decide on possible actions to take.
b. They asked the King of England to do away with laws that the colonists thought were unfair.
c. They asked that the British troops leave.

On the next page, write the sentence that states the main idea of each paragraph. Then write the supporting details in your own words.

1. The American Revolution began in 1775 in Massachusetts with confusing encounters between British troops and bands of American rebels. In April of that year, the rebels refused to let British troops march through Lexington. No one knows who fired first, but the untrained colonials soon managed to chase the British back to Boston. In June, the Americans occupied two hills outside Boston. The British eventually took both hills, but they lost nearly half their men in the process.

2. That same year, a new congress, the Second Continental Congress, decided to end British rule and govern the colonies itself. It formed an army to fight the British and made George Washington commander-in-chief. It issued and borrowed money. It set up a postal system and created a navy.

3. The idea of independence spread throughout the colonies. *Common Sense*, written by Thomas Paine, convinced the colonists that they must fight. The colonists in Massachusetts, New Jersey, and South Carolina rebelled against their British governors. A committee set to work on a statement telling the King of England why the colonies believed that they must break away from England. Thomas Jefferson, with suggestions from the committee, wrote this statement—the Declaration of Independence.

4. A young Frenchman named Lafayette offered to help the colonial army. Later France declared war on Great Britain. In 1780, France sent 6,000 soldiers to the colonies. The British kept them in Newport Harbor for eleven months. The following spring, the French sent a large squadron of ships and a lot of money. The French had come to the aid of the colonists.

5. In 1781, the colonists won the battle at Yorktown. The British General Cornwallis had marched his soldiers to Yorktown, Virginia. Knowing of Cornwallis's movements, the colonists put into action a plan that ended the Revolutionary War in their favor. Washington and his French allies pretended to move to New York, but marched to Yorktown instead. Meanwhile the French fleet took control of the waters off Yorktown so that Cornwallis could not get help from the British fleet. Surrounded by these forces, Cornwallis had no choice but to surrender.

Paragraph 1   Main Idea: _____

_____

Supporting Details:

a. _____

b. _____

c. _____

Paragraph 2   Main Idea: _____

_____

Supporting Details:

a. _____

b. _____

c. _____

Paragraph 3   Main Idea: _____

Supporting Details:

a. _____

b. _____

c. _____

Paragraph 4   Main Idea: _____

Supporting Details:

a. _____

b. _____

c. _____

d. _____

Paragraph 5   Main Idea: _____

_____

Supporting Details:

a. _____

b. _____

c. _____

d. _____

Skill: Making Inferences

If you read carefully and think about what you read, you can **infer**, or figure out, information that is not stated directly in a selection.

Use the following steps to make inferences as you read.

1. Read carefully.

2. Think about what you have read. Be sure that you understand the information that is stated.

3. Read again and look for clues to information that is not stated.

4. Put together the information stated with information that you already know. Use clues to help you make inferences.

As you read the following selection about Phillis Wheatley, pay close attention to the facts. Use the facts to infer information that is not directly stated in the selection.

Phillis Wheatley

1. The year was 1761. Mrs. Wheatley walked out of her large house on an upper-class Boston street. The wife of a successful tailor, she was headed for a slave ship that had docked in Boston harbor. Although the Wheatleys had a few elderly slaves in their household, Mrs. Wheatley wanted a slave who would serve as her personal maid for years to come.

2. Mrs. Wheatley boarded the slave ship. She found hundreds of people cramped in small, dark, stuffy rooms. As she looked around, she was drawn to a thin, frightened-looking girl in a corner. The girl had been kidnapped from her home in West Africa to be sold in America. The long journey had been difficult for her. Mrs. Wheatley paid a small amount for this sickly girl. The ship's captain was pleased because he was afraid she was too sick to sell.

3. The sad life of the young girl was about to undergo a complete change. The girl reminded Mrs. Wheatley of a tiny tree in need of warmth, food, and care. Mrs. Wheatley named her Phillis, which means "a green branch of a tree." Although the girl spoke only the language of her West African group, Mrs. Wheatley explained to her the meaning of her new name. Phillis was pleased with it.

4. Phillis learned quickly. Although she was a servant in the Wheatley home, she was treated more like a member of the family. Instead of doing hard chores, Phillis learned to read English and Latin. She hungrily studied the Bible, mythology, ancient history, and eighteenth-century English poetry. Gradually Phillis became a well-read woman.

5. Phillis started to write poetry as a teenager. Her first poem, written in 1767, was about the death of George Whitefield, a famous English preacher. When it was published three years later, Phillis became the first African American woman and only the second woman of any race to publish in the colonies. Soon all of Boston knew of her. Her fame spread to England and the rest of Europe, as well.

6. Phillis became ill in the early 1770s, and the Wheatleys' family doctor recommended a change in climate. Phillis accompanied Mr. Wheatley on a business trip to England. She met the best of British society and was well received. With the help of her English friends, her book *Poems on Various Subjects, Religious and Moral* was published.

7. George Washington became commander-in-chief of the Revolutionary army in 1775. Phillis was

delighted that the colonists finally had a strong leader in the fight against England. To express how she felt, Phillis wrote a poem about Washington. She sent it to him with a letter. Much to Phillis's surprise, George Washington sent her a thank-you note praising her for her beautiful verses and inviting her to visit him. Phillis accepted his invitation.

8. After Mr. and Mrs. Wheatley died, Phillis was left alone. She married John Peters, a freed slave like herself. However, he was never able to support the family. Phillis tried to raise money by publishing a second book. She put an advertisement in the newspaper seeking buyers for the book. Much to her disappointment, almost no one showed interest in her work. Shortly thereafter, at the age of 31, she died. Despite all of her hardships, Phillis Wheatley earned great fame as a poet in her time.

Put a ✔ next to the following statements that can be inferred from each paragraph. On the lines that follow, write the phrase or sentence from the paragraph that is a clue that helped you make the inference. Then explain how you inferred the information.

Paragraph 1 (check two):

a. _____ The Wheatleys were wealthy.

b. _____ The Wheatleys had several children.

c. _____ Mrs. Wheatley was looking for a young maid.

Clue: _____

Explanation: _____

Clue: _____

Explanation: _____

Paragraph 2 (check two):

a. _____ Many of the slaves died on the trip to America.

b. _____ The slave ship carried its passengers as if they were cargo.

c. _____ The healthy-looking slaves brought higher prices.

Clue: _____

Explanation: _____

Clue: _____

Explanation: _____

Paragraph 4 (check two):

a. _____ Phillis was not very good at doing household chores.

b. _____ Phillis had an excellent mind and was eager to learn.

c. _____ The Wheatleys allowed Phillis to read many books in their home.

Clue: _____

Explanation: _____

Clue: _____

Explanation: _____

A **suffix** is a word part that is added to the end of a word to change its meaning. Study eight suffixes and their meanings in the chart below.

Suffix	Meaning	Suffix	Meaning
-ity	condition or quality	-ous	having or full of
-let	small, little	-ship	condition of or state of
-ly	like or every	-ure	act or result
-or	person or thing that	-ward	toward

A. Read each word below and the meaning that follows it. Write the correct suffix after each word.

1. month_____ happening every month

2. back_____ toward the back

3. acid_____ condition of being acidic

4. courage_____ having courage

5. direct_____ person who directs

6. book_____ little book

7. fail_____ act of failing

8. week_____ every week

9. friend_____ state of being friends

10. invent_____ person who invents

11. west_____ toward the west

12. partner_____ state of being partners

B. Use one of the words from the chart above to complete each sentence below.

1. Karen looked _____ to see if she had dropped anything.

2. Tabitha Babbit, the _____ of the circular saw, got the idea for it while watching her spinning wheel.

3. Because a _____ is little, it often has a paper cover.

4. The _____ between Joe and Ben started in second grade.

5. Jumping into the water to save a frightened child is a _____ act.

6. The author was discouraged by his _____ to write a successful novel.

7. The drink's _____ made it taste sour.

8. Every Friday, Pete bought a _____ supply of groceries.

9. The _____ watched the play from backstage.

10. On the first month, the employees had their _____ meeting.

11. Bill and Pat formed a _____ in order to buy a toy business.

12. The wind was blowing in a _____ direction.

To locate a book in the library quickly and easily, use the **library catalog**. In most cases, the catalog will be a computer database. Although formats may vary, most library databases are set up to give the same basic information. You find information by choosing items from a **menu**, or list. The main menu often lists other resources as well as the library catalog. When you choose the catalog, a second menu will appear. You can then search for a book by its title, by the author's last name, or by its subject. If you do not have exact information about the book, you may be able to search using **keywords**. The computer will search its database using one or two important words that you give it.

A library catalog gives more information than just the subject, author, and title of a book. Usually an entry for a book gives a summary of the book's contents, a description (size, number of pages, kind of illustrations), the publisher and date it was published, and a list of related subjects. It may tell how many copies of the book the library owns, which branches of the library have the book, and whether the book is currently available.

Subject Search

Suppose you want to read a true story about survival in the wilderness. First you select *Subject* from the catalog menu to do a **subject search**. Then enter a phrase such as *wilderness survival*. A list of subjects will appear. Choose one that is the same as, or close to, the phrase that you entered. A list of books about that topic will appear. Then choose a particular book to find out more about it.

Author Search

If you want to find out which books by a particular author are in the library, you can do an **author search**. Choose *Author* from the catalog menu, and enter the author's name, last name first (for example: Miller, Dorcas). A list of the author's books will appear. You can then choose a particular book to find out more about it.

Title Search

If you already know what book you want, you can do a **title search**. Choose *Title* from the catalog menu, and enter the exact title. Information about the book will appear on the screen.

In each kind of search, the last step is to select a particular book. When you do, a screen similar to the screen in the left column appears.

Notice the **call number** at the top of the screen. This number appears on the spine, or narrow back edge, of the book. Every nonfiction book has its own call number, which tells where it is shelved in the library. Nonfiction books are kept in numerical order. This book would come before a book with the number 613.7 and after one numbered 612.06. The letters immediately following the number are the first two or three letters of the author's last name. Across from the call number is the word *status*. The information there tells you whether the book is on the shelf or is checked out.

Public Library

HOME   SEARCH AGAIN

Call Number 613.69 Mi	Nonfiction	Status: Checked Out

Author:	Miller, Dorcas (editor)
Title:	Rescue: Stories of Survival From Land and Sea
Publisher:	New York: Thunder's Mouth Press, ©2000
Description:	376 pages; ill.; 8.94 in.
Summary:	17 true stories and 2 fictional ones of people rescued from shipwrecks, avalanches, plane crashes, and other dangerous wilderness situations.
Subjects:	Wilderness Survival
	Survival
	Rescues

A. **Use the screen on page 90 to do the following.**

1. Circle the year that the book was published.

2. Is this book illustrated? Put two lines under the information that tells you.

3. If you wanted to find more books like this one, what subjects might you search under? Draw a box around each.

B. **Circle the kind of search that you would do in order to answer each question.**

1. Who wrote the book *Cowboy: An Album*?
   author search   title search   subject search

2. Which of Virginia Hamilton's books does the library have?
   author search   title search   subject search

3. Does the library have any new books about World War II?
   author search   title search   subject search

4. What is the call number for *The Forgotten Heroes: The Story of the Buffalo Soldiers*?
   author search   title search   subject search

5. Does the library have books on martial arts?
   author search   title search   subject search

6. Does the library have Laurence Yep's latest book?
   author search   title search   subject search

C. **Use the information on the computer screen below to answer each question.**

1. When was this book published? _____

2. The summary mentions survival in the desert. Under what subject could you look for more information on this topic? _____

3. Would this book be shelved before or after one with call number 613.5 FAR?

   _____

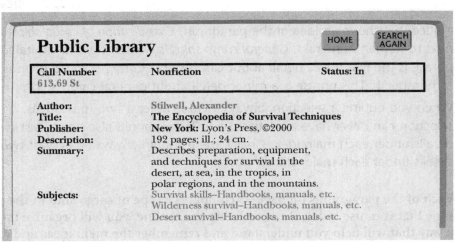

Public Library   HOME   SEARCH AGAIN

Call Number 613.69 St	Nonfiction	Status: In

Author: Stilwell, Alexander
Title: **The Encyclopedia of Survival Techniques**
Publisher: New York: Lyon's Press, ©2000
Description: 192 pages; ill.; 24 cm.
Summary: Describes preparation, equipment, and techniques for survival in the desert, at sea, in the tropics, in polar regions, and in the mountains.
Subjects: Survival skills–Handbooks, manuals, etc.
Wilderness survival–Handbooks, manuals, etc.
Desert survival–Handbooks, manuals, etc.

Skill: Outlining

> Sometimes you write a summary of a selection or of a chapter in a textbook to help you understand or study it. Another good way to understand and remember what you read is to make an **outline** of it. An outline can be written quickly and read easily. A good outline shows how the main ideas and supporting details in a selection are organized and related.

In a paragraph, the most important idea is the **main idea**. In an outline of a selection or chapter, the main idea of each paragraph is restated in a few words and written next to a Roman numeral: I, II, III, and so on.

The details that give important supporting information about the main idea are the **major details**. The major details are written next to capital letters: A, B, C, and so on. These letters are indented, or moved a little to the right, underneath the Roman numerals.

The details that give information about the major details are the **minor details**. The minor details are written next to numbers: 1, 2, 3, and so on. These numbers are indented underneath the capital letters.

Read the following paragraph. Then look at the outline next to it.

Cargo ships are classified into three groups according to the kinds of cargo they carry. Ships that carry packaged goods are called *general cargo ships*. Packaged goods include such items as chemicals, food, and furniture. *Tankers* carry liquid cargo. This might include petroleum—the thick, natural oil that fuel oil and gasoline are made from—or molasses. *Dry bulk carriers* haul products, such as iron ore and coal, that can be loaded loose on the vessels.

Cargo Ships
I. Classification of cargo ships
   A. General cargo ships
      1. Carry packaged items
      2. Examples—chemicals, food, furniture
   B. Tankers
      1. Carry liquid cargo
      2. Examples—petroleum, molasses
   C. Dry bulk carriers
      1. Carry loose items
      2. Examples—coal, iron ore

Notice that the main idea of the paragraph, *Classification of cargo ships*, is written next to Roman numeral I. *General cargo ships* is written next to capital letter A. This phrase is the first major detail about cargo ships. *Carry packaged items* is written next to number 1. This phrase is a minor detail about general cargo ships.

When you outline a selection, always include at least two main ideas. An outline of a selection can never have a I without a II. There should also be at least two major details under each main idea. Finally, there should always be at least two minor details under each major detail.

Each of the paragraphs on page 93 compares a type of cargo ship of the past with a type that is in use today. By completing the outline, you will organize information in a way that will help you understand and remember the main ideas and details.

In the early 1900s, most general cargo ships had three areas, called *islands*. The first island was called the forecastle. It held the crew's quarters. The bridge was the second island, located in the middle of the ship. The crew steered and navigated the ship from the bridge. The poop, which held the officers' cabins, formed the third island. Today freighters have one island for the bridge and the crew's quarters. This arrangement leaves extra room for hatches. With bigger hatches, it is easier to load and unload cargo.

The first oceangoing tanker, the *Gluckauf*, was launched in 1885. Built in Great Britain for a German oil company, it was 300 feet (91 meters) long and 37 feet (11 meters) wide. The *Gluckauf* carried 2,300 tons (2,090 metric tons) of oil. It could travel at a speed of 9 knots (9 sea miles per hour). Large tankers are often called supertankers today. The largest tankers carry about 555,000 deadweight tons. They can travel at a speed of about 15 knots.

During the 1800s, the first dry bulk carriers hauled iron ore on the Great Lakes. Like tankers, they could carry only one kind of cargo. Unlike tankers, however, the ore carriers hauled solid cargo. For this reason, loading and unloading were more complicated than for tankers. Tankers needed only house connections and pumps for loading and unloading. Today oceangoing bulk carriers are much larger. Most of them are loaded with more than 100,000 short tons (91,000 metric tons) of cargo. These ships need motor-driven equipment on board to quickly remove enormous hatch covers so that the cargo can be reached easily.

II. General cargo ships

   A. Early 1900s—three islands

      1. _____

      2. _____

      3. _____

   B. Today—one island

      1. _____

      2. _____

III. _____

   A. _____

      1. _____

      2. _____

      3. _____

      4. _____

   B. _____

      1. _____

      2. _____

IV. _____

   A. _____

      1. _____

      2. _____

      3. _____

   B. _____

      1. _____

      2. _____

Skill: Reading Drug Labels

Medicine can be helpful in curing an illness but dangerous if taken incorrectly. It is very important to read the **label** on the bottle or box *before* taking any medication. The label states the medical problems that the medication may help. It gives the **dosage**—how much medicine should be taken and how often. A label may also provide certain **warnings** to help prevent the wrong use of the medicine. Anyone using medication should read the label carefully to be familiar with the proper dosage and use.

Read the labels below from two different medications.

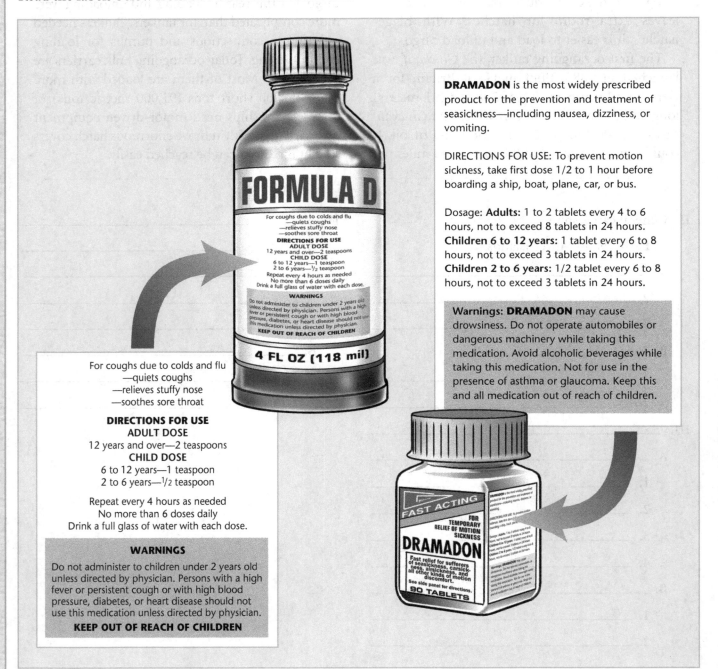

FORMULA D

For coughs due to colds and flu
—quiets coughs
—relieves stuffy nose
—soothes sore throat

DIRECTIONS FOR USE
ADULT DOSE
12 years and over—2 teaspoons
CHILD DOSE
6 to 12 years—1 teaspoon
2 to 6 years—½ teaspoon
Repeat every 4 hours as needed
No more than 6 doses daily
Drink a full glass of water with each dose.

WARNINGS
Do not administer to children under 2 years old unless directed by physician. Persons with a high fever or persistent cough or with high blood pressure, diabetes, or heart disease should not use this medication unless directed by physician.
KEEP OUT OF REACH OF CHILDREN

4 FL OZ (118 mil)

For coughs due to colds and flu
—quiets coughs
—relieves stuffy nose
—soothes sore throat

DIRECTIONS FOR USE
ADULT DOSE
12 years and over—2 teaspoons
CHILD DOSE
6 to 12 years—1 teaspoon
2 to 6 years—¹/₂ teaspoon

Repeat every 4 hours as needed
No more than 6 doses daily
Drink a full glass of water with each dose.

WARNINGS
Do not administer to children under 2 years old unless directed by physician. Persons with a high fever or persistent cough or with high blood pressure, diabetes, or heart disease should not use this medication unless directed by physician.
KEEP OUT OF REACH OF CHILDREN

DRAMADON is the most widely prescribed product for the prevention and treatment of seasickness—including nausea, dizziness, or vomiting.

DIRECTIONS FOR USE: To prevent motion sickness, take first dose 1/2 to 1 hour before boarding a ship, boat, plane, car, or bus.

Dosage: **Adults:** 1 to 2 tablets every 4 to 6 hours, not to exceed 8 tablets in 24 hours.
Children 6 to 12 years: 1 tablet every 6 to 8 hours, not to exceed 3 tablets in 24 hours.
Children 2 to 6 years: 1/2 tablet every 6 to 8 hours, not to exceed 3 tablets in 24 hours.

Warnings: **DRAMADON** may cause drowsiness. Do not operate automobiles or dangerous machinery while taking this medication. Avoid alcoholic beverages while taking this medication. Not for use in the presence of asthma or glaucoma. Keep this and all medication out of reach of children.

DRAMADON
FAST ACTING
FOR TEMPORARY RELIEF OF MOTION SICKNESS
Fast relief for sufferers of seasickness, carsickness, airsickness, and all other kinds of motion discomfort.
See side panel for directions.
90 TABLETS

A. Use the information on the labels on to page 94 to complete each sentence.

1. The medication used to prevent seasickness is _____.

2. The medication used to quiet coughs is _____.

3. You can tell that Formula D is not a tablet because the directions tell how many _____ to take.

4. Each container of Dramadon contains _____ tablets.

5. The symptoms—or signs—of seasickness are _____.

6. To prevent seasickness from occurring, you should take Dramadon _____.

7. The Dramadon label warns against driving an automobile while using the medication

   because the medication may cause _____.

8. If an adult uses the maximum number of Dramadon tablets recommended for one day,

   then a container of Dramadon will last for _____ days.

9. The medication that should be taken with a glass of water is _____.

10. If an 11-year-old takes the maximum number of recommended doses of Formula D in

    one day, then he or she will take _____ teaspoonfuls of the medication. If a 4-year-old

    takes the maximum number of doses in a day, he or she will take _____ teaspoonfuls.

11. A 1-year-old should not be given Formula D unless a _____ has recommended it.

12. "No more than 6 doses daily" means no more than 6 doses in _____.

B. Circle the letter next to one, two, or three answers to each question.

1. Which warning(s) is (are) given on both medications?
   a. Keep out of reach of children.
   b. Do not drive an automobile while using medication.
   c. Do not use if you have glaucoma.

2. Both medications have different dosages for which age group(s)?
   a. children 2 to 6 years old   b. children 6 to 12 years old   c. adults

3. How many teaspoonfuls of Formula D can an adult take every 4 hours?
   a. 1   b. 8   c. 2

4. What is the most Formula D an adult should take in one day?
   a. 2 teaspoonfuls   b. 12 teaspoonfuls   c. 8 teaspoonfuls

5. What are the benefits of Formula D cough syrup?
   a. It helps to quiet a cough.   b. It relieves a stuffy nose.   c. It makes a sore throat feel better.

Mountains to Climb

LESSON 33

Skill: Setting

BACKGROUND INFORMATION

"Triumph and Tragedy" is the true story of a young man who, in 1865, became the first person to climb the Matterhorn, one of the highest mountains in Europe. Today mountaineers use high-tech equipment and benefit from experienced guides and teachers. In the mid-1800s, however, the sport of mountain climbing was new—and very dangerous.

SKILL FOCUS: Setting

Setting is the time and place in which story events occur. Sometimes you may have to figure out the setting from clues in the story.

To identify a setting and its effect on story characters, ask yourself the following questions as you read.

- Where and when do the story events occur?
- What details about setting does the author use?
- What difficulties does the setting create?
- How do the characters overcome the difficulties that arise because of the setting?
- What overall effect does the setting have on the characters?

▶ Think of a story you have read in which characters struggled against forces in the setting. On the chart below, describe the story's setting and its effect on the characters.

Effects of Setting	
Title of story	
Time of setting	
Place of setting	
Difficulties caused by setting	
How characters overcame difficulties	

CONTEXT CLUES: Word Groupings

When you see an unfamiliar word, study the **word groupings** around it. They may name more familiar items that can serve as clues to the meaning of the new word.

Read the following sentence. Look for a word grouping that can help you figure out the meaning of the underlined word.

> *Young Edward Whymper grew up in England among hills and farmlands filled with crags and* **_moors_**.

If you don't know the meaning of *moors*, the words *hills* and *farmlands* can help you. *Moors* is grouped with other things in the same category, so you can figure out that moors are a type of landform.

▶ Read the following sentences. Circle the word groupings that are clues to the meaning of *besiege*.

> *His plan was "to return with a companion and* **_besiege_** *the mountain for so long that either it or we will be beaten." He wanted to attack and conquer the mountain, almost as if it were an enemy in battle.*

As you read the next selection, use word groupings to figure out the meanings of the underlined words *sheer*, *grappling*, and *catastrophe*.

> **Strategy Tip**
>
> As you read "Triumph and Tragedy," look for details that describe the setting. Notice how the time and place of events cause difficulties for the characters.

Triumph and Tragedy

Young Edward Whymper grew up in England among hills and farmlands filled with crags and moors. He had never seen a mountain or even climbed a hill. That is, not until he came to the Alps at the age of 20. These famous mountains stretch through several European countries, including France, Italy, Switzerland, and Austria.

Whymper made illustrations for books. He had an assignment to make pictures of tall mountains. Since there are no large mountains in England, he came across the English Channel and journeyed over land to see the mountains for himself. These towering, snowcapped peaks were like nothing in England. Out of green valleys and clear lakes, the majestic mountains seemed to reach for the sky.

It was 1860, and mountaineering was just becoming a sport. A hundred years earlier, Horace Bénédict de Saussure, a scientist from Geneva, offered a reward to whomever could climb the highest peak of the Alps. This peak was Mont Blanc, at 15,771 feet (4,808 meters). More than 25 years later, Michel Gabriel Paccard and his guide, Jacques Balmat, succeeded. Before Mont Blanc was conquered, mountain climbing was almost unheard of. By the 1850s, however, at least a hundred large peaks in the Alps had been climbed for the first time.

The sheer peaks of the Alps attracted many climbers eager to conquer these steep, towering, challenging mountains. However, the surge of interest in climbing led one concerned climber to ask sadly in 1854, "Will our grandsons succeed in the future in conquering the last of all the alpine peaks?" The "Golden Age" of alpinism, the climbing of the Alps, had begun. So many English climbers came to explore the peaks of Europe that the Alps became known as the "Playground of Europe." By the 1870s, nearly all the important peaks had been conquered.

As difficult as it may be to believe today, the earliest alpine hikers didn't realize that climbing was dangerous. They had no experience that alerted them to the particular dangers of the sport. Attempts to climb the Matterhorn finally helped people understand the dangers of mountaineering. That is where Edward Whymper returns to the story.

Located on the Swiss-Italian border, the Matterhorn looks like a sharp, pointed pyramid. Its steep face challenges even the most experienced climbers today.

After journeying in the Alps for almost a year, Whymper first saw the Matterhorn in the summer of 1861. Though he had never climbed a hill before coming to the Alps, he decided to climb the Matterhorn. His first attempt failed. Whymper was inexperienced, and the equipment he had was not good enough for climbing such a steep mountain. Even the best mountaineers said that the Matterhorn was impossible to climb. That did not stop Whymper. He resolved to succeed in his climb someday. His plan was "to return with a companion and besiege the mountain for so long that either it or we will be beaten." He wanted to attack and conquer the mountain, almost as if it were an enemy in battle.

Climbing the Matterhorn is a challenge to even the most experienced mountain climbers.

Whymper thought he had found his companion in Giovanni Antonio Carrel. Carrel grew up in Italy, at the foot of the Matterhorn. It had been his dream since he was a young boy to be the first person to climb it. Back in 1857, he had tried to climb it with his brother and another mountaineer, but the mountain proved overwhelming. Still Carrel was determined to climb the Matterhorn, and he knew in his heart that he would succeed.

The two determined men could surely make it together. Whymper went back to England, where he devoted his time to planning for the trip. He created a mountaineer's tent that could be carried. By using it, the climbers could bivouac (BIV ə wak)—make a camp—with some protection from the wind, snow, ice, and cold. A bivouac allows climbers to spend nights on steep rock faces when getting to a flat space would take more than one day. Whymper built new kinds of equipment, such as a <u>grappling</u> iron that could help the climbers grab onto the impossibly steep rock faces. He also built two ladders that could be folded up, which the climbers could carry with them.

In 1863, Whymper was ready. He and Carrel had decided that their best route up would be the Italian ridge. However, they had to wait for conditions that were suitable for climbing. There is snow on these high peaks year-round, but summer offers the best chance for success. Finally in the summer of 1865, all signs indicated that it was time. When Whymper arrived in Italy, he spoke with Carrel. He found out that his would-be companion had decided to go up with some Italian climbers instead. What had been a partnership had turned into a rivalry.

Whymper was disappointed but not beaten. He had come this far. There was no way he would turn back now. He found other companions and used his special equipment to climb the mountain. As it turned out, Whymper and his party reached the top first. Whymper is considered the first person ever to climb the Matterhorn. Finally he had realized his dream! The young man who, until five years earlier, had never rested his eyes on a mountain peak had climbed a mountain most people said was impossible to climb.

According to one account by Whymper, his cries of triumph were heard by Carrel and his party on the Italian side of the peak. Whymper said that he and another climber sent rocks sliding down the mountain to be sure that the Italians knew of their victory.

It didn't take long for Whymper's great joy to turn to grave <u>catastrophe</u>. On the way down the mountain, disaster struck. One of the men in his party slipped. Three of his companions who were attached to the same rope were pulled off the mountain with him. When the rope snapped and the four men fell from the mountain, Whymper could only watch in horror. Afterward, he described the tragic accident: "For a few seconds we watched our unfortunate companions tumble down the slope, fighting with outstretched hands for some kind of finger-hold. They were still unhurt as one by one they disappeared from view and crashed from cliff to cliff down a drop of almost 4,000 feet."

No one knows whether the rope broke in midair or whether it was cut as it slid against a rock. Some people have even suggested that a member of the

In spite of the dangers of mountaineering, most of the important peaks of Europe had been conquered by the 1870s.

party cut the rope or gave the climbers who fell a weaker rope. Historians do not believe these stories. They point out that until this time, climbers weren't really aware of just how dangerous the sport could be.

Although there had been other deaths and accidents, this disaster quickly changed what people thought about mountain climbing. People all over the world heard about the accident. Climbers and nonclimbers began to realize how truly dangerous the pursuit of mountain peaks could be.

The more people climbed mountains, the more accidents happened. People died from slipping off footholds or from pieces of mountain breaking off the main rock face. They were killed by exposure to the wind and cold and by equipment failures. Accidents in which people were injured but not killed made the trip much more dangerous for those in the party who had to carry the injured person. Climbing down a sheer rock wall was already a life-risking course of action. Trying to do it while carrying a badly hurt climber was even more dangerous.

In 1896, near Vienna, Austria, three climbers were buried by an avalanche. After this tragedy, the first mountain-rescue service was founded. The service responds to climbers all over the world, and its members have been called "The Angels of the Mountains."

Today's climbers wear up-to-date safety equipment. They train and practice before attempting to climb great peaks. Lightweight but warm clothes, shoes with spikes, and belts that help hold hikers to the mountain are just some of the modern inventions that now help climbers. In addition, climbing clubs and schools around the world teach people proper safety techniques. In the United States, there are even indoor climbing clubs, where people can practice climbing with the safety of soft mats to cushion their falls.

Of course, climbing remains dangerous. Avalanches, snowstorms, equipment failures, and carelessness still cause injuries and deaths. However, the sport has come a long way since Whymper's climb of triumph and tragedy.

COMPREHENSION

1. Who was Edward Whymper?

_____

_____

2. Who was Whymper's rival from Italy?

_____

_____

3. Explain why Whymper's first attempt to climb the Matterhorn was unsuccessful.

_____

_____

4. Why did Whymper need years of preparation before he was ready to return to the Matterhorn?

_____

_____

5. Describe the kind of equipment that Whymper built to help him in his climb.

_____

_____

_____

6. Tell what Whymper and his party did when they reached the top of the Matterhorn.

_____

_____

_____

7. Circle the word that best describes the mood or atmosphere in this story.

adventurous   humorous   peaceful

8. Answer each question by writing *yes* or *no* on the line provided.

   a. Should a beginning skier learn to ski on a mountain's <u>sheer</u> slopes? _____

   b. Could a sailor use a <u>grappling</u> tool to anchor his boat to another boat? _____

   c. Would a wonderful birthday party be a <u>catastrophe</u>? _____

CRITICAL THINKING

1. Explain why you think Whymper thought that Carrel was his rival.

_____

_____

2. Tell why mountain climbers might tie ropes around themselves that attach them to one another.

_____

_____

3. Describe how you think Whymper felt when he returned from climbing the Matterhorn.

_____

_____

4. Whymper had resolved "to return with a companion and besiege the mountain for so long that either it or we will be beaten." Describe which happened.

_____

_____

5. Circle three character traits demonstrated by Edward Whymper in his climb of the Matterhorn.

   determination   laziness   shyness

   inventiveness   resolve   fearfulness

6. **a.** Using the illustration on page 98, describe in one sentence the clothing climbers wore in the mid-1800s.

_____

_____

   b. Using details from the story, how do you think modern climbers would be dressed?

_____

_____

7. Do you think that Edward Whymper would have wanted to climb the Matterhorn again? Explain your answer.

_____

_____

SKILL FOCUS: SETTING

Use information in the story, the photograph on page 97, and the illustration on page 98 to answer the following questions.

1. Identify where and when Edward Whymper's climb took place.

_____

_____

2. **a.** Using details from the story, describe the setting in one sentence.

_____

_____

b. Using details from the photograph, describe the setting in one sentence.

_____

_____

3. What difficulties did the setting create for Whymper and his party?

_____

_____

4. Explain how Whymper prepared for the setting.

_____

_____

5. Describe the effect the setting had on Whymper and his party.

_____

_____

Reading-Writing Connection
Think of a sport that can be dangerous. On a separate sheet of paper, write a paragraph describing some of the safety equipment recommended for this sport.

Skill: Reading a Map

BACKGROUND INFORMATION

"The Great Mountain Ranges of the World" describes eight of Earth's major mountain ranges. To be a mountain, a landform must rise at least 2,000 feet (600 meters) above sea level. Usually mountains rise together in groups called ranges. Life in high mountains is hard. For one thing, the air is thinner than at sea level, making breathing more difficult. In addition, many high mountains are snow-covered year-round and support little plant life.

SKILL FOCUS: Reading a Map

There are many types of maps. You may be familiar with road maps, bus or train maps, or even maps of a mall. Social studies textbooks have many types of maps. Some are political maps, showing the cities and states of a country. Others show population, rainfall, or the products of a region.

A **relief map** is another type of map. It shows the differences in height of various parts of the earth's surface. Some landforms, such as mountains, rise high into the air. Other landforms, such as valleys and plains, are low. A relief map shows these differences.

The height of a landform is called its **elevation**. Elevation is measured in feet or meters above sea level. The elevation at sea level is zero feet or meters. Relief maps use different colors to show different elevations. Each relief map has a **key** that shows these colors. The key indicates the range of elevations that each color on the map stands for.

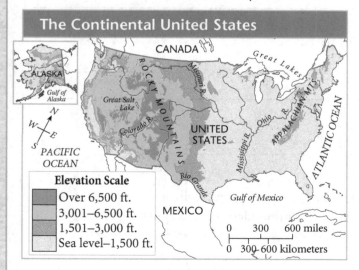

The Continental United States

Elevation Scale
- Over 6,500 ft.
- 3,001–6,500 ft.
- 1,501–3,000 ft.
- Sea level–1,500 ft.

An **elevation illustration** is another way to compare the heights of landforms. This type of illustration makes it possible to compare landforms that are not close together geographically. An elevation illustration has a **vertical elevation scale**. At the bottom of the scale is sea level. Landforms, such as mountains, are drawn to their proper heights according to the scale.

▶ Look at the map of the United States on this page. What type of map is it? How do you know?

_____

_____

CONTEXT CLUES: Details

Details in surrounding sentences often serve as clues that can help you figure out the meanings of new words. In the sentences below, look for details that show the meaning of the underlined word.

The Rockies were formed millions of years ago when there was a great __upheaval__ in the earth's crust. Hot, liquid rock inside the earth pushed the crust upward thousands of feet above sea level, forming the Rockies.

The meaning of *upheaval* in the first sentence is explained by details in the sentence that follows it.

▶ Circle the details below that help show the meaning of *obstacle*.

The Rockies were an __obstacle__ for settlers in the East who wanted to move to the West. The difficulty of crossing this huge wall of mountains discouraged the settlers.

As you read the selection, use details to figure out the meanings of the underlined words *avalanche*, *moderate*, and *eke*.

Strategy Tip

As you read "The Great Mountain Ranges of the World," study the elevation illustration and the relief map. Using them along with the text will help you to compare the elevations of various landforms.

The Great Mountain Ranges of the World

During the long history of Earth, the mighty forces of nature have been tirelessly at work. These natural forces have shaped the landscape of our world. Among nature's greatest works of art are mountains. Eight major mountain ranges crown the continents of Earth. To the people who live among them, these mountains are things of both beauty and danger.

The Rocky Mountains

The largest mountain range in North America is the Rocky Mountains. This range stretches for more than 3,000 miles (4,800 kilometers) from Canada's Yukon Territory to New Mexico. In places, the Rockies are 350 miles (560 kilometers) wide. The highest peak is Mount Elbert in Colorado. It rises 14,433 feet (4,399 meters) above sea level. (See elevation illustration below.)

The Rockies were formed millions of years ago when there was a great upheaval in the earth's crust. Hot, liquid rock inside the earth pushed the crust upward thousands of feet above sea level, forming the Rockies. Glaciers, wind, and rain have, over time, carved them into a variety of shapes and sizes. The Rockies form a huge, high wall. For this reason, they are called the **Continental Divide**. On one side of the Divide, rivers flow east toward the Gulf of Mexico and the Atlantic Ocean. On the other side, rivers flow west toward the Pacific.

The Rockies were an obstacle for settlers in the East who wanted to move to the West. The difficulty of crossing this huge wall of mountains discouraged the settlers. When the South Pass was discovered, however, wagons could cross the mountains more easily, opening the West to settlement.

SOCIAL STUDIES

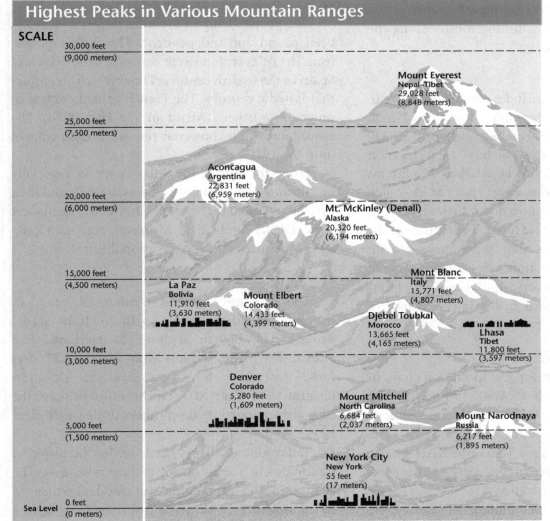

Highest Peaks in Various Mountain Ranges

The highest mountain in the world, Mount Everest, towers over the peaks of other ranges.

The Appalachian Mountains

The Appalachian (AP ə LAY chee ən) Mountains stretch through eastern North America from Quebec in the north to Alabama in the south. This mountain range is more than 1,500 miles (2,400 kilometers) long. The Appalachians are a relatively low range. Their highest point is Mount Mitchell in North Carolina, 6,684 feet (2,037 meters) above sea level. (See elevation illustration.)

The Appalachians also stood as a barrier to early pioneers as they tried to settle the continent. In the late 1700s, Daniel Boone led a group of settlers through the Cumberland Gap in Kentucky to open up for settlement the land west of the Appalachians.

Today hikers can walk 2,000 miles (3,200 kilometers) through the range on the Appalachian Trail. This trail is a marked footpath that stretches from Maine to Georgia, running mostly along the crest of the mountains.

The Alaskan Mountains

The Alaskan range includes the highest peak in North America, Mount McKinley, also called Denali (də NAHL ee). McKinley reaches a height of 20,320 feet (6,194 meters) above sea level (see elevation illustration on Page 103). The Alaskan Mountains are truly Arctic mountains. Huge rivers of ice, called **glaciers** (GLAY shərz), move down their slopes and fill the valleys with great ice fields. The climate of the range is so threatening that some areas remain unmapped. The Alaskan mountains contain some of the most beautiful scenery in the world. Mount McKinley National Park is in the northern part of the range.

The Andes Mountains

The Andes form the longest mountain chain in the world. It stretches 4,500 miles (7,200 kilometers) from the northern tip to the southern tip of South America along its west coast. The highest peak is Aconcagua (ah kawn KAH gwah), which stands 22,831 feet (6,959 meters) above sea level. (See elevation illustration.)

The Andes were formed millions of years ago by a great uplift of the earth's crust. Many active volcanoes in the Andes can still spread disaster when they explode with fire and liquid rock.

The native people of South America live in many of the high regions of the Andes. Because of the altitude, the air is very thin. These native South Americans have adapted to their environment over the centuries. They have larger-than-average lungs to take in more air. They also have 20 percent more blood than a lowlander, which allows them to carry more oxygen to their body cells.

The Atlas Mountains

The Atlas range in northwest Africa is rich in legend and history. Ancient Greeks believed that the mountains were the home of a giant, or Titan, named Atlas. Atlas was thought to hold up the heavens on his mighty shoulders. For many centuries, the Atlas Mountains were a mystery because they were impossible to cross.

The people living in the Atlas range have always been proud and independent. The Berber people from the Atlas region swept across North Africa and Spain in the twelfth century. They created an empire that lasted a century. The French gained control of much of northern Africa in the late 1800s. The mountain people, however, resisted French control until the 1930s.

From the north, the Atlas range is especially beautiful. The mountains begin as foothills and then climb higher and higher on the horizon. The highest peak, Djebel Toubkal in Morocco, reaches 13,665 feet (4,165 meters). (See elevation illustration.)

The Alps

The Alps are the largest mountain range in Europe, extending from northern Italy across Austria, the Balkan regions, Switzerland, and France. The highest peak is Mont Blanc, 15,771 feet (4,807 meters) above sea level(see elevation illustration on Page 103). The beautiful peaks of the Alps are separated by deep valleys dotted with clear lakes.

Today alpine villages nestle under the towering mountains in scenes out of picture postcards. The beauty of the mountains can suddenly turn to terror, however. In winter and spring, an avalanche is a common occurrence. During an avalanche, tons of snow and ice suddenly break off the mountains

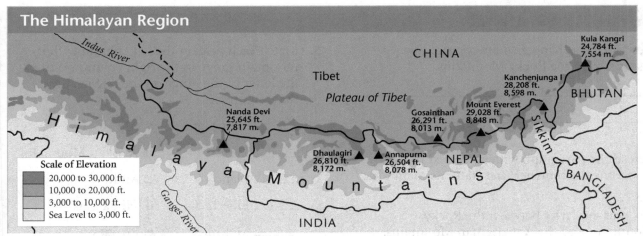

The Himalayan Region

Kula Kangri
24,784 ft.
7,554 m.

CHINA

Tibet

Kanchenjunga I
28,208 ft.
8,598 m.

BHUTAN

Plateau of Tibet

Nanda Devi
25,645 ft.
7,817 m.

Gosainthan
26,291 ft.
8,013 m.

Mount Everest
29,028 ft.
8,848 m.

Sikkim

H i m a l a y a

Dhaulagiri
26,810 ft.
8,172 m.

Annapurna
26,504 ft.
8,078 m.

NEPAL

BANGLADESH

M o u n t a i n s

Indus River

Ganges River

INDIA

Scale of Elevation
20,000 to 30,000 ft.
10,000 to 20,000 ft.
3,000 to 10,000 ft.
Sea Level to 3,000 ft.

The Himalayas rise sharply from the plains of India and the Plateau of Tibet.

and slide into the valleys below. The force of the snow can destroy everything in its path. To protect themselves, villagers plant trees and erect snow fences around their homes. Mountain roads are sheltered by snow sheds. Still, avalanches claim many lives every year in the Alps.

The Ural Mountains

The Ural Mountains stretch for about 1,500 miles (2,400 kilometers) through Russia and Kazakhstan. The Urals form a north-to-south line that is often considered the dividing point between Europe and Asia. Because the Urals are very old mountains that have been worn down by time, they are of only <u>moderate</u> height. Their rounded hills are generally low and rolling, with steeper slopes on the eastern side. In the north, they average 3,300 to 3,600 feet (1,000 to 1,100 meters) high. The highest point is Mount Narodnaya at 6,217 feet (1,895 meters) above sea level. (See elevation illustration.)

Much of the Ural range is covered by thick forests. Within the mountains are rich mineral deposits. As early as the 1500s, miners found salt, silver, and gold in the Urals. In the 1800s, the mountains became a famous source of gemstones. Takovaya emeralds are especially prized. During World War II, the Urals supplied the Soviet Union with such valuable resources as iron, copper, asbestos, and potash. Today the Ural range is a leading industrial region.

The Himalaya Mountains

The Himalayas are truly the giants of Earth. They form the highest mountain range in the

world. Located in Asia, the Himalayas stretch across parts of Pakistan, Kashmir, India, China, Nepal, and Bhutan. The Himalayas are also the world's youngest mountain range. They are still being pushed higher by earthquakes and other forces.

The Himalayas are a complex and beautiful group of mountains. There are many famous peaks in the range, but the most famous of all is Everest. Mount Everest is the highest mountain in the world. It reaches an altitude of 29,028 feet (8,848 meters). (See elevation illustration.)

The name *Himalaya* comes from the Sanskrit language and means "house of snow." For several different groups of people, the Himalayas are home. In some areas of the mountains, holy men of the Hindu and Buddhist religions live in mountain monasteries. In the Tibetan Himalayas, **nomadic** (noh MAD ik), or wandering, groups live as herders of yaks. Yaks provide them with wool, leather, milk, cheese, meat, and transportation. On the lower slopes of the Himalayas in Nepal, native Sherpas <u>eke</u> out a living as herders and farmers. They have a difficult time raising crops. The farmers cut terraces, like huge steps in the mountainside, to make room for the crops. Rice, wheat, corn, and lentils are the chief terrace crops. They also grow barley, jute, pepper, and tobacco. Sherpas are often among the climbers on Mount Everest.

All the great mountains of the world have now been conquered by mountaineers. Even Everest, the roof of the world, has been scaled many times.

1. Describe what happened after a pass was discovered in the Rocky Mountains.

   _____

   _____

2. Reread the paragraph with an ✘ next to it. Underline the sentence that states its main idea.

3. List one similarity between the Rocky Mountains and the Appalachian Mountains.

   _____

   _____

4. List one similarity and one difference between the Berbers group and the Sherpa herders.

   _____

   _____

   _____

   _____

5. Match each peak in the left column with its mountain range in the right column. Write the letter of the range on the line next to the mountain.

   _____ Aconcagua   **a.** Alps

   _____ Everest   **b.** Alaskan Mountains

   _____ Blanc   **c.** Andes

   _____ Elbert   **d.** Himalayas

   _____ McKinley   **e.** Rockies

6. Complete each sentence with the correct word below.

   avalanche   moderate   eke

   a. Actors without acting jobs often _____ out livings as waiters.

   b. A(n) _____ amount of rainfall is neither very great nor very small.

   c. The mountain was closed to skiers because of a(n) _____.

1. **a.** Which of the eight great mountain ranges is farthest north? _____

   b. How does its location affect its climate?

   _____

   _____

2. Explain why mountains no longer prevent travel as they used to do.

   _____

   _____

3. Many peoples living on mountains have lived the same way for hundreds of years. Give a reason why their lives might not have changed as much as those of other people.

   _____

   _____

4. Reread the paragraph with a ✔. Write a sentence stating its main idea.

   _____

   _____

A. Study the relief map of the Himalayas on page 105. Read the map key. Then answer the questions that follow.

1. How many elevation ranges are shown on this map? _____

2. **a.** What is the highest elevation range shown? _____

   b. What is the lowest elevation range shown? _____

3. In which elevation range is Mount Everest? _____

4. Which area has the higher elevation, the Tibetan plateau to the north of the Himalayas or the Indian plain to the south of the Himalayas? _____

5. How many peaks shown are higher than 25,000 feet? _____

B. Turn to the elevation illustration on page 103. Study the elevation scale and the mountain peaks. Then answer the questions that follow.

1. Which mountain shown has the lowest elevation? What is its elevation?

   _____

2. Which mountain has an approximate elevation of 20,000 feet (6,000 meters)?

   _____

3. Which two mountains are close in elevation to Mount Elbert?

   _____

4. What is the approximate difference of elevation between Mount Everest and Aconcagua?

   _____

5. Which city shown in the illustration is closest to sea level?

   _____

6. Which city shown in the illustration has the highest elevation?

   _____

Reading-Writing Connection

Research facts about mountain ranges in or near your own state. On a separate sheet of paper, write a paragraph describing the highest peaks in the range, and explain how the mountains affect the climate and economy of surrounding areas.

Skill: Cause and Effect

BACKGROUND INFORMATION

"The Theory of Plate Tectonics" describes a scientific theory that explains why the continents and oceans have their present shapes. Scientists believe that the oceans and continents lie on giant slabs of rock called tectonic plates. These plates, scientists say, move between 1 and 5 centimeters (0.39 and 1.97 inches) each year. This movement causes earthquakes and volcanoes.

SKILL FOCUS: Cause and Effect

A **cause** is an event that makes something happen. An **effect** is what happens as a result of a cause. To find an effect, ask, "What happened?" To find a cause, ask, "Why did it happen?" The words *because*, *since*, *due to*, and *as a result* often signal cause-and-effect relationships.

Often a single cause has more than one effect.

Cause

Hot liquid rock erupts out of underwater volcanic mountains.

Effect 1

The eruption pushes the earth's plates apart.

Effect 2

The liquid rock cools and hardens into new crust.

Sometimes an effect can be the result of more than one cause.

Cause 1

Scientists observed that continents look as if they could fit together like a jigsaw puzzle.

Cause 2

Scientists observed similar rocks and fossils on continents that are now far apart.

Effect

Scientists created a theory that all the continents had once been joined together as one landmass.

▶ Read the following sentences. Circle the two effects. Underline the one cause.

When two tectonic plates pull apart, an earthquake can result. This movement can also cause volcanic eruptions.

CONTEXT CLUES: Antonyms

Antonyms are words with opposite meanings. As you read, you can sometimes find a nearby antonym to help you figure out the meaning of a new word.

In the following sentence, look for an antonym that can help you figure out the meaning of *debatable*.

*Although scientists are certain of the boundaries of the plates, the question of how the plates move is still **debatable**.*

If you do not know the meaning of *debatable*, the word *certain* can help you figure it out. *Debatable* and *certain* are antonyms. *Debatable* means "open to debate" or "not certain."

▶ Read the following sentences. Circle the antonym that helps you figure out the meaning of *segmented*.

*It begins with the idea that the crust of the earth is not continuous, but **segmented**. According to the theory, the earth is made up of seven major plates, or sections, and several smaller plates.*

In the selection, use antonyms to figure out the meanings of the underlined words *rifts*, *advocated*, and *gradually*.

Strategy Tip

As you read "The Theory of Plate Tectonics," look for cause-and-effect relationships. The maps and diagrams in the selection, along with the text, will help you recognize causes and effects.

The Theory of Plate Tectonics

A theory is an explanation of observed facts. Scientists base their theories on facts that have been observed or examined. Theories are always subject to change if new evidence is found that contradicts them. The most recent theory about the movement of the earth's crust is the theory of **plate tectonics** (tek TAHN iks). It begins with the idea that the crust of the earth is not continuous but segmented. According to the theory, the earth is made up of seven major plates, or sections, and several smaller plates. These plates make up the topmost, solid part of the earth. The topmost part of the earth is called the **lithosphere** (LITH ə sfir). It covers the floor of the oceans and all the continents.

The seven major lithospheric plates are the Pacific, the North American, the South American, the Eurasian, the African, the Antarctic, and the Australian. The boundaries of the continents are not necessarily the same as the boundaries of the plates. For example, the eastern edge of North America and the western edge of Europe are not the boundaries of plates. The plates that these continents rest on extend into the Atlantic Ocean. These plates include part of the ocean floor. (See Figure 1.)

Two of the smaller plates are the Caribbean and the Arabian. The Arabian plate includes the Arabian Peninsula, the Red Sea, and the Persian Gulf. The Caribbean plate lies between North America and South America.

Although scientists are certain of the boundaries of the plates, the question of how the plates move is still debatable. Many scientists believe that the lithospheric plates float like rafts on the **asthenosphere** (as THEN ə sfir), the layer of the

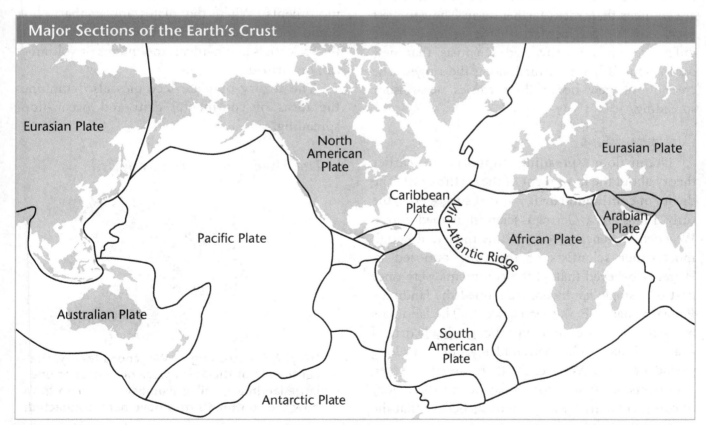

Major Sections of the Earth's Crust

Eurasian Plate

North American Plate

Eurasian Plate

Caribbean Plate

Mid-Atlantic Ridge

Arabian Plate

Pacific Plate

African Plate

Australian Plate

South American Plate

Antarctic Plate

FIGURE 1. **This map shows the seven major lithospheric plates and two smaller plates. The Mid-Atlantic Ridge is one of the midocean ridges.**

SCIENCE

earth beneath them. The asthenosphere is made up of hot, liquid rock. The hot liquid and gases flow outward from the inner part of the asthenosphere. This flow of hot, liquid rock below the lithosphere causes the plates to move.

Ocean-Floor Spreading

Mid-ocean ridges are large systems of underwater volcanic mountains. They are found in all the oceans. Deep <u>rifts</u> run through the center of these otherwise solid ridges. When hot, liquid rock flows up from the asthenosphere, it erupts, or explodes upward out of the rifts. This action pushes the plates apart. When the liquid rock, or lava, cools and hardens, new crust is formed. The eruption of lava from between plates can cause the opposite edges of the plates to be pushed down into the asthenosphere. (See Figure 2.) This process is called **ocean-floor spreading**. The theory of plate tectonics resulted in part from scientists' discovery of ocean-floor spreading.

In the 1950s, scientists discovered that rocks directly next to the mid-ocean ridges on either side are younger than rocks farther away. The youngest rocks are in the center of the ridges. These differences in age convinced scientists that new ocean floor is being formed along the ridges. The creation of new ocean floor causes ocean-floor spreading.

Continental Drift

Ocean-floor spreading supports an earlier theory about the movement of the earth's crust. The theory of **continental drift** was first suggested in the early 1900s by a German scientist named Alfred Wegener. Wegener <u>advocated</u> this theory, although most other scientists of the time opposed it. Wegener believed that all the continents were once part of a single landmass. He named the landmass **Pangaea** (pan JEE ə). (See Figure 3.) The landmass broke into separate continents that <u>gradually</u> drifted apart. This did not happen suddenly, but over a long period of time. As a result, there are now seven continents. Most scientists today accept the theory of continental drift. Many scientists believe that the continents are still drifting.

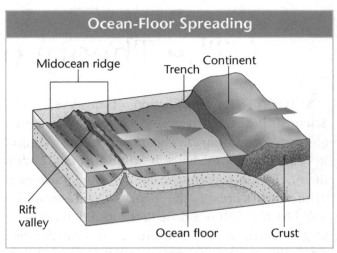

FIGURE 2. **This diagram shows the process of ocean-floor spreading. This discovery, in part, brought about the theory of plate tectonics.**

The theory of plate tectonics is of great interest to scientists today because it helps explain many natural events. For example, earthquakes can be caused by crustal plates sliding past each other, moving apart, or colliding. Volcanic activity and mountain building are also related to such movements. When the plates move apart, hot, liquid rock can erupt from the asthenosphere. As the rock cools and hardens, mountains or volcanoes can be formed.

The theory of plate tectonics also combines the ideas of continental drift and ocean-floor spreading.

The Theory of Continental Drift

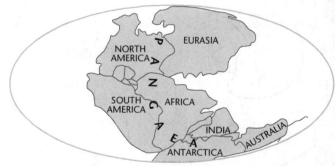

FIGURE 3. **According to Wegener's theory, the continents of the Earth were once part of one large landmass, called Pangaea. This map shows how the continents may have been connected.**

1. What is a theory?

   _____

2. Define the term *lithosphere*.

   _____

3. How many major plates make up Earth's crust?

   _____

4. Tell what the asthenosphere is made up of.

   _____

5. What are mid-ocean ridges?

   _____

6. What natural events can be explained by the movement of crustal plates?

   _____

   _____

7. Decide if each statement is true or false. Write *T* or *F* on the line.

   _____ **a.** Lightning hitting a wooded area could result in <u>rifts</u> in trees.

   _____ **b.** If you <u>advocated</u> building a new library, you would be against it.

   _____ **c.** A patient who <u>gradually</u> recovered from sickness is now healthy.

CRITICAL THINKING

1. The fact that some of the continents look as if they could fit together like a jigsaw puzzle supports the idea that
   a. the continents were once of equal size.
   b. the continents can float on water.
   c. the continents were once joined together.
   d. the continents were once hit by meteors.

2. The hot, liquid rock and gases in the asthenosphere flow
   a. from a hot area to a cooler area.
   b. from a cold area to a warmer area.
   c. from a high area to a lower area.
   d. from a low-pressure area to a high-pressure area.

3. The volcanic mountains that make up the mid-ocean ridges
   a. are made up of shells and coral.
   b. are made up of the skeletons of deep-sea fish.
   c. are made of dinosaur bones.
   d. are made up of lava from the asthenosphere.

4. Ocean-floor spreading does not cause the crustal plates to become larger because
   a. parts of them evaporate.
   b. parts of them are pushed down into the asthenosphere.
   c. parts of them burn up.
   d. parts of them become mountains.

1. Explain what process in the asthenosphere causes the movement of lithospheric plates.

    _____

    _____

2. What causes the lithospheric plates to be pushed apart?

    _____

    _____

3. List one effect of scientists' discovery of ocean-floor spreading.

    _____

    _____

4. What was the effect of the breakup of Pangaea?

    _____

    _____

5. Identify the three movements of crustal plates that can cause earthquakes.

    _____

    _____

6. What effect can occur when crustal plates move apart?

    _____

    _____

7. Underline two effects of ocean-floor spreading.
    a. heats up the asthenosphere
    b. pushes apart crustal plates
    c. pushes opposite edge of plates into asthenosphere
    d. causes movement of icebergs
    e. makes oceans deeper

Reading-Writing Connection

Research a particular geographic feature in your state. On a separate sheet of paper, write a paragraph explaining what caused the geographic feature and what effect it has on the land around it.

Skill: Reading Percents

BACKGROUND INFORMATION

In "How to Read Percents," you will learn about percents, a very useful mathematical tool. You make use of percents all the time. When a store announces a 40 percent off sale, you might go shopping. When there is an 80 percent chance of rain, you might grab an umbrella. When unemployment rises to 8 percent, you know that jobs are getting harder to find. Knowing about percents helps you understand many different kinds of information.

SKILL FOCUS: Reading Percents

The symbol % stands for **percent**. The word *percent* refers to a certain number compared to 100. For example, 83% means 83 parts out of 100.

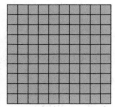

100%

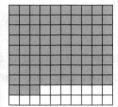

83%

Percents are very useful for comparing amounts. For example, you might read that 3 of every 7 mountains in the world are taller than 8,000 meters. You might also read that 5 of every 9 mountains are snow-covered during the summer. Comparing these two amounts is difficult, however. Which is more: 3 out of 7 or 5 out of 9?

Using percents makes the comparison easier. Another way to write 3 out of 7 is 43%. Another way to write 5 out of 9 is 56%. Comparing these percentages lets you see at a glance that the

number of snow-covered mountains is greater than the number of peaks over 8,000 feet.

▶ Each grid below has 100 squares. Fill in the first grid to represent 43%. Fill in the second grid to represent 56%.

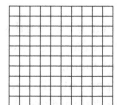

Percentage of mountains over 8,000 meters

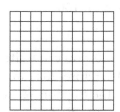

Percentage of snow-covered mountains in summer

WORD CLUES

The word *percent* comes from two Latin words, *per centum*, meaning "per one hundred" or "for each hundred." Knowing the origin of *percent* will help you understand how to use percents.

When reading the selection, also look for the important words *fraction*, *decimal*, and *change*.

Strategy Tip

Note that "How to Read Percents" has four headings. The information under each heading will teach you how to carry out an important mathematical operation. Be sure that you understand how to do each operation before going on to the next section.

How to Read Percents

The word *percent* refers to a certain number compared to a hundred. Many facts about the mountain ranges of Earth can be stated using percentages. One is below.

Mountains cover about 20 percent of Earth's surface.

The statement above means that if the earth's surface were divided into 100 equal sections, mountains would cover about 20 of them.

The symbol % stands for percent. Twenty percent can be written as 20%. You can think of the percent symbol as two zeros separated by a one. These are the same digits that make up 100.

$$\% = 100$$

Because 20% means 20 out of 100, you can write the same value as the **fraction** $\frac{20}{100}$. Therefore, 20% and $\frac{20}{100}$ are the same. You can also write the fraction $\frac{20}{100}$ as a **decimal**. Because $\frac{20}{100}$ means 20 one-hundredths, you can write the same value as 0.20. Therefore, 20%, $\frac{20}{100}$, and 0.20 all express the same value.

What are three ways to explain the following percentage value?

North America makes up about 16 percent of the earth's land surface.

16 percent can be written as 16%.

$$16 \text{ out of } 100 = \frac{16}{100}$$

$\frac{16}{100}$ written as a decimal is 0.16.

$$16\% = \frac{16}{100} = 0.16$$

The number in the next example can also be stated as a percent, a fraction, or a decimal.

Approximately 75 percent of all active volcanoes lie in one area of the world.

$$75\% = \frac{75}{100} = 0.75$$

Changing a Percent to a Decimal

To **change** a percent to a decimal, move the decimal point *two places to the left*. Then remove the % sign.

$$92.6\% = \underset{\smile}{.92.6\%} = 0.926$$

Sometimes you have to put in one or more zeros.

$$3.7\% = \underset{\smile}{03.7\%} = .037$$

Often a decimal point is not shown in the percent. You then have to put a decimal point at the end of the number and then move it two places to the left to make it a decimal.

$$27\% = \underset{\smile}{27.\%} = 0.27$$
$$9\% = \underset{\smile}{09.\%} = 0.09$$

Changing a Decimal to a Percent

To change a decimal to a percent, move the decimal point *two places to the right*. Then add the % sign.

$$.132 = \underset{\smile}{.132} = 13.2\%$$

Sometimes you have to put in one or more zeros.

$$.7 = \underset{\smile}{.70} = 70\%$$

Sometimes a decimal point is not shown.

$$3 = 3. = \underset{\smile}{3.00} = 300\%$$
$$17 = 17. = \underset{\smile}{17.00} = 1,700\%$$

Changing a Percent to a Fraction

To change a percent to a fraction, remove the percent sign to form the numerator, and add the denominator 100.

$$93\% = \frac{93}{100}$$

The numerator of the above fraction is 93. The denominator of all percent fractions is 100.

$$8\% = \frac{8}{100}$$
$$137\% = \frac{137}{100}$$
$$16\% = \frac{16}{100}$$

Changing a Fraction to a Percent

Two different types of fractions may be changed to a percent. If the denominator of the fraction is 100, just remove the denominator and add a percent sign.

$$\frac{29}{100} = 29\%$$
$$\frac{7}{100} = 7\%$$

If the denominator is not 100, it must first be changed to 100. You need to multiply the numerator and denominator by a number that will change the denominator to 100. For example, to change $\frac{3}{4}$ to a percent, multiply both the numerator and the denominator by 25 to change the fraction to $\frac{75}{100}$.

$$\frac{3}{4} \times \frac{25}{25} = \frac{75}{100} = 75\%$$

To change $\frac{1}{5}$ to a percent, do the following.

$$\frac{1}{5} \times \frac{20}{20} = \frac{20}{100} = 20\%$$

Study these four rules.

1. To change a percent to a decimal, move the decimal point two places to the *left*. Remove the % sign. Add a decimal point and zeros when they are needed.

2. To change a decimal to a percent, move the decimal point two places to the *right*. Add a percent sign and zeros when they are needed.

3. To change a percent to a fraction, first remove the percent sign. Then write the number over the denominator 100.

4. To change a fraction to a percent, remove the denominator if it is 100, and add a percent sign. If the denominator is not 100, multiply both the numerator and the denominator by a number that will change the denominator to 100. Then remove the denominator and add a percent sign to the numerator.

COMPREHENSION

1. Define the word *percent*.

_____

_____

_____

2. Explain how to change a percent to a decimal.

_____

_____

_____

3. Explain how to change a percent to a fraction.

_____

_____

_____

4. Explain how to change a fraction to a percent.

_____

_____

_____

CRITICAL THINKING

1. Explain why moving the decimal point two places changes a percent to a decimal and a decimal to a percent.

_____

2. Give two or three examples to show how percents might be used in ads.

_____

3. Explain why percents are used to score tests.

_____

4. What part of something is 100% of it?

_____

MATHEMATICS

A. Fill in the blanks. The first one is done for you.

1. 15% = $\frac{15}{100}$ = .15
2. 13% = _____ = _____
3. 137% = _____ = _____
4. 36% = _____ = _____
5. 8% = _____ = _____

6. 34.7% = _____ = _____
7. 1.1% = _____ = _____
8. 3% = _____ = _____
9. 75% = _____ = _____
10. 50% = _____ = _____

B. Change the percents to decimals and the decimals to percents.

1. 14% = _____
2. 73% = _____
3. 5% = _____
4. 100% = _____
5. 83.9% = _____

6. .16 = _____
7. .84 = _____
8. .03 = _____
9. 1.04 = _____
10. .752 = _____

C. Change the fractions to percents and the percents to fractions.

1. $\frac{79}{100}$ = _____
2. $\frac{7}{100}$ = _____
3. $\frac{3.7}{100}$ = _____
4. $\frac{1}{4}$ = _____
5. $\frac{3}{5}$ = _____

6. 67% = _____
7. 29% = _____
8. 2% = _____
9. 125% = _____
10. 43% = _____

D. Write the percent, fraction, and decimal for the following amounts.

1. twenty-five and nine tenths percent _____

2. eight twenty-fifths _____

3. twelve tenths _____

4. forty-two hundredths _____

Reading-Writing Connection

Where do you read percents in your daily life? On a separate sheet of paper, describe three places where you have seen numbers written as percents recently.

Skill: Evaluating Opinions

What is the difference between a fact and an opinion? A **fact** is a statement that can be checked and proven. An **opinion** is a statement that tells how someone feels or what someone thinks about something. Some opinions may be more valid, or reliable, than others because they have one or more facts to back them up. When you find an opinion in your reading, decide how valid it is.

Read the following selection.

The Sierra Nevada

The Sierra Nevada is a huge mountain range in eastern California. *Sierra Nevada* means "snowy, saw-toothed mountain" in Spanish. The Sierra Nevada is the site of three national parks—Yosemite, Sequoia, and Kings Canyon—and beautiful Lake Tahoe. Donner Memorial State Park, a historic landmark, is also in this mountain range.

The Sierra Nevada is like a granite wall extending north and south for 430 miles (692 kilometers) through California. It is about 70 miles (110 kilometers) wide. At one time, the earth's crust lifted and tilted to the west to make a long, gentle slope on the mountain's western side and a steep slope on its eastern side. The highest point of the Sierra Nevada is Mount Whitney. Its elevation, or height, is 14,494 feet (4,418 meters). In fact, Mount Whitney is the second-highest point in the United States. Several other peaks of the Sierra Nevada are almost as high as Mount Whitney.

Many rivers, such as the Feather, American, and San Joaquin, flow in the Sierra Nevada. Rushing mountain waters have cut deep canyons in the long western slope of the mountain range. Yosemite Valley is the most outstanding of these canyons. Yosemite was originally cut by streams. Later, glaciers moved down the valley, eroding it further. The glaciers created the Sierra Nevada's granite cliffs and impressive landscapes. On the shorter, steeper eastern slope, many creeks descend and join the Owens, Walker, Carson, and Truckee rivers. The cliffs, meadows, evergreen forests, lakes, and waterfalls make the Sierra Nevada a beautiful mountain range.

In the Sierra Nevada, rainfall increases as elevation increases. This is true up to about 4,500 feet (1,350 meters). From there to the top, the rain decreases. In a typical winter, 30 to 40 feet (9 to 12 meters) of snow accumulates at Lake Tahoe and Donner Pass, but as much as 60 feet (18 meters) of snow can fall in some years. It is no wonder that skiers are attracted to this region.

A variety of vegetation grows on the Sierra Nevada at different elevations. Shrubs and grasses grow near the Sacramento and San Joaquin valleys at the western base of the Sierra Nevada. From 3,000 to 4,000 feet (900 to 1,200 meters) are forests of yellow pine, sugar pine, cedar, and fir. These trees are a valuable source of timber. Within the forest are sequoia trees, the largest plants on Earth. At 6,000 to 7,000 feet (1,800 to 2,150 meters), lodgepole pine, Jeffrey pine, and red fir grow. Above the timberline is rocky land that is barren except for scattered evergreens. The rivers of the western slope of the mountain range supply water for irrigation. The farms in the Sacramento and San Joaquin valleys and the Tulare Basin receive this water. The largest cities in California receive their water supply from these rivers, too. Hydroelectric plants on the rivers generate the power for farmlands and cities.

The Sierra Nevada forms a barrier to east-west travel. However, cars, trucks, and buses can cross the mountains through several passes. Major highways use six passes, each at a different elevation. A road at 9,625 feet (2,935 meters) over Tioga Pass connects Yosemite Valley and Mono Lake. Unfortunately this road is usually closed nine months of the year because of snow. Railroads also travel over the Sierra Nevada. Hikers and pack trains, or groups of mules, use the various trails to cross the mountain range.

The gold rush of 1849 began when gold was discovered in the Sierra Nevada. This attracted many people to the foothill region in the mid-1800s.

Mining of gold and other metals is no longer important, however. Now tourism is the area's chief industry. All kinds of camping and recreational facilities are located throughout the Sierra Nevada for people who enjoy summer or winter sports. Other industries in the region are fruit-growing, lumbering, and grazing.

Read the opinions about the Sierra Nevada in the left column. Then select none, one, or two of the facts in the right column that support each opinion. Write the letter of each supporting fact on the line. Write *none* if the opinion has no supporting facts.

Opinions	Facts
1. _____ The Sierra Nevada is a huge mountain range.	a. Each year, the Sierra Nevada receives 30 to 40 feet (9 to 12 meters) of snow.
2. _____ Lake Tahoe is one of the most beautiful lakes in the world.	b. The range has meadows, cliffs, and forests.
3. _____ Yosemite Valley is the most outstanding canyon in the United States.	c. At 4,000 feet (1,200 meters) is yellow pine, sugar pine, cedar, and fir.
4. _____ The Sierra Nevada is a beautiful mountain range.	d. The Sierra Nevada is over 400 miles (640 kilometers) long.
5. _____ The best skiing in the West is in the Sierra Nevada.	e. Rivers on the western slope supply California's largest cities with water.
6. _____ No forests can offer as large a selection of timber as those of the Sierra Nevada.	f. The Sierra Nevada is about 70 miles (110 kilometers) wide.
7. _____ Visitors to California should spend their time seeing the Sierra Nevada rather than Disneyland.	g. Some winters, 60 feet (18 meters) of snow falls.
8. _____ Some of the best fruit in the United States is grown in the Sierra Nevada.	h. Glaciers moved down the Yosemite Valley and created cliffs and impressive landscapes.
9. _____ If not for the rivers of the Sierra Nevada, California would be without water.	i. The peak of Mount Whitney is 14,494 feet (4,418 meters) high.
10. _____ Mount Whitney seems very high.	j. Rivers on the western slope irrigate farmlands.
	k. At 7,000 feet (2,150 meters) is lodgepole pine, Jeffrey pine, and red fir.
	l. The range has waterfalls, such as those in Yosemite Valley.

Skill: Improving Reading Rate

People have so much to read today that the ability to read quickly has become important. The typical reader of a century ago had fewer books, newspapers, and magazines to read. For this reason, you may read more in a week than your great-grandparents did. Having a rapid **reading rate** helps you to read more in a short period of time. However, it is always important to keep in mind that to read material without understanding it is a waste of time, no matter what the speed.

A rapid rate of reading has no particular value in itself. A good reader is able to read at several speeds, depending on the type of material being read. When reading materials are difficult or unfamiliar, a good reader reads more slowly. For example, social studies, science, and mathematics may be more difficult to read than literature. Therefore, these materials are read more slowly. Even literature can be difficult. Sometimes a reader needs to slow down when words or sentences are difficult or unfamiliar, or reread a paragraph to understand a complex idea. A good reader also stops to read diagrams and maps. This requires increased attention, making a slower reading rate necessary.

The best way to increase your reading rate is to get rid of bad reading habits. If you have any of the habits below, practice these suggestions for overcoming them.

Lip moving	Hold your finger over your lips, or hold a piece of paper between your lips.
Finger pointing	Hold your book with both hands, one on each side of the book.
Head moving	Rest your chin in the palm of one hand and hold it still.
Reading one word at a time	Work hard at trying to take in several words at each glance.

The following paragraph is marked off into word groups. See if you can read it by taking in each group of words in one glance.

> Bertela lives / on an island / that belongs / to Denmark. / There are / beech trees / in the woods / near her home. / Every fall / she gathers beech nuts / in these woods. / The squirrels gather / the nuts, too. / The nuts are so plentiful / that there are / enough of them / for both Bertela / and the squirrels.

On the next page is a selection that can be used in checking your reading rate. Use a watch or a clock with a second hand to time yourself. Start right on a minute, such as four minutes past ten o'clock. Write your starting time at the beginning of the selection. Then read the selection. Write your ending time at the end of the selection.

At the top of the hill, the three riders reined their horses to a stop. They wore blue coats, tan trousers, high boots, and three-cornered hats. The tallest of the riders lifted a pair of field glasses to his eyes and looked out over the fields and woods.

"Tell us, General Washington, what do you see? British soldiers? Campfires?" asked one of the riders.

Washington smiled. "Remember, Lafayette, it will take the British a few days to reach this area from the Delaware River."

Lafayette looked disappointed. Then General Greene, the third rider, spoke. "General Washington, we have ridden all over this land today, and we still have not found a good place for battle against the British."

"True enough," Washington sighed.

Greene looked up at the darkening sky. "Look, sir, it's going to storm."

The three riders started toward a field below them. Black clouds raced across the sky. It began to thunder.

"There's a house ahead!" shouted Lafayette. "Let's stop there."

"Yes, hurry!" Washington led the dash to the farmhouse.

Just as the riders reached the barn near the house, the rain came pouring down. They got off their horses and looked around. A farmer was staring at them. "Why, it's General George Washington. Here on my farm! General, sir, welcome. Come into my house and have some food. My son, Tom, will look after your horses. Our name is Small."

Washington smiled and went into the house with the farmer. Lafayette followed the general. Greene stayed with the horses. He was worried. Suppose these were friends of the British. The boy might hide their horses, and they would be trapped. Finally, however, he decided to follow the others.

Inside the warm house, Washington sat at the table, talking with the farmer. Lafayette was pacing from window to window. Washington looked out the window and said, "Mr. Small, I see this storm will last for hours. I wonder if you would let us stay the night?"

Both Lafayette and Greene looked worried. Greene whispered to the general, "Sir, we can't stay. We don't know if these people are friends or enemies. We might be in British hands by morning!"

Washington said coldly, "We will stay."

Dinner was good, and even Greene enjoyed it. For a while, he felt at ease and almost forgot his fears. Lafayette also seemed to relax and was talking happily. When they went upstairs, however, all of Greene's fears returned. Without undressing, he lay on top of the bed with his eyes open. He jumped up with each new sound.

Just before sunrise, Greene heard a horse whinny and a dog bark. Silently he went downstairs and out to the barn. The horses seemed safe. He put his hand on his gray horse.

"Don't do it, sir." A low voice cut the darkness.

"Who's there?" Greene whirled around.

"Me! Tom Small! Don't run away. The general needs you."

"Run away? What do you mean?" asked Greene.

Tom looked at his feet. "I've been standing watch because I was afraid you were going to slip away with your horse."

"Fool!" shouted Greene. "You think me a traitor?"

Tom looked uneasy. "Well, you acted so strange, sir. I just thought....There have been lots of deserters—traitors, too."

Suddenly Greene laughed. "Tom, we're a pair! We both were worried about the same thing. I came down here because I heard some noise and thought the British had trapped us."

Two hours later, at breakfast, Washington looked at Greene and said, "You look like you didn't sleep all night. What's wrong?"

Greene winked at Tom. "Nothing, sir. Tom and I just stood watch all night."

Washington looked from one to the other but said nothing. Later, after they had left the Smalls', they stopped to rest. Washington broke the silence. "You know, you were right. I did take a risk last night. I was quite wrong."

Greene could only nod. But Lafayette held out his hand to Washington. "Ah, my general, only a great man will say, 'I was wrong.'"

To find the total time that it took to read the selection, do the following:

1. Subtract your beginning time from your ending time.

2. Divide the number of words in the selection by your reading time expressed in seconds. For example, if it took you 3 minutes and 5 seconds ($3 \times 60 + 5 = 185$ seconds) to read the selection, you would have read 3.7 words per second ($692 \div 185 = 3.7$).

3. To find the number of words per minute (WPM), multiply your rate per second (WPS) by 60. Your answer would be 222 WPM.

Words in selection: 692

	Hr.	Min.	Sec.
Ending time:	_____	_____	_____
Starting time:	_____	_____	_____
Total time:	_____	_____	_____

No. seconds (min. × 60 + sec.): _____

Rate (sec.): 692 ÷ _____ sec. = _____ WPS

Rate (min.): _____ WPS × 60 = _____ WPM

Circle the letter next to the correct answer to each question.

1. Where do the three riders stop the first time?
   a. at a farmhouse
   b. under a tree
   c. at the top of a hill
   d. on a battlefield

2. Who looks through the field glasses?
   a. General Greene
   b. General Washington
   c. Lafayette
   d. Tom Small

3. How do you know that Greene does not sleep very much at the Smalls'?
   a. He doesn't undress.
   b. He sits on the bed.
   c. He keeps his eyes open.
   d. He hears a dog bark.

4. Who looks after the riders' horses?
   a. General Greene
   b. General Washington
   c. the farmer
   d. Tom Small

5. Why is Lafayette pacing from window to window?
   a. He is hungry.
   b. He is afraid of thunder.
   c. He is worried about the British.
   d. He wants to go home.

6. What does Tom mean when he says, "There have been lots of deserters"?
   a. Many American soldiers stole horses.
   b. Many farmers hid American soldiers.
   c. Many American soldiers ran away.
   d. Many American soldiers were spies.

Skill: Taking Notes

When reading new information that you need to remember, it is a good idea to take notes. **Taking notes** will help you remember the information as you read it. Taking notes is especially helpful in recording the information from several references before writing a report.

It is not necessary to remember every minor detail you read. When taking notes, write down only the important information, especially main ideas and major supporting details. Following are some suggestions to help you take notes.

1. Find the main idea of each paragraph, and include it in your notes.

2. Look for major details that answer such questions as *who, what, where, when, why,* and *how*. Write these details under the main ideas. Leave out minor details, or information that is not needed.

3. Arrange your notes in the same order in which the information appears in the selection. Group each main idea and its supporting details together.

4. Label your notes by writing the subject at the top of the page. Write your notes in your own words. Do not copy entire sentences, but do write down key words and phrases. Be brief so that you can read your notes quickly.

The following selection is written in chronological order, the order in which the events take place. Using the space provided on page 123, take notes as you read the selection. Make sure your notes show the correct sequence of the visits of the Spanish explorers to the New World.

Explorations to the New World

Columbus's voyages to the New World led the way to further exploration of North and South America. By the Treaty of Tordesillas, Spain claimed the right to most of the New World. Early Spanish explorers heard stories of wealthy kingdoms in the Americas. Such reports encouraged new expeditions. Until 1519, Spanish control of the New World was limited to small settlements in the West Indies. With the many Spanish expeditions that followed Columbus's, Spain gradually gained control of most of South and Central America and parts of North America.

Hernando Cortés

In 1519, Hernando Cortés, a clever fighter and skillful leader, landed on the coast of Mexico in search of gold. He soon heard about the powerful Aztec Empire that demanded huge payments from the people it conquered. Cortés sought out the support of the many native groups who hated their Aztec rulers. He marched his small army of about 400 soldiers and 16 horses into the crowded Aztec capital of Tenochtitlán, where he confronted the Aztec ruler, Montezuma.

After months of negotiations, Montezuma agreed to become a subject of the Spanish king. In 1520, the Aztecs revolted against the Spanish. Cortés and his army barely escaped with their lives. However, with the help of his allies, Cortés surrounded Tenochtitlán. In 1521, he attacked and destroyed the Aztec capital. Within a few years, the Aztec Empire crumbled.

Francisco Pizarro

Nine years later, in 1530, Francisco Pizarro, another Spanish explorer, received permission to explore the Inca Empire, located in what is now Peru. With 180 metal-clad soldiers—less than half of Cortés's force—Pizarro marched into the Inca kingdom. Luck was with him. When he arrived, the Incas were caught up in a civil war.

Pizarro launched a surprise attack, imprisoned the Inca leader, Atahualpa, and killed most of his attendants. The attack stunned the Incas, weakening their resistance to the Spanish. By 1535, Pizarro had captured Cuzco, the Inca capital, and crushed nearly all opposition.

Francisco Coronado

In 1540, Francisco Coronado led an expedition in search of the "seven cities of gold" reportedly nestled in the hills of what is now New Mexico. For about two years, Coronado, along with many Spanish soldiers, searched in vain for these cities of gold, which did not really exist. In the process, he explored much of what would become the southwestern United States. One of his lieutenants was the first European to see the Grand Canyon.

Hernando de Soto

While Coronado was looking for gold in the West, Hernando de Soto led another gold-hunting expedition into what would become the southeastern United States. From 1539 to 1542, his army wandered as far north as the Carolinas and as far west as present-day Oklahoma. When de Soto died, the expedition returned without having found any large supplies of gold. Even before de Soto's death, the Spanish had begun to concentrate on settling the area to the south, in what is now Mexico, the Caribbean, and South America.

Notes on Early Exploration

_____

_____

_____

_____

_____

_____

_____

_____

Taking notes can help you remember and review what you have read. Use the information from your notes to complete the chart. The name of the first explorer has been provided.

Explorer	Areas Explored	Dates	Importance
Cortés			

Skill: Reading a Road Map

It is a good idea to have a **road map** in your car at all times. A road map shows how to get from one place to another by car and how far it is between places. It also shows the location of points of interest.

Look at the road map below. It shows the Great Smoky Mountains National Park and some of the surrounding areas.

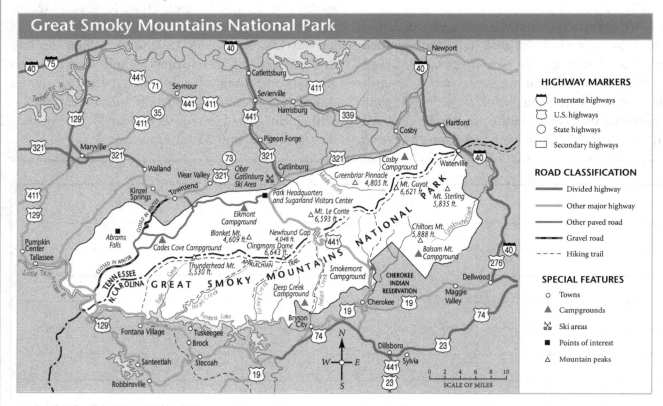

Great Smoky Mountains National Park

Notice the **key** to the right of the map. A key explains the symbols used on a map. The **scale of miles** in the lower-right corner of the map helps you figure out the distance from one place to another. The **road classification** symbols identify different kinds of roads. **Special symbols** also mark such features as towns, campgrounds, ski areas, and other points of interest. Maps usually include a direction symbol known as a **compass rose**. The compass rose indicates north, south, east, and west with the abbreviations N, S, E, and W. Notice the compass rose at the bottom of this map.

A. Read the definitions in the left column. Then read the words in the right column. On the line next to each definition, write the correct word.

1. _____ explains map symbols
2. _____ indicates directions
3. _____ shows distance from one place to another
4. _____ identifies different kinds of roads
5. _____ show campgrounds, ski areas, mountain peaks

a. scale of miles
b. road classification
c. key
d. special features
e. compass rose

B. Decide if each of the following questions can be answered using the map on the opposite page. Write *yes* if you can find the answer on the map. Write *no* if the map cannot provide the answer to the question.

_____ **1.** Are there hiking trails in Great Smoky Mountains National Park?

_____ **2.** What towns are south of the park?

_____ **3.** How long does it take to drive through the park?

_____ **4.** Are there campgrounds inside the park itself?

_____ **5.** Are there hotels and motels near the park?

_____ **6.** Which roads are closed in the winter?

_____ **7.** Which rivers run through the park?

_____ **8.** How high is Newfound Gap?

_____ **9.** How many miles is it from the park to New York City?

_____ **10.** How can you get from Gatlinburg to the Cherokee Indian Reservation?

C. Circle the letter next to the phrase that correctly completes each sentence.

1. The Great Smoky Mountains National Park is in the states of
   a. North Carolina and South Carolina.
   b. Tennessee and North Carolina.
   c. Tennessee and Kentucky.
   d. Kentucky and North Carolina.

2. If you travel south through the park from Gatlinburg, you will first reach
   a. Park Headquarters and Sugarland Visitors Center.
   b. Newfound Gap.
   c. Smokemont Campground.
   d. Pigeon Forge.

3. To get from Gatlinburg to Cosby, you can travel on
   a. US 441.   **b.** Route 339.   **c.** Route 73.   **d.** US 321.

4. The interstate highway that is closest to the park is
   a. Interstate 82.   **b.** Interstate 75.   **c.** Interstate 40.   **d.** Interstate 80.

5. The highest point in Great Smoky Mountains National Park is
   a. Newfound Gap.   **b.** Clingman's Dome.
   c. Mt. Le Conte.   **d.** Thunderhead Mountain.

6. A large body of water on the southern border of the park is called
   a. Rainbow Falls.   **b.** Fontana Lake.   **c.** Forney Creek.   **d.** Eagle Creek.

The Struggle to Win

LESSON 41

Skill: Conflict and Resolution

BACKGROUND INFORMATION

"The Campaign for Kate" is a play about a young woman who must decide whether or not to devote herself totally to swimming in order to make the U.S. Olympic team. Training for the Olympics takes time, energy, and total commitment. Many young competitors begin training as early as age five. They practice their sport many hours daily and often give up other activities they enjoy to achieve their dreams.

SKILL FOCUS: Conflict and Resolution

The main character of a story usually has a goal or faces a problem. The struggle to achieve this goal or to solve this problem is called **conflict**.

Story characters face three main types of conflict.

1. A character may have a **conflict with self**. Such a character struggles with feelings within himself or herself. This struggle is called an **internal conflict**. An example is a person overcoming a fear of water after nearly drowning.

2. A character may have a **conflict with another character**. For example, two story characters may have an argument or compete against each other in a race. This type of struggle is called an **external conflict**.

3. In some stories, there is a **conflict with an outside force**. A character may struggle against nature or society. An example is a firefighter trying to save people inside a burning house. This type of struggle is also called an **external conflict**.

By the end of a story, the main character succeeds or fails at solving the problem or achieving the goal that is causing the conflict. The way a conflict is settled is called the story's **resolution**.

▶ Read each conflict on the chart at the top of the next column. Write which of the three types of conflict each character faces.

Character's Problem	Type of Conflict
Tai's mother wants her to go to college, but Tai wants to get a job instead.	
Carlo wants to ask Anita to the prom, but he feels too shy.	
The apple trees in Hannah's orchard are dying from a strange new disease.	

CONTEXT CLUES: Using a Dictionary

Sometimes there are no clues to help you figure out a new word's meaning. To understand some new words, look them up in a dictionary.

Think about the underlined word in this sentence.

Besides, my eyes are always red from the <u>*chlorine*</u> *in the pool.*

You can tell from the context that *chlorine* is something in the pool. However, there are not enough clues to help you figure out exactly what chlorine is.

▶ Read the following sentence. Look up the underlined word in a dictionary, and write its definition on the lines.

And for what—so I can someday say I'm a great swimmer in the <u>*butterfly*</u> *event?*

_____

_____

In the play, use a dictionary to find the meanings of the underlined words *clamber*, *priority*, and *fatigue*.

> **Strategy Tip**
>
> As you read "The Campaign for Kate," think about the conflict the main character faces as she tries to achieve her goals.

The Campaign for Kate

Cast

Kate Fenton, member of a swim team
Maria Cortez, member of a swim team
Mr. Meacham, coach of the swim team

Scene 1

Late in the afternoon at the Hillside High School pool. Mr. Meacham stands at the edge of the pool, stopwatch in hand. When Mr. Meacham speaks, the team stops doing laps. Everyone leaves the pool but Kate and Maria, who hang on to the edge and talk.

Mr. Meacham *(loudly):* All right, team, that's enough for today. I'll see you all tomorrow, bright and early. Remember, be here no later than 6:30 A.M.

Kate *(to Maria):* He'll see me, but I won't see him. I'll be swimming, but I'll probably nap through my first four laps! I don't know if I can keep this up.

Maria: Mr. Meacham says it's important to work out every day for several hours, especially with the all-county meet coming up on Saturday.

Kate: Well, I'm beginning to get tired of this stuff. Besides, my eyes are always red from the chlorine in the pool. It doesn't do my hair any good, either. Furthermore, practicing five hours a day doesn't leave me time or energy for anything else.

All this so I can someday say I'm a great swimmer in the butterfly event?

Maria: I know. I'm tired, too, but now I take Mr. Meacham's advice and go to bed an hour earlier. Maybe you should try that.

Kate: Agh! I go to bed early as it is. I need some time to myself, to do other things. If I go to bed any earlier, I'll sleep away my whole life. You know, I used to love swimming. I had dreams *(pause)* … dreams of becoming an Olympic champion. Now it's more like a nightmare than a dream.

Maria: I heard Mr. Meacham say you have the talent to make the Olympic team someday.

Kate: He did—but I keep wondering if I can throw myself into swimming and train the way he wants me to. I don't know if I'm ready to give up everything just to try for it.

Maria: Here comes Mr. Meacham. We'd better talk about this later.

Mr. Meacham *(very enthusiastic):* Good workout, Maria. Your time is improving. *(turns toward Kate, showing concern)* Kate, you've just got to think about your kick as you finish each lap. It's cutting down your speed. You could lose a race that way. Tomorrow morning we'll work on it. I think you're either daydreaming or not getting enough sleep.

Kate: I'll be all right, Mr. Meacham.

Mr. Meacham: Well, you'd better hit the showers and then go home to hit the books. I want my team to get decent grades, too!

Kate and Maria clamber out of the pool and head for the showers.

Kate *(takes off her swimming cap):* By the way, some of the kids want me to run for the student senate. What do you think?

Maria *(throws a towel over her shoulders):* It sounds great, but do you have the time? Mr. Meacham says swimming has top priority.

Kate: I'll just have to make the time. Anyway, Maria, you take Mr. Meacham too seriously. Just because you want to be a swim coach someday.

Maria: I have to work harder than you, Kate! *(getting angry)* You have a natural talent that I could never match. I'll be glad if I can be a coach someday.... You can set your sights even higher. I get angry when you won't!

Kate: Okay! Okay! Sorry. Friends?

Maria *(pause):* Friends.

Scene 2

Saturday. Kate and Maria sit on a bench in the locker room before the swim meet begins.

Maria *(concerned):* You look tired, Kate.

Kate *(fatigue shows in her voice):* I'm beat. I was at a campaign meeting until 11:00 last night. We were painting posters and writing slogans. How does this one sound? "Get in the swim—vote for Kate!"

Maria: Sounds great! Now let's get in the swim ourselves. Let's go out there so you can beat me and everyone else without even trying, as usual!

Kate and Maria rise and walk toward the locker room doors.

Scene 3

Maria and Kate cling to the edge of the pool after the race.

Kate *(despite her disappointment):* Congratulations, Maria! First place, and your best time ever! You even beat my best time!

Maria *(happy and relieved):* I can hardly believe it myself, beating you and everyone else in the pool! I've never done that before!

Kate: You deserve it. You work hard, Maria.

Mr. Meacham *(walks toward Maria and Kate):* Maria! That was great! Congratulations! *(turns to Kate and becomes very serious)* Now, Kate, I want to talk to you. You've got to work on your kick as you make the turn.

Kate *(raises her voice; becomes angry):* Mr. Meacham, can't you leave me alone? I hate my kick! I hate this pool! I'm not meant for this. I'll never be an Olympic athlete! I can't even win a high school race! *(gets out of the pool and walks over to the starter's table)*

Mr. Meacham *(follows Kate):* You certainly won't make the Olympic team with that attitude.

Kate: Well, you saw today that I haven't got what it takes.

Mr. Meacham *(very calmly):* All I saw today was a swimmer who wasn't concentrating. Kate, you have a natural talent. It's far greater than that of any other member of the team. Maria knows it. Today was a lucky break for her. It may not come again. Maria knows her best shot is to study to be a coach. However, you could be a star if you work to develop your talent.

Kate: I don't know if I can work that hard at swimming. You said it was important to be well-rounded. Some kids want me to run for a place as representative in the student government. On a day like today, that sounds like a good idea. Why shouldn't I do it?

Mr. Meacham *(very patiently)*: For most kids, it would be a great idea. However, your talent is special, Kate. You shouldn't give up your chance at an Olympic medal someday by trying to do too many other things at the same time. *(pause)* I have an idea. You continue to come to practice, but don't compete for the next three weeks. Run for the student senate. However, you must make up your mind by the end of the three weeks. If you decide to swim in the meet on the fourteenth, you've committed yourself to swimming. If you don't race on the fourteenth, you're off the team.

Kate: Okay. *(walks slowly toward the locker room)* I can accept that.

Scene 4

The following week. Kate and Maria chat in the pool.

Maria: Did you hear, Kate? I won again yesterday! Our whole team won.

Kate: I heard! I heard! Mr. Meacham must be pleased.

Maria: Oh, sure, but he misses you. I even miss swimming four strokes behind you!

Kate: Maria, you put yourself down too much. You work hard. You deserve to win.

Maria: Speaking of winning, how is your campaign coming?

Kate: I have until the fourteenth to officially begin my campaign.

Maria: That's the day of the next race!

Kate: I know. I know.

Kate and Maria swim to the end of the pool to start their laps.

Scene 5

The fourteenth. Hillside High School pool, less than 20 minutes before the swim meet. Kate is nowhere in sight.

Mr. Meacham: Maria, have you seen Kate? Is she coming?

Maria *(sits on the bench near the locker room door)*: I don't know. Last night on the phone she said something about showing us her new campaign posters.

Mr. Meacham *(his disappointment is obvious)*: Then she's decided.

Kate *(bursts into the pool area)*: I thought you'd like to take a look at these. Here's one for you, coach. *(Mr. Meacham slowly takes the poster from Kate)* Here's one for you, Maria.

Maria *(eagerly reads)*: "Get in the swim with Kate—and vote for someone else!"

Mr. Meacham: Great, Kate! Let's get ready for the Olympics!

Curtain

COMPREHENSION

1. Explain how Kate's goal is different from Maria's.

   _____

   _____

   _____

2. Discuss why Maria feels that she is not as good a swimmer as Kate.

   _____

   _____

   _____

3. Tell why Kate is so tired the day of the first swim meet.

   _____

   _____

   _____

4. What does Mr. Meacham say was the cause of Kate's loss at the swim meet?

   _____

   _____

   _____

5. Explain why Kate says that Maria deserves to win first place.

_____

_____

6. Circle the word that correctly completes each sentence.

   a. Very young children _____ on a jungle gym.

   swim   clamber   somersault

   b. Something considered more important than other things is a _____.

   lap   campaign   priority

   c. Someone who is extremely tired is suffering from a feeling of _____.

   fatigue   disgust   failure

CRITICAL THINKING

1. How are Maria and Kate different?

_____

_____

2. Tell why Kate and Maria argue if they are friends.

_____

_____

3. Explain why training as a swimmer is so demanding.

_____

_____

4. Describe how you think Kate feels when she hears about Maria's second victory.

_____

_____

5. From the stage directions in Mr. Meacham's dialogue, describe what kind of person you think Mr. Meacham is.

_____

_____

6. What is the message of this play?

_____

_____

1. Of the three kinds of conflict described on page 126, which kind of conflict does Kate face? _____
_____

2. Discuss Kate's conflict with swim training. _____
_____

3. Explain how Mr. Meacham, the coach, helps Kate with her problem. _____
_____
_____

4. Describe how the conflict is finally resolved. _____
_____

5. Is Kate's conflict internal or external? Explain. _____
_____

6. There is also a minor conflict in the story. It is an external conflict. Circle the letter of
   the statement that identifies this minor conflict. Then tell how it is resolved on the
   lines below.
   a. Maria has to deal with being second best.
   b. Maria gets angry with Kate over her unwillingness to work hard.
   c. Maria does not get along with her coach.
   d. Maria is jealous of Kate's swimming ability.
   _____
   _____

7. Maria also has a conflict with herself about her love of swimming and her knowledge that
   she is not a first-class swimmer. Explain how she resolves this conflict.
   _____
   _____

Reading-Writing Connection

On a separate sheet of paper, write a paragraph describing a recent conflict in your life or in
the life of someone you know. Explain how the conflict was resolved.

Skill: Reading a Timeline

BACKGROUND INFORMATION

"Swifter, Higher, Stronger" is a brief history of the Olympic Games. The history of the Olympics is divided into two parts. The original games were held in ancient Greece and went on for 1,200 years. They finally ended in A.D. 390. The modern Olympics did not begin until 1896. Now in their second century, the modern Olympics promote peace and understanding among nations.

SKILL FOCUS: Reading a Timeline

A **timeline** is a chart that lists events in chronological order—the time order in which they occurred. Some timelines show major historical events over a long period of time. Others show events that occur during just a few hours or days.

Each section on a timeline stands for a specific period of time. It could be one year, ten years, a century, or some other length of time. When you read a timeline, look at how much time each section stands for. Then look for the dates and times of specific events.

A timeline shows a sequence of events in a brief, clear form. It helps you understand when an event happened in relation to other events. A timeline can also give you a quick overview of the history of a topic, region, or period.

▶ Use the following timeline to answer the questions at the top of the next column.

Notable Early Events in the Modern Olympics

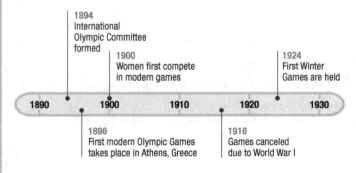

How much time does each section of the timeline stand for?

_____

When did women first compete in the Olympic Games?

_____

CONTEXT CLUES: Appositive Phrases

Sometimes the meaning of a new word follows the word and is set off by commas or dashes. This type of context clue is called an **appositive** if it is one word. If it is more than one word, it is called an **appositive phrase**.

Read the sentences below. Find the appositive that explains the meaning of the underlined word.

The Olympics started in ancient Greece. They began so long ago that their <u>origin</u>, or beginning, is not recorded in history.

If you do not know the meaning of *origin*, the appositive *or beginning* can help you. *Origin* means "beginning."

▶ In the sentence below, circle the appositive phrase that helps you figure out the meaning of the underlined word.

Other events, including <u>chariot-racing</u>— races between horse-drawn, two-wheeled cars— came later.

As you read the selection, use appositives and appositive phrases to help you understand the meanings of the underlined words *sound*, *pentathlon*, and *decathlon*.

> ### Strategy Tip
>
> As you read "Swifter, Higher, Stronger," pay attention to the timeline on pages 133–134. It will help you understand the sequence of events that the text describes.

SWIFTER, HIGHER, STRONGER

Gifted athletes from around the world gather to compete against each other as individuals. They are also **representatives** (REP ri ZENT ə tivz) of their countries. These men and women are Olympic athletes.

The Olympic Games have a history reaching back to ancient Greece. Many people think that the modern Olympics are the most exciting of sports events. Athletes the world over devote their lives to training for the games. Like the early Greeks, these athletes have as their goal the motto *Citius, altius, fortius,* meaning "swifter, higher, stronger."

The oldest event in the Olympic Games is track and field. It was, and still is, the heart of the games. Even the Olympic motto is directed to the track-and-field athlete. The Latin words encourage the athlete to run faster, jump higher, and throw harder.

The Beginning of the Olympics

The Olympics started in ancient Greece. They began so long ago that their origin, or beginning, is not recorded in history. The ancient Greeks believed in excellence in every area of life. A Greek citizen was expected to be <u>sound</u>, or healthy, in both mind and body. The Olympics were a celebration of the human body and what it could achieve.

The first Olympics recorded in history took place in 776 B.C. The Greeks have left us a picture of what the event was like. The games took place in the beautiful valley of Olympia. This was a sacred place where the Greeks came to worship their gods.

The grassy slopes of the valley served as a stadium for the games. In 776 B.C., more than 45,000 Greeks watched and cheered the athletes in the games. The first person ever to have his name put in an Olympic record was Coroebus (kə REE bəs). Coroebus was a cook from the city of Elis (EE lis). He was the winner of a footrace of about 200 yards (180 meters).

An Olympic winner became a great hero in ancient Greece. He was crowned with an olive wreath. The people of his city welcomed him home with parades. Poems were written about him, and statues were built in his honor.

The Greeks admired physical strength and skill because they were often at war. Warfare at the time meant hand-to-hand battle, and young Greek men might be called upon at any time to defend their country.

SOCIAL STUDIES

The Modern Olympic Games

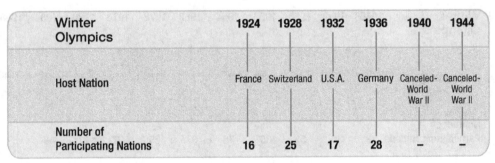

Winter Olympics	1924	1928	1932	1936	1940	1944
Host Nation	France	Switzerland	U.S.A.	Germany	Canceled- World War II	Canceled- World War II
Number of Participating Nations	16	25	17	28	–	–

Summer Olympics	1896	1900	1904	1908	1912	1916	1920	1924	1928	1932	1936	1940	1944
Host Nation	Greece	France	U.S.A.	England	Sweden	Canceled- World War I	Belgium	France	Netherlands	U.S.A.	Germany	Canceled- World War II	Canceled- World War II
Number of Participating Nations	13	22	12	23	28	–	29	44	46	37	49	–	–

The Early Games

✔ In the first Olympic Games, there were only footraces. The <u>pentathlon</u> (pen TATH lon)—a contest consisting of five events—was later added to the games. The pentathlon tested an athlete in the long jump, javelin throw, footrace, discus throw, and wrestling. Wrestling soon became a favorite event in the games. Other events, including chariot racing—races between horse-drawn, two-wheeled cars—came later.

One of the stories of outstanding Greek athletes is about the famed Milo (MY loh) of Croton (KROHT ən). He won the wrestling crown in six Olympic Games. He developed his great strength, it is said, by lifting a baby calf on his shoulder every day until it was a huge bull.

The Olympics began when the Greek empire was at the height of its power. When Greece declined as a world power, the games lost their noble spirit. The last of the early games was held about A.D. 390. Then in A.D. 393, they were outlawed by the Christian Emperor Theodosius I. After about 1,200 years, the Olympics ended. During that long time, they had not been interrupted once, not even by war. Though the games were no longer played, their memory and spirit lived on.

The Modern Olympic Games

In 1896, the Olympics were reborn. For the first time in 1,506 years, an Olympic winner was crowned with an olive wreath. Once again, athletes met to find out who was swifter, higher, and stronger.

The credit for the **revival** of the Olympics belongs to one person, Baron Pierre de Coubertin of France. Coubertin believed that the Olympic Games could serve the modern world as they had ancient Greece. The games would encourage physical fitness in young people. They would also promote world understanding and peace.

Alone, Coubertin began a campaign to revive, or bring back, the Olympics. Finally in 1894, he gained support for his idea. Two years later, the first modern Olympic Games were held. Fittingly, the first modern Olympics took place in Athens, Greece. The games created excitement and enthusiasm throughout the world. At first, the United States did not support the Olympics. After the 1896 games, however, the country caught Olympic fever. A major reason for the sudden interest was the success of American athletes. They competed in the track-and-field events in 1896 and won nine out of the twelve events.

The Modern Olympic Games

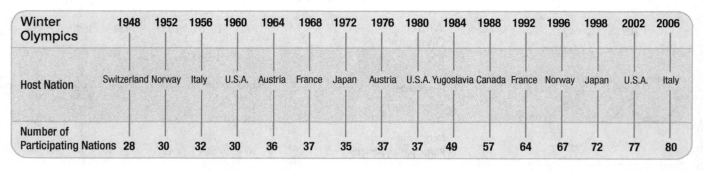

Winter Olympics	1948	1952	1956	1960	1964	1968	1972	1976	1980	1984	1988	1992	1996	1998	2002	2006
Host Nation	Switzerland	Norway	Italy	U.S.A.	Austria	France	Japan	Austria	U.S.A.	Yugoslavia	Canada	France	Norway	Japan	U.S.A.	Italy
Number of Participating Nations	28	30	32	30	36	37	35	37	37	49	57	64	67	72	77	80

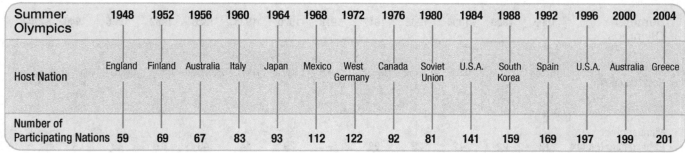

Summer Olympics	1948	1952	1956	1960	1964	1968	1972	1976	1980	1984	1988	1992	1996	2000	2004
Host Nation	England	Finland	Australia	Italy	Japan	Mexico	West Germany	Canada	Soviet Union	U.S.A.	South Korea	Spain	U.S.A.	Australia	Greece
Number of Participating Nations	59	69	67	83	93	112	122	92	81	141	159	169	197	199	201

Many new games were included in the Olympics in 1896. These included gymnastics, shooting, swimming, fencing, and weight lifting.

In 1912, the challenging <u>decathlon</u>—a track-and-field contest of ten events—was added to the Olympics. Athletes compete in this contest for two days. There are five events the first day. These include the 100-meter dash, long jump, shot put, high jump, and 400-meter run. Five more events follow on the second day. They are the 110-meter hurdles, discus throw, pole vault, javelin throw, and 1,500-meter run.

In 1908, ice skating was first included in the Summer Games in London. Many people wanted Winter Games to be organized. However, Coubertin believed that winter sports were snobbish activities enjoyed only by the rich. The first Winter Games were finally held in 1924. They included figure skating, speed skating, skiing, and a bobsled race.

The Winter Games were an immediate success and have remained so ever since. From 1924 to 1992, both the Summer Games and the Winter Games were held every four years in the same years. Since 1994, however, the Summer and Winter Games have alternated every two years.

Over the years, the number of participants and the number of events in the Summer Games and Winter Games have grown. Women as well as men compete in today's Olympics. At their best, the Olympics reach the goal that the Baron de Coubertin had in mind when he revived them. In 1896, Coubertin wrote these words about the games: "The important thing in the Olympic Games is not to win, but to take part, just as the important thing in life is not the triumph but the struggle. The essential thing is not to have conquered but to have fought well."

COMPREHENSION

1. Number the following events in the order in which they happened.

   _____ **a.** The first Winter Games were held.

   _____ **b.** Coroebus set an Olympic footracing record.

   _____ **c.** The first modern Olympic Games were held in Athens, Greece.

   _____ **d.** Theodosius outlawed the Olympics.

   _____ **e.** Wrestling was added to the games.

2. Tell what effect the decline of the Greek empire had on the early Olympic Games.

   _____

   _____

3. Identify where the early Olympics and the first modern Olympics were both held.

   _____

   _____

4. List the new events that were added to the Olympics in 1896.

   _____

   _____

5. Explain why Baron de Coubertin revived the Olympics.

   _____

   _____

   _____

6. Reread the paragraph in the selection marked with an ✘. Underline its main idea. Then circle two or more details that support the main idea.

7. Draw a line to match each word with its meaning.

   sound   a contest of five events

   decathlon   healthy

   pentathlon   a contest of ten events

1. Write the cause for the effect described below.

   Cause: _____

   _____

   Effect: Many of the early Olympic events tested physical skills needed by Greek soldiers.

2. The ancient Greeks believed in both a sound body and a sound mind. Compare their beliefs with the feelings of Americans today.

   _____

   _____

   _____

   _____

3. During what large time period were the Olympic Games *not* held?

   _____

   _____

   _____

4. Explain why the events in the Olympics changed over the years.

   _____

   _____

   _____

5. Reread the paragraph in the selection that has a ✔ next to it. Write a sentence that expresses its main idea.

   _____

   _____

   _____

6. Do you think Baron de Coubertin's statement on page 135 about the Olympics is still true of the Olympics today? Explain.

   _____

   _____

   _____

7. **a.** Is Baron de Coubertin's statement a fact or an opinion?

   _____

   b. In two sentences, tell why you agree or disagree with the statement.

   _____

   _____

   _____

8. Do you think the Olympic motto "swifter, higher, stronger" is still fitting for today's Olympic Games? Explain.

   _____

   _____

   _____

9. Explain how the Olympic Games have always been democratic in spirit.

   _____

   _____

   _____

10. Tell why the decathlon might be considered the most challenging Olympic event.

    _____

    _____

    _____

Use the timeline on pages 133 and 134 to answer the following questions.

1. How frequently were the Olympic Games held until 1992? _____

2. In what year did the greatest number of nations participate in the games? _____

3. **a.** In what three years were the Olympic Games canceled? _____

   b. Why were the games canceled?

   _____

   _____

   _____

4. Where were the Summer and Winter Olympics held in the first games after World War II?

   _____

5. Where and when were the first Winter Olympic Games held? _____

6. In what year were both the Summer and the Winter games held in Germany? _____

7. As of 2006, how many games, Summer and Winter, had been held in the United States? _____

8. In which two countries have the most Olympic Games been held? _____

9. Look at the number of nations participating in the Summer Olympics.

   What trend do you see from 1896 to 2004?

   _____

   _____

10. Have the Winter Olympics ever been held in Greece? Explain why this might be so.

   _____

   _____

   _____

Reading-Writing Connection

On a separate sheet of paper, write a paragraph describing your favorite sport in the Summer or Winter Olympics. Explain why it is your favorite.

Skill: Following Directions

BACKGROUND INFORMATION

"Work and Machines" describes two simple machines, the lever and the pulley, and explains how these machines make work easier for people. In all, there are six simple machines: the lever, the pulley, the inclined plane, the wedge, the screw, and the wheel and axle. Complex machines are made up of different combinations of these simple machines.

SKILL FOCUS: Following Directions

Following directions is an important skill in science. To perform any science experiment, you must follow the steps of the directions exactly. The directions for many experiments are divided into five parts.

1. **Problem** The problem is often a question that you should be able to answer at the end of the experiment.

2. **Aim** The aim is a description of what will be done during the experiment.

3. **Materials** Materials are the objects and equipment needed to perform the experiment.

4. **Procedure** The procedure lists the steps you must carry out in order to do the experiment.

5. **Observations or Conclusions** At the end of the experiment, you should make observations or draw conclusions based on its outcome.

Use the following four steps to help you read a selection with directions for an experiment.

1. Read the paragraphs that explain the ideas on which the experiment is based.

2. Read the five parts of the directions carefully.

3. Study any pictures or diagrams.

4. Reread and be sure that you understand the Problem, Aim, Materials, Procedure, and Observations or Conclusions.

▶ Think about a science experiment you completed in school recently. On the lines, write the problem and the aim of the experiment.

Problem: _____

Aim: _____

CONTEXT CLUES: Diagrams

A **diagram** is a drawing that helps explain a thing by showing all the parts, how it is put together, and how it works. A diagram shows in pictures what a text is describing in words. Be sure to read the title, the caption, and the labels on the diagram to help you interpret what you see.

The diagram below shows a man using a simple machine called a lever to lift a weight. What does the diagram show you about the meaning of the term *resistance force*?

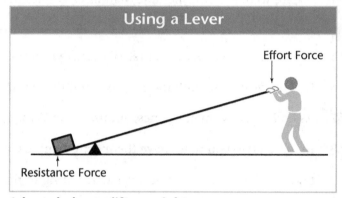

Using a Lever

Effort Force

Resistance Force

A lever helps to lift a weight.

By looking at the diagram, you can figure out that the resistance force is the force or weight that the lever must lift.

▶ Look at the diagram and write a sentence that tells what *effort force* means.

_____

As you read the selection, use the diagram on page 139 to help you understand the meanings of the words *fulcrum*, *effort arm*, and *resistance arm*.

Strategy Tip

After you read "Work and Machines," study the directions for the experiment on page 140. Use the steps described in the Skill Focus on this page to help you understand the experiment.

Work and Machines

People use machines every day. Some machines are complicated and have many moving parts. Others are so simple that most people don't think of them as machines. A **machine** is any invention that makes work easier or faster.

What Is Work?

To a scientist, *work* has a special meaning. *Work* means "the use of force to move an object through a distance." The object is moved in the direction of the force. This meaning for work can be expressed in an equation.

$$\text{Work} = \text{Force} \times \text{Distance}$$

To move an object, a machine must overcome the force that resists the movement of the object. This force is the **resistance**. The distance through which the machine moves the object is called the **resistance distance.**

How Do Machines Make Work Easier?

When a machine is used, some work goes into making the machine function. The force applied by the user to a machine is called the **effort.** The distance through which the user applies the effort is called the **effort distance.** Some machines make work easier by increasing the amount of force that is applied to them and using it against the resistance force. The amount by which a machine increases a force is called the **mechanical advantage** of the machine.

$$\text{Mechanical Advantage} = \text{Resistance} \div \text{Effort}$$

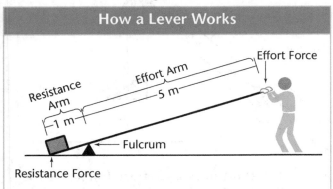

How a Lever Works

Resistance Arm

Effort Arm

Effort Force

5 m

1 m

Fulcrum

Resistance Force

FIGURE 1. **A lever makes moving a heavy object easier.**

Like a seesaw, a lever rocks on a fixed point.

Levers

A **lever** is a simple machine that can multiply a small effort force to overcome a large resistance force. A lever is like a seesaw. It has a rigid arm that rocks back and forth on a fixed point called the <u>fulcrum</u>. Figure 1 shows a simple lever. What is the resistance? How is the effort being applied?

The rigid arm of every lever has two parts. The <u>effort arm</u> is the distance between the fulcrum and the effort force. The <u>resistance arm</u> is the distance between the fulcrum and the resistance force. You can figure out the mechanical advantage of a lever by dividing the length of the effort arm by the length of the resistance arm.

$$\text{Mechanical Advantage of Lever} = \text{Effort Arm} \div \text{Resistance Arm}$$

In Figure 2, the resistance arm is 1 meter, and the effort arm is 5 meters. The mechanical advantage of this lever, then, is 5. On a seesaw, the effort arm and the resistance arm are equal. Therefore, the mechanical advantage of a seesaw is 1.

You can figure out how much effort is needed to move an object if you know the mechanical advantage of a machine. To do this, you divide the resistance by the mechanical advantage.

$$\text{Effort} = \text{Resistance} \div \text{Mechanical Advantage}$$

SCIENCE

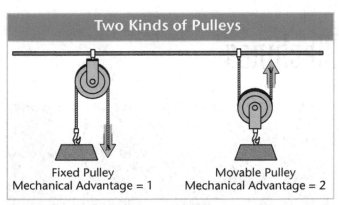

Two Kinds of Pulleys

Fixed Pulley
Mechanical Advantage = 1

Movable Pulley
Mechanical Advantage = 2

FIGURE 2. **A fixed pulley is held in place by a support beam. A movable pulley moves freely.**

Pulleys

A **pulley**, another highly useful simple machine, is a form of a lever. A pulley makes work easier by changing the direction of a force. (See Figure 3.) A pulley is a grooved wheel over which runs a cord. To lift an object with a pulley, you pull on the cord. Your pull is the effort. The object that is pulled is the resistance. A pulley attached to a wall, a beam, or any other support frame is called a **fixed pulley**. Window shades and flagpoles often have fixed pulleys. Fixed pulleys do not multiply the effort force put into them. They only change the direction of the force. Often it is easier to pull against a resistance than to lift it.

A greater advantage is gained through using a movable pulley. A **movable pulley** is hung on a rope attached to a support frame. The rope runs through the pulley. The pulley itself moves up the rope as the rope is pulled. A movable pulley makes it easier to lift a heavy weight. You can figure out the mechanical advantage of a pulley by dividing the resistance distance by the effort distance.

Mechanical Advantage of Pulley =
Resistance Distance ÷ Effort Distance

EXPERIMENT

The following experiment will show the advantage of a fixed pulley.

PROBLEM
What mechanical advantage can you obtain by using a fixed pulley?

AIM
In this experiment, you will measure the mechanical advantage of a fixed pulley.

MATERIALS
You will need a support frame, a single lightweight pulley, a length of cord, a 2-kilogram weight, a spring balance, and a meter stick.

PROCEDURE
1. Attach the weight to the spring balance. What is the weight of the load, or the resistance?

2. Remove the weight from the spring balance. Tie the weight to one end of the cord. String the free end of the cord over the pulley. Hang the pulley on the support frame and attach the top of the spring balance to the free end of the cord. Pull slowly on the spring balance. Read the spring balance to determine the value of this effort. How does the effort compare to the resistance? Was it easier to lift the weight by hand or to lift it with the use of the pulley? Why?

3. Use the meter stick to see how far you must pull down the cord to lift the weight 1 meter. Then compare the two distances. What is the mechanical advantage of a fixed pulley?

OBSERVATIONS OR CONCLUSIONS
The mechanical advantage of a fixed pulley is 1. Think about what this means. Why is a fixed pulley useful?

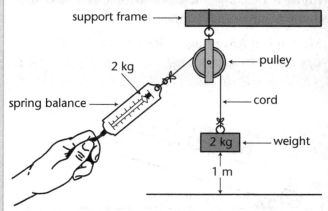

Measuring the Mechanical Advantage of a Fixed Pulley

support frame

2 kg

spring balance

pulley

cord

2 kg — weight

1 m

Compare the effort force and effort distance to the resistance force and resistance distance.

1. Define *machine.* _____

_____

2. Describe the mechanical advantage of a

machine. _____

_____

3. In Figure 1, what object is the fulcrum?

_____

4. Draw a line to match each term with its explanation.

fulcrum

a. distance between the fulcrum and the effort force

effort arm

b. distance between the fulcrum and the resistance force

resistance arm

c. fixed point over which a lever rocks

CRITICAL THINKING

1. If a lever has an effort arm of 4 meters and a resistance arm of 2 meters, what is the mechanical advantage of the machine?

_____

_____

2. Tell which tool is not a lever: a bottle opener, a nutcracker, a crowbar, an axe.

_____

3. A pair of scissors is a kind of lever. Explain where the fulcrum is on a pair of scissors.

_____

_____

4. **a.** On a pair of scissors, where is the effort applied? _____

_____

b. What provides the resistance? _____

_____

5. How far must you raise the cord of a movable pulley in order to lift a load 2 meters?

_____

6. Explain how you could make a seesaw work better as a lever. _____

_____

_____

_____

This experiment should show how much force it would take to lift an object of a certain weight with two different levers. Complete the directions, using the experiment on page 140 as a model. Use a ruler or a meter stick for the arm, a block of wood for the fulcrum, a weight for the resistance, other weights to measure the effort needed to lift the resistance, and a spring balance. Number the steps in the Procedure part. In the box, draw and label a diagram to show this experiment. The Problem and Aim have been completed.

EXPERIMENT

PROBLEM
Compare the effort needed to lift an object of a certain weight with two different levers.

AIM
In this experiment, you will compare the effort force needed to lift a resistance of a certain weight with two different levers. The effort arm of one lever should be twice the length of the resistance arm. The effort arm of the other lever should be four times the length of the resistance arm.

MATERIALS
_____

_____

PROCEDURE
_____

_____

_____

_____

_____

_____

_____

_____

_____

_____

OBSERVATIONS AND CONCLUSIONS
_____

_____

_____

_____

Reading-Writing Connection
On a separate sheet of paper, write a paragraph describing a kind of pulley or lever that you use daily. Include an explanation of how the pulley or lever works.

Skill: Reading a Graph

BACKGROUND INFORMATION

"Costs of World War II" provides information about the long struggle to win World War II (1939–1945). The war killed more people, cost more money, and damaged more property than any other war in history. During the war, the Allies—led by the United States, the Soviet Union, Great Britain, and France—struggled against the Axis nations. The Axis nations included Germany, Japan, and Italy. As a result of the war, there were far-reaching changes in Asia, Europe, and the United States.

SKILL FOCUS: Reading a Graph

A **graph** shows numerical information visually. You can find information in a graph more quickly than you can in a paragraph of text. Graphs also make it easier to compare information. Newspapers, magazines, and textbooks often present information in the form of graphs.

Different types of graphs are used for different purposes. **Circle graphs** are used to show parts of a whole. For that reason, circle graphs usually show percents. For example, a circle graph might show the results of a public-opinion poll. By looking at a graph, you can see at a glance the percentage of people who approve, disapprove, or have no opinion on an issue.

To use a circle graph, first read its **title**. The title tells what kind of information is shown on the graph. Also pay attention to the **labels** on each section of the circle. The labels will help you find the information you need. Be sure to compare the sizes of the sections on a circle graph to see what part of the whole each section represents.

Reading the paragraphs that come before and after a circle graph is important, too. These paragraphs might explain the purpose of the graph. They might also include background information that will help you understand and use the facts shown on the graph.

▶ Look at the circle graph below. Then answer the questions.

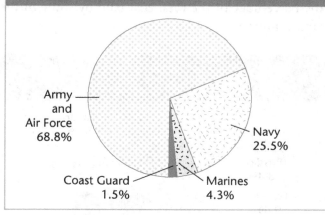

What is the title of the circle graph?

_____

In World War II, what percentage of the U.S. armed forces were in the Marines?

_____

WORD CLUES

Look for the important words *sectors*, *label*, and *data* in "Costs of World War II." Knowing these words will help you understand circle graphs.

Strategy Tip

In "Costs of World War II," read the title of each graph before studying the graph itself. Also take time to understand what the labels mean. Understanding the title and the labels will help you interpret the information the graph presents.

COSTS OF WORLD WAR II

According to one estimate, World War II cost $1,154,000,000,000 to fight. That is more than one trillion dollars. Dozens of nations took part in the war and paid part of the cost. Circle Graph 1 shows the percentage of the total cost paid by some of the largest nations.

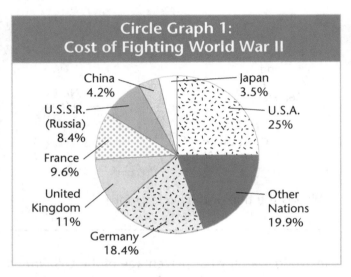

Circle Graph 1:
Cost of Fighting World War II

As you can see, the title of the graph is *Cost of Fighting World War II, by Country.* Also notice that the graph is divided into eight sections, or **sectors.** Each sector has a **label.** The labels tell you what each sector stands for. The labels also identify the **data**, or numerical information, represented by each sector. On Circle Graph 1, each label names a country. It also tells the percentage of the total cost paid by that country.

You can use the sectors in Circle Graph 1 to compare how much of the total cost different nations paid. You can see, for example, that the United States paid about 25 percent, or $\frac{1}{4}$, of the total cost of the war. Germany was the second-largest spender. France and the United Kingdom each spent about 10 percent of the total. Notice that one of the sectors has the label *Other Nations.* This sector shows the total percentage of the cost that dozens of smaller nations paid.

At the peak of World War II, more than 70 million people were in uniform. They fought for more than 50 countries. Circle Graph 2 lets you compare the sizes of the armed forces of different nations during the war. The labels tell the names of major countries that fought. They also tell the percent of the total number of soldiers that each country supplied.

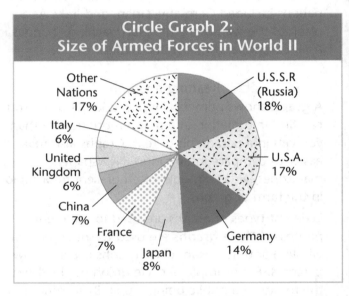

Circle Graph 2:
Size of Armed Forces in World II

The graph shows that the U.S.S.R., now Russia, supplied 18 percent of all the armed forces in World War II. The United States supplied almost as many, 17 percent. You can also see from the graph that China and France, for example, each supplied about 7 percent.

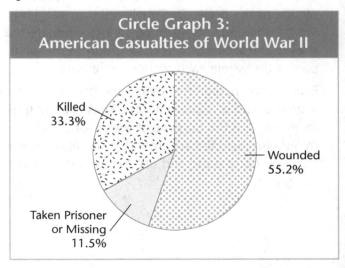

Circle Graph 3:
American Casualties of World War II

During World War II, the United States suffered many casualties. In all, about 1,216,000 soldiers were killed, wounded, taken prisoner, or declared missing. Circle Graph 3 shows the percentage of the total casualties represented by each of these groups.

Circle Graph 3 shows that about one-third, or 33.3%, of the American casualties were killed. It does not, however, show the actual number of soldiers who were killed. If you know the total number of American casualties, however, you can figure out how many Americans were killed. Use the following numerical sentence.

$$33.3\% \text{ of } t = k \text{ or } \frac{1}{3} \times t = k$$

The symbol t stands for the total number of casualties. The symbol k stands for the number of Americans who were killed.

Since the paragraph at the top of this column mentions that there were 1,216,000 casualties in all, you can solve the sentence:

$$\frac{1}{3} \times 1,216,000 = k$$

$$\frac{1,216,000}{3} = k$$

$$405,333.3 = k$$

The figure of 405,333.3 is not an exact number because percents on circle graphs are usually rounded. Rounding your answer, you can say that about 405,333 Americans were killed during World War II.

If the labels on a circle graph do not include percents, you can still compare the size of the sectors just by looking at them. You can see which sector represents the largest percentage. You can see which one represents the smallest percentage. You can also see which sectors represent about the same amount.

You can also estimate the amounts represented by each sector by using fractions. If a sector takes up about a quarter of the circle, for example, it represents about $\frac{1}{4}$, or 25%, of the total amount.

When the labels include percents, you can figure out how much larger one sector is than another. Also, if you know the total amount represented by the whole circle, you can figure out the amount represented by each sector. Just multiply the total amount by the fraction or decimal represented by each sector.

COMPREHENSION

1. Look at Circle Graph 1. What percentage of the total cost of the war was paid by the United States, the United Kingdom, and France together?

_____

2. Look at Circle Graph 2. What percentage of the armed forces in the war were supplied by Germany?

_____

3. How can you figure out the amount represented by each sector if you know the total amount represented by the circle?

_____

_____

_____

_____

CRITICAL THINKING

1. Tell what determines the size of a sector in a circle graph.

_____

2. State what would happen to the other sectors if the size of one sector of a circle graph were increased.

_____

3. Put a ✔ next to the idea that could best be shown in a circle graph.

_____ **a.** the reasons that World War II began

_____ **b.** how many Americans were in favor of, opposed to, or had no opinion about entering World War II in 1940

_____ **c.** political changes that occurred in Europe after World War II

_____ **d.** annual increases in U.S. government spending for the years 1939-1945

SKILL FOCUS: READING A GRAPH

Use the following paragraph and circle graph to answer the questions.

The four major air powers in World War II were the United States, Germany, Japan, and the United Kingdom. In all, these four nations lost about 240,000 military airplanes during the war. The circle graph on this page shows what percent each lost.

Losses of Military Aircraft of Major Air Powers in World War II

Germany 40%
United States 25%
Japan 20%
United Kingdom 15%

1. What is the title of this circle graph?

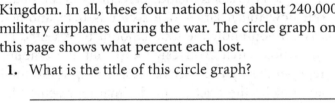

2. How many sectors are shown on the graph?

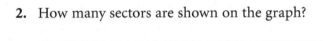

3. What are the labels of the sectors?

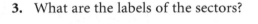

4. What is the sum of the percents given in the labels?

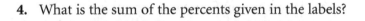

5. Which country shown on the graph lost the fewest airplanes?

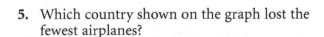

6. What percentage of the airplanes shown on the graph was lost by the United States?

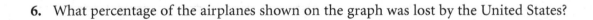

7. How many of the 240,000 airplanes did the United States lose?

_____

Reading-Writing Connection

Take a poll of your classmates to find out their opinions on a current issue. On a separate sheet of paper, make a circle graph to show the results of your poll.

A word may have a different meaning in literature, social studies, science, mathematics, or music. Study the following words with **multiple meanings**.

band	change	crop	legend	pupil
cell	cone	yard	power	plot

Read the two definitions for each word below. Choose a word from the list above that fits those two definitions. Write the word on the line above the definitions.

1. _____

   Mathematics: a measure, 36 inches in length

   Social Studies: an open place used for a business or special purpose

2. _____

   Music: a group of musicians playing instruments together

   Social Studies: a group of people joined to do something

3. _____

   Social Studies: a small room in a prison or jail

   Science: the basic unit of living matter, usually very small

4. _____

   Mathematics: a solid object that narrows evenly from a flat circle at one end to a point at the other

   Science: the part of evergreen trees that bears seeds

5. _____

   Mathematics: money returned when one has paid more than the amount owed

   Social Studies: places or conditions that become different as time passes

6. _____

   Literature: the action, or series of events, in a story

   Social Studies: a secret plan, in politics or during a war, to gain power or harm an enemy by misleading people, usually by dishonest methods

7. _____

   Science: energy or force that has the ability to do work

   Social Studies: a person or group that has authority, right, or control over others

8. _____

   Science: the dark opening in the center of the eye

   Social Studies: a person being taught by a teacher

9. _____

   Social Studies: the full amount of produce grown by a farmer in one season

   Science: a pouch in a bird's gullet where food is softened for digestion

10. _____

   Literature: a story handed down through the years and connected with some real events, but probably not true in itself

   Social Studies: a key or brief explanation accompanying a chart or map

Skill: Using an Index

A quick way to find information in a textbook or reference book is to use the **index** at the back of the book. An index lists all the important subjects included in the book.

On the following page is part of an index from a science textbook. The **topics** are arranged in alphabetical order. Find the topic *Oil*. Below it, three subtopics are listed alphabetically: *pollution from*, *source*, and *use*. **Subtopics** list the specific kinds of information given in the book about the topic. Notice that some subtopics have such words as *in* and *of* before them. These short words do not affect the alphabetical order of the subtopics.

The numbers after each topic or subtopic are the page numbers on which information is found. Numbers separated by dashes indicate that information begins on the page before the dash and ends on the page after the dash. Numbers separated by commas show that information appears on only the pages for which numbers are given.

Study the index on page 149. Then answer the following questions.

1. On what page(s) would you find information about mud? _____

2. How many subtopics are listed under the topic *Moon*? _____

3. On what page(s) would you find information about craters on the moon? _____

4. How many pages does the book have on nuclear energy? _____

5. On what page(s) would you find information about the moons of Pluto? _____

6. How many pages does the book have on the Milky Way? _____

7. On what page(s) would you find information about nitrogen in the soil? _____

8. What two planets' moons are discussed on the same page? _____

9. If you wanted information on life in the oceans, which page would you *not* read between pages 250 and 256? _____

10. On what page(s) would you find information about nickel in the earth's core? _____

11. What five subtopics about the moon are discussed on page 105?

    _____

12. What topic comes between nickel and nuclear energy? _____

13. If the book had information about mold, after which topic would it be listed? _____

14. If the book had information about fish farms in the oceans, before which subtopic would it be listed? _____

Methane, 475
  in atmosphere, 262
  in outer planets, 75, 77
Milky Way, 25–28, 38–41, 47, 57
Minerals:
  chemical weathering of, 320–324
  conservation of, 473–474
  crystals, 138–140, 161–162
  deposits, 171–172
  gems, 143–145
  identification of, 138, 145–153
  in lithosphere, 29
  in rocks, 158, 161, 168, 323
  soil and, 324–327, 330
  sources of, 141–142, 470–472, 489
Mining, 471–474
Moho, 187–188
Mohs scale, 148–149
Molecules, behavior of, 122–125
Moon:
  age of, 103, 444–446
  atmosphere of, 104
  axis, rotation of, 102–103
  craters on, 79, 104–105
  eclipses, 108–109
  gravity of, 102
  marias, 103–105
  orbit of, 105
  phases, 105–108
  revolution of, 105
  size, 102
  tides and, 109–111
Moons:
  of Jupiter, 75
  of Mars, 74
  of Neptune, 77
  of Pluto, 78
  of Saturn, 76
  of Uranus, 77
Moraines, 345–346
Mountains, 200–202, 452, 454
  belts, 202
  earth's mantle and, 367–368
  erosion and, 30, 201
  faults and, 372
  folds and, 375–376
  magma and, 377
  oceanic, 240, 248–250, 404–406
  ores in, 333
  ranges, 201–202, 402–403, 411,
      453, 456
  soils, 332–333
  system of, 202
  weathering and, 30
Mud, 165

N

Nebulae, 40
Nekton, 251–253
Neon:
  in atmosphere, 94
  in meteoroids, 81
Nickel:
  in the earth's core, 192–193
  in meteoroids, 81
Nitrogen:
  in atmosphere, 30, 94, 263–265, 275
  from carbon, 14, 443
  living things and, 264–265, 481–482
  in oceans, 242
  in soil, 324, 469
Nuclear energy, 492–494
Nucleus, 127

O

Oceans:
  basins, topography of, 244–250,
  255, 257
  continental margins, 245–246
  depths, 238, 241, 243, 245–246, 250–254
  gases in, 242
  life in, 250–254, 256, 426
  minerals in, 490
  oceanography, 13, 239, 241, 254–257
  salinity, 239–242, 251, 256
  spreading of floor, 404–407, 454
  temperatures and, 241–243
      256, 309
  trenches, 249, 406–407
Oil:
  pollution from, 482–483
  source, 474–475
  use, 324, 476
Orbit, 24, 69
  of planets, 68–69, 70–76
  of satellites, 87–89
Orbital velocity, 87–89
Ores, 141–143, 333, 470–471
  mining, 471–472
  refining, 472–473
Oxidation, 320–321

Skill: Comparing Travel Packages

In planning a vacation, people need to decide where they will go, how long they will stay, where they will stay, what they want to see, and how much money they will need to spend. **Travel packages** are arrangements made by a travel agent or travel company to cover vacation plans. These arrangements may include air travel, hotels, meals, and extras such as sightseeing. Before making a decision on travel plans, many people look into several travel packages to compare what they offer.

Read and compare the following travel packages.

Experience Relaxation
while exploring the historic past.

GALVESTON: A 19th-Century Island City

The historic Gulf Inn Resort combines gracious charm with comfort. Overlooking the Gulf of Mexico, the resort is within walking distance of the city's finest shops and historic homes. Dimly lit dining is provided in the Gulf Room Restaurant. In addition, a pool, an indoor gym, and tennis courts offer relaxing recreation for our guests.

$100 per person per night, double occupancy

PACKAGE INCLUDES:
- Deluxe room with balcony
- Half-day bus tour of city
- Full breakfast
- Half-day walking tour of historic homes
- Relaxing massages
- Free use of recreation facilities
- Free "Historic Galveston Travel Guide"
- Free parking

PHONE your travel agent
or call the Gulf Inn Resort at
713-555-8686

Enjoy FAMILY FUN in historic
WILLIAMSBURG!
THREE-NIGHT SPECIAL
(includes, hotel, breakfast, sightseeing)
$150 per adult, double occupancy
Mon.–Thurs., excluding holiday periods

Stay
at the Colonial Motel
- Up to two children under 15 stay free
- Free breakfast
- Free parking
- Free swimming pool and game room

Visit
the Historic Past
- Free full-day guided tour of Williamsburg
- Sights include the capitol building, Bruton Parish Church, Governor's Palace, and restored homes on Duke of Gloucester Street

Dine
in Historic Williamsburg
- Midweek Special includes one dinner for two at any of three fine restaurants. (Up to $25.00 per person)

Enjoy
Other Family Attractions
- For just $30 a day, you can rent a car with unlimited mileage to visit nearby family attractions and amusement parks.

MAKE YOUR RESERVATIONS *NOW!*
PHONE "Sunstar Travel Group" TOLL-FREE
800-555-3742

A. Circle the letter next to the phrase that correctly completes each sentence.

1. The Galveston package stresses
   a. family fun.   **b.** sightseeing.   **c.** relaxation.   **d.** bargain prices.

2. The Williamsburg package stresses
   a. family fun.   **b.** sightseeing.   **c.** relaxation.   **d.** bargain prices.

3. The rates for both packages are based on "double occupancy." This means that
   a. the charge is the same for two people in the room as it is for one person.
   b. the actual price is half the quoted rate.
   c. the room rate changes with each additional person in the room.
   d. the per-person charge is based on two people in a room, so the price of the room is actually twice the quoted rate.

4. If a family wants to save money, it may prefer the Williamsburg package because
   a. up to two children can stay free in the motel in Williamsburg.
   b. Williamsburg offers a holiday discount.
   c. the Galveston package does not offer a free breakfast.
   d. the Galveston package does not include free tours.

5. For three nights, the Galveston package costs
   a. $300.00 per person.   b. $300.00 per room.   c. $100.00 per person.   d. $600.00 per person.

6. Both the Galveston and Williamsburg packages include
   a. a special three-day rate for rooms.
   b. a room rate based upon double occupancy.
   c. a car rental.
   d. special holiday discounts.

B. Compare the two travel packages by completing the chart below. If no information is given for a particular item, write *no information*. Then answer the questions below the chart.

Travel Package Information	Galveston	Williamsburg
price per night per adult		
number of people per room		
days available		
children's rates		
meals included		
free recreation facilities		
number of tours		
car rental		
how to reserve		

1. Which package is less expensive per night? _____

2. Which package includes more free recreation facilities? _____

3. Which package has a special children's rate? _____

4. Which package is available on weekends? _____

The Computer Age

LESSON 48

Skill: Point of View

BACKGROUND INFORMATION

"The Principal Problem" is a story told through a student's journal entries. Carmen's life changes dramatically when a computer arrives at her school. As computers have become more common, people have criticized them for different reasons. Workers fear they will lose their jobs to the machines. People complain about computer errors and how hard they are to correct. Whatever their drawbacks, however, computers are here to stay.

SKILL FOCUS: Point of View

Point of view is the eye through which a story is written. Some stories are told from the first-person point of view. Others are told from the third-person point of view.

In the **first-person point of view**, a character in the story tells the story. This character uses the first-person pronouns *I*, *me*, and *we* to tell the story. A **first-person narrator** tells his or her own experiences and thoughts. This type of narrator cannot enter the minds of other characters or describe events that he or she has not seen.

In the **third-person point of view**, the narrator is outside the story. The narrator uses the third-person pronouns *he*, *she*, and *they* to tell what the characters think and do. A **third-person narrator** can tell what different characters are thinking and doing.

▶ Read the following sentences. On the lines below, write the narrator's point of view and how you determined it.

Walking home, I heard someone running toward me. I was frightened. A tall man ran by me. He raced to an emergency police phone.

_____

_____

CONTEXT CLUES: Using a Dictionary

When you read a new word, context clues might give you a general idea of the word's meaning. If you want a detailed definition of the word, however, you need to look it up in a dictionary.

Read the following sentence, and think about the meaning of the underlined word.

> ___Technicians___ *have been trying to put together the six computer pieces so that our new principal can start functioning properly.*

The context clues suggest that technicians work on computers. A dictionary might say that a technician is an expert on a technical subject.

▶ Think about the meaning of *policy* below.

> *Mr. Alioto must have announced six different big changes in school **policy** over the public-address system today. Twice he changed a policy that had been set only yesterday.*

What do you think a policy is?

_____

Now look up *policy* in a dictionary. Write its definition on the lines.

_____

_____

As you read, use a dictionary to define *coincidence*, *aerobics*, and *malfunctioned*.

> **Strategy Tip**
>
> As you read "The Principal Problem," think about who is telling the story. Is the information you learn limited to the narrator's own thoughts, feelings, and observations?

THE PRINCIPAL PROBLEM

September 10 It had to happen, of course. Summer vacation has come to an end. Today, I, Carmen Soares, began my last year at Gloria Willis Junior High. I wish it were my last week, though I'm relieved to have Miss James for my homeroom teacher. She's got potential; she just has to be trained right. Seat assignments were handed out, and I'm right in front of Harry Seely. How's that for luck? He asked to borrow a pencil, and I very coolly said, "Keep it, Harry; I've got zillions of them." Definitely a good start!

September 11 A weird thing happened at our first assembly of the year. Mr. Alioto, the assistant principal, announced that Mrs. Uxley would not be returning as principal. I guess she's retiring or something. When one of the kids asked about Mrs. Uxley's replacement, Mr. Alioto didn't say anything for a moment. Then he answered, "Her replacement will be delivered next week."

September 14 I've done nothing for the last three days but wonder about our new principal. How do you "deliver" a principal?

September 19 Well, I got my answer today—you deliver a principal in boxes. Our principal was delivered in six boxes, to be exact. It's a computer—talk about new ideas! It's a good thing that I'm heading for high school after this year. Yet Luis Garcia says that won't make a bit of difference. He told me that once they get a bad idea in one school, they usually take it around to all the others.

September 23 Technicians have been trying to put together the six computer pieces so that our new principal can start functioning properly. They've been running in and out of the principal's office. Rumors are racing around the school, but no one really knows what's happening. Harry Seely borrowed another pencil. That makes three. What does he do with them?

September 24 Two items of interest! First they put a suggestion box in each classroom. Then they gave everyone, even teachers, a form to complete. In the top part, you had to write your hobbies, your favorite television shows, even the kinds of food that you like best. Also they wanted you to suggest how life at Gloria Willis could be improved. They also handed out this funny note.

GLORIA WILLIS JR. HIGH
OFFICE OF THE PRINCIPAL

HELLO,

MY NAME IS T12H2679DELTA. CALL ME DELLIE. I AM YOUR NEW PRINCIPAL. ALL NEW DELTA COMPUTERS ARE PROGRAMMED FOR TOP PERFORMANCE IN A SPECIFIC TYPE OF JOB, AND I AM NO EXCEPTION. A SUGGESTION BOX HAS BEEN PLACED IN YOUR CLASSROOM. PLEASE USE IT OFTEN SO THAT YOU CAN HELP ME IN MY JOB. I THINK WE CAN HAVE FUN TOGETHER, DON'T YOU?

September 26 As if things weren't bad enough, I just saw a magazine article about my new principal. It said that there were two Delta computers now in use: ours and one that's working as a town manager out in some small Midwestern town. The article talked about how the other Delta has to be a diplomat, which means it has to consider everybody's opinion before it makes any decisions. Our Delta principal, on the other hand, is supposed to act like a dictator. It makes decisions without considering anyone's opinion. I think we're in big, big trouble at Gloria Willis—really gigantic trouble!

September 27 I detest Harry Seely—he's been borrowing Rita Korngold's pencils, too.

September 28 All's well that ends well. Rita Korngold was shipped off to the other side of the room. I don't think it had anything to do with my suggestion, although it was really a very funny coincidence. I dropped another suggestion into the box just to be sure.

October 1 That'll teach me. I thought I was safe telling Milos Kelly, the track star, about the suggestion box, but that just shows how smart I really am! When Miss James said gym was being replaced by <u>aerobics,</u> I knew whose suggestion that was. I just hope he keeps his promise not to tell anyone else.

October 2 Now I know what Milos Kelly's promises are worth! When I walked into class this morning, there was a long line of kids waiting to drop suggestions into the box. To make things worse, when I went to my seat, I found out that Harry Seely was no longer sitting in back of me. He'd been moved to the other side of the room, to a seat next to—guess who? They put Ronnie Franks behind me in Harry Seely's place. What a trade that was! Now I'll have to stop wearing my hair in a braid. Ronnie Franks is that kind of neighbor. After I finish writing this, I'm going to spend at least two hours writing suggestions.

October 3 Things are getting weird, to say the least. There's a ten-minute wait at just about every suggestion box in school—at any time of day! Mr. Alioto must have announced six different big changes in school policy over the public-address system today. Twice he changed a policy that had

been set only yesterday. I wonder who suggested that we be allowed to bring our pets to school.

October 5 War was declared in school today, and it's our class against 9C. They started it. Just after we sat down in the auditorium, Mr. Alioto said, "It's been suggested that some of the classes change places at assembly." He said, "some of the classes," but he changed only two. Guess which two? What hurt was the way the kids in 9C laughed as we walked to the rear of the auditorium.

October 6 Every kid in class suggested that we change assembly places again. Later, during hide and seek, Mr. Alioto announced that there wouldn't be homework anymore. Everybody shouted and clapped, but I felt kind of sad. I wonder what's wrong with me.

October 7 I told my mother that I wanted to move to a new school. When she asked me why, I didn't know what to say. How could I explain that I was tired of seeing movies and playing games all day? She'd take me to a doctor; I'm sure she would.

October 9 I spent most of the day in the nurse's office. Cindy Marshall's snake bit me. Looking over the magazines that they have at the nurse's office now, I happened to see a story about that Delta computer that's running a town out in the Midwest. It seems the people in that town are having a lot of trouble with their computer. It makes them stand in lines according to their height and punishes them when they are late. In a way, I wish that our principal was more like the town manager.

October 12 A quiet day: our clown phoned in sick, and the movie projector exploded. I dropped six suggestions into the box, suggesting that we be allowed to do plain old schoolwork again. No one can ever know about those suggestions! We still didn't get our old seats back in assembly.

October 13 Miss James told us there would be an election in school next month. When we asked her what the election was for, she became very upset. Ronnie Franks tapped me on the shoulder and threatened, "You better vote for me next month, or you'll be sorry!" When I asked him what he was running for, he answered, "Homeroom teacher."

October 16 9C was sent down to the basement for a fire drill. They were the only class to go, so you can guess whose idea the whole thing was. They didn't come back until the afternoon relay races. I think I know why we never got our assembly seats back, and why we still haven't been given plain old schoolwork, as I suggested. It's simple mathematics. There are 32 kids in 9C, and 31 kids in our class. We were outnumbered and outsuggested!

October 19 What a day! First our water balloon fight was called off. Then at eleven o'clock, people from the board of education broke down the front door and took over the school. At first they thought that our computer principal had <u>malfunctioned</u>, but, as it turns out, we were sent the wrong computer. We should have gotten the one that went out to the Midwest, and they should have gotten ours. *We* got the diplomat, and *they* got the dictator! Nobody would have discovered the mistake if our principal hadn't ordered ten tons of popcorn for the hot-lunch program.

November 14 The last three weeks have been great! I love doing math, history, and English again. I feel as if the first month of school was all a bad dream. I'd better save this journal, or else no one will ever believe what happened. Of course, I can always show people the scar where Cindy's snake bit me.

November 16 Something's wrong again. I saw Miss James crying, and she wouldn't tell me why.

November 18 I found out why.

GLORIA WILLIS JR. HIGH
OFFICE OF THE PRINCIPAL

IN A SURPRISE MOVE, THE NEW PRINCIPAL OF THE GLORIA WILLIS JUNIOR HIGH SCHOOL FIRED ALL OF THE SCHOOL'S TEACHERS. WHEN ASKED WHY THE TEACHERS WERE FIRED, T12H2679-DELTA ANSWERED, "I HAD TO. ALL THEY DID FOR THE PAST MONTH WAS PLAY GAMES, WATCH MOVIES, EAT COTTON CANDY, AND CAMPAIGN FOR THEIR JOBS." WHEN ASKED IF REPLACEMENTS COULD BE FOUND QUICKLY, T12H2679-DELTA ANSWERED, "WITHOUT A DOUBT! MANY OF THEIR REPLACEMENTS HAVE ALREADY BEEN DELIVERED."

COMPREHENSION

1. Describe the setting of the story.

_____

_____

2. Explain why Gloria Willis Junior High School was getting a new principal.

_____

_____

3. Tell how the new principal arrives.

_____

_____

4. Where and how is the second Delta computer being used?

_____

_____

5. Are the two Delta computers alike or different? Explain your answer.

_____

_____

_____

_____

6. Draw a line to match each word with its meaning.

coincidence   **a.** failed to work as programmed

aerobics   **b.** events happening at about the same time that seem to be connected but really are not

malfunctioned   **c.** physical exercises that improve the circulation of the blood

1. Explain why Carmen is sorry after she tells Milos about the suggestion box.

   _____

   _____

2. Describe the ways that life at Gloria Willis Junior High School changes with the delivery of the new principal.

   _____

   _____

3. Identify the following statements as facts or opinions. Write *F* or *O* on the lines provided.

   _____ a. Once they get a bad idea in one school, they usually take it around to all the others.

   _____ b. There will be an election in school next month.

   _____ c. I think we're in big, big trouble at Gloria Willis—really gigantic trouble.

   _____ d. The last three weeks have been great! I love doing math, history, and English again.

4. a. Describe how Carmen feels about Dellie when it first arrives.

   _____

   _____

   b. Describe how Carmen feels about Dellie a few weeks later.

   _____

   _____

   c. How does Carmen feel after the board of education discovers that the wrong computer was delivered to the school?

   _____

   _____

5. Explain why Miss James is fired.

   _____

   _____

6. Do you think a computer could be a good assistant to a principal? Give reasons.

   _____

   _____

1. Who is the narrator of the story?

_____

_____

2. Is the narrator a participant in the story's events or an outsider? Explain.

_____

_____

3. Why is the first person a good point of view from which to tell this story?

_____

_____

4. In her journal entries, the narrator reveals thoughts and feelings about what is going on at Gloria Willis. List two or three of the narrator's thoughts about having a computer principal.

_____

_____

5. Why does the reader not know how the other students feel, or what they think, about the computer?

_____

_____

6. Why is it not possible for Carmen to tell in her journal entry how Miss James felt?

_____

_____

Reading-Writing Connection

On a separate sheet of paper, write two paragraphs describing how you would feel if the teachers in your school were replaced by computers. Use the first-person point of view.

Skill: Making Generalizations

BACKGROUND INFORMATION

"From the Abacus to the Personal Computer" traces the historical development of the computer. Only in the last 70 years have amazing developments in electronics made the idea of computers a reality. The computer is only the latest development in people's centuries-old quest to find more efficient ways to calculate. The ancient Chinese developed a calculator called the abacus, for example. The abacus is more than 2,500 years old.

SKILL FOCUS: Making Generalizations

A **generalization** is a broad statement that applies to many examples or events. You can make a generalization by thinking about related facts and what they have in common.

Read the following group of related facts.

- At school, Tasha does research on a computer.
- Ryan's favorite pastime is playing computer games.
- Mrs. Curtis pays her bills on the Internet.
- At his after-school job, Ramón uses a computer to design and print posters.

Based on these facts, you could make the following generalization: Computers play an important role in many areas of everyday life.

Certain words can signal generalizations. They include *all, most, many, few, always, everyone, overall,* and *generally.* These signal words show that the generalization is a broad statement that many examples support.

▶ In the chart below, write a generalization based on the three facts.

CONTEXT CLUES: Using a Glossary

Many social studies and science selections include specialized vocabulary words. Often these words are organized in a glossary at the end of a chapter or book. A **glossary** is an alphabetized list of words and their meanings.

Suppose you read the following sentence in a selection that includes a glossary.

*In 1833, he tried to build the first **digital** computer.*

If you do not know the meaning of the word *digital,* and there are no context clues to help you figure it out, look up the word's meaning in the glossary. *Digital* means having data in number form.

▶ Read the sentence below. Then use the glossary on page 162 to find the meaning of the underlined word. Write the meaning on the line.

*They could work so fast that their operation was measured in **nanoseconds.***

_____

As you read the selection, use the glossary on page 162 to find the meanings of the underlined words *computer, data, binary,* and *CD-ROM.*

> ### Strategy Tip
>
> As you read "From the Abacus to the Personal Computer," try to make generalizations about the development of the modern computer.

Fact 1	Fact 2	Fact 3
The first British computer was called Colossus because it was so big.	In 1946, the first American computer, called ENIAC, filled a huge room.	All the computers NASA used in 1969 to send astronauts to the moon had about as much power together as one of today's personal computers.

Generalization

FROM THE ABACUS TO THE PERSONAL COMPUTER

The computer revolution (REV ə LOO shən) has been underway for some time. It has brought about more changes than the **Industrial Revolution** did. What makes this revolution so amazing is that the computer did not exist 70 years ago.

In that sense, the computer is a modern invention. However, many of the ideas used in computer design date back several hundred years. There has always been a need for efficient and accurate counting. In the beginning, people used their fingers for counting. As their needs became more complex, however, they needed help from machines.

The Abacus

At least 2,500 years ago, the Chinese invented an efficient way of counting. Their invention, the abacus, is still in use. This early mechanical calculator consists of a handheld rectangular frame. In the frame are many fixed rods strung with movable beads. Numbers are recorded by moving the beads. A skilled abacus operator can easily keep pace with a person using a modern calculator.

The abacus has been in use since ancient times.

Machine Arithmétique

In 1642, the French mathematician Blaise Pascal invented the world's first calculating machine that could add and subtract. He called his device *Machine Arithmétique*. Pascal's machine used gear-driven counterwheels to record amounts. It worked something like the speedometer in a car. Over the next 300 years, many types of mechanical calculators used a similar technique.

Pascal's *Machine Arithmétique* (1642) was the world's first calculating machine.

The Analytical Engine

Charles Babbage was an English mathematician born in 1791. He was the first person who tried to make a calculator that could do more than just add and subtract. In 1833, he tried to build the first digital computer. He called this machine the Analytical Engine. It had all the features of a modern computer, including memory, control, and input/output abilities. In one minute, it could do 60 additions or subtractions. More important, the Analytical Engine could actually be **programmed** to carry out different kinds of processes.

Unfortunately Babbage could not get the support he needed to continue his project. He died in 1871, frustrated and unhappy. However, his ideas would make him famous long after his death.

Punched Cards and the Tabulating Machine

The needs of the U.S. Census Bureau led to the development of punched cards and the **tabulating** (TAB yoo lay ting) machines that read them. In 1880, the Census Bureau did its survey of the American population, as it does every ten years. By 1885, however, the Bureau was still struggling to count the results. It became clear that this job might actually take longer than the ten-year span between censuses. A faster way of doing the job was needed.

Herman Hollerith, a worker at the Census Bureau, figured out a way of recording the census data on strips of paper. His method was quite simple. Information was coded on strips of paper by means of a series of punched holes in a planned pattern. Each hole had a specific meaning.

This coding system proved to be an efficient way of recording information. The paper strips were soon replaced by three-by-five-inch cards. Each card contained punches that coded the entire record of an individual or a family. To process these coded cards, Hollerith made a tabulating machine that could read the codes of about 65 cards per minute.

The use of the punched card and tabulating machine saved the government a great deal of time and money. It was so successful that Hollerith decided to make similar machines that businesses could use. To manufacture his invention, he formed the Tabulating Machine Company. This successful company would eventually merge with other companies. It became the giant company we know today as the International Business Machines Corporation, or IBM.

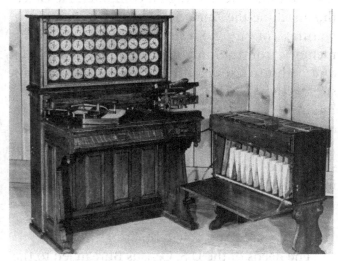

Hollerith's punched card tabulating machine was first used for a U.S. census.

The First Computers

In 1944, a scientist named Howard H. Aiken worked with IBM to make a new computing device. It performed arithmetic on <u>data</u> input on punched cards. This machine, MARK I, was an early form of today's digital computer.

✔ By 1947, the University of Pennsylvania had built the Electronic Numerical Integrator and Computer, ENIAC. It was built in 1945 by J. P. Eckert, Jr. and J. W. Mauchly. ENIAC was made up of 40 separate units. It weighed about as much as four adult African elephants. ENIAC filled a space as large as a two-car garage, and it gobbled up 140,000 watts of electricity. However, ENIAC could add 5,000 numbers in 1 second. This means it took ENIAC about 20 seconds to solve problems that took one person days to solve. While ENIAC worked 1,000 times faster than MARK I, it had one major weakness. To perform different operations, it had to be rewired by hand. This task could take several days. Only one ENIAC was ever built. It worked for nine years.

A scientist named John Von Neumann suggested feeding data into the computer through a keyboard. The first computer to have this input device was UNIVAC I, the Universal Automatic Computer. In 1951, UNIVAC I became the first mass-produced, commercially available computer.

✗ The most important contributions to the development of computers were made by John Von Neumann. His work resulted in improvements in areas from the computer's design to its electronic circuits. With others, he developed the ideas of the stored program and the <u>binary</u> number system. These concepts are still used in most modern computers.

Modern Computer Generations

In recent years, computer developments have been far-reaching and numerous. Because of this rapid progress, computers have been categorized by **generations**. Each generation of computers features an important advance over the previous generation.

First Generation (1942-1959)

These computers used vacuum tubes for the storage of data. Vacuum tubes were bulky and caused major overheating problems. They were also unreliable. These "maxi," or mainframe, computers, such as ENIAC, were large and expensive.

Second Generation (1959-1965)

These computers replaced vacuum tubes with **transistors** (tran ZIS tərz). A transistor is a small electronic device made up of crystals that control the flow of electric currents. Second-generation computers were smaller and worked faster. They could perform a single operation in one-tenth the

The first computers, such as ENIAC (left), were large mainframe computers that took up entire rooms. The first type of mouse (right) was wooden and had wheels.

time it took computers that used vacuum tubes. With the second generation of computers, manufacturers began producing business computers with more efficient storage and faster input/output abilities. These mini-computers were smaller, more reliable, and cost less than earlier models.

Third Generation (1965-1970)

These computers had tiny integrated circuits on a chip, or plate, as small as a dime and as thin as paper. The parts on the chip were so small that they were hardly visible to the naked eye. These computers also had tremendous memory capacities. They could work so fast that their operation was measured in nanoseconds.

In addition, new input/output devices could communicate with computers over great distances, using telephone lines. They could display pictures on a screen and accept voice input. Before there was such a thing as a mouse, input was given by touching a light pen to the computer screen. Computer scientists experimented to find an input tool that was easier to use than a light pen. The first mouse was developed in 1965 by scientists at Stanford Research Institute. This mouse had two wheels on the bottom. As the mouse was pushed or pulled along a surface, it moved a pointer on the screen.

Fourth Generation (1970-present)

These computers brought the microprocessor into use. A microprocessor uses a chip that contains the integrated circuits and the whole central processing unit (CPU) of a simple computer.

This generation of computers also brought the Internet into wider use. The first software for finding and viewing documents on the Internet was developed in 1990. Tim Berners-Lee wanted to make it easier for scientists to share and find information. He called the software World Wide Web. The software made finding information on the Internet easier. Now a person could use a mouse to click on text and view different documents. Each document appeared in a separate window. The documents had text that was formatted. They had images, sounds, and even movies.

The Future Is Now

About 70 years ago, there were just a few slow, garage-sized computers available only to scientists. Today there are millions of small, lightning-fast personal computers available to everyone. Thanks to <u>CD-ROM</u> drives and modems, a tremendous amount of information is now available to us at the click of a mouse.

Glossary

binary   having a two-number system consisting of the digits 0 and 1

calculator   machine that rapidly adds, subtracts, multiplies, and divides, often by electronic means

CD-ROM   (Compact Disc Read-Only Memory) an optical disk containing text and multimedia data that can be retrieved by a laser beam

central processing unit   (CPU) control center for an entire computer system

computer   electronic device used to calculate, store, and select data

data   information or instructions that a computer can interpret

digital   having data in number form

input   data inserted or fed into a computer

integrated circuit   a tiny unit that combines many electronic parts and the connections between them in one small slice of material

Internet   a worldwide computer network with millions of subscribers

mainframe computer   largest and most powerful of the early computers

microprocessor   a chip having the capabilities of a simple computer

modem   a device for sending data, usually over telephone lines, between computers

nanosecond   one-billionth of a second

output   information that has been processed through a computer

stored program   series of commands that directs what the computer does

COMPREHENSION

1. Number the following events in the order in which they occurred.

    _____ **a.** construction of Babbage's Analytical Engine

    _____ **b.** invention of the abacus

    _____ **c.** creation of ENIAC

    _____ **d.** invention of Pascal's *Machine Arithmétique*

    _____ **e.** production of UNIVAC I

    _____ **f.** development of Hollerith's punched cards

2. What did the first mouse look like?

    _____

    _____

3. Reread the paragraph marked with an ✗. Underline its main idea. Then circle two details that support the main idea.

4. Write three sentences, each using one or more vocabulary words from the glossary listed below.

    computer   data   binary   CD-ROM

    a. _____

    _____

    b. _____

    _____

    c. _____

    _____

CRITICAL THINKING

1. The ancient Chinese needed efficient and accurate counting. Their need resulted in the invention of the abacus. Compare their need with present-day needs.

    _____

    _____

2. Reread the paragraph with a ✔ next to it. Then circle the letter of the statement that best states the main idea of the paragraph.

a. ENIAC worked faster than the earlier MARK I.

b. The first fully electronic digital computer worked much faster than earlier types, but it was large and difficult to program.

c. The early electronic computers contained thousands of vacuum tubes.

d. ENIAC required so much energy that it could only work for nine years.

SKILL FOCUS: MAKING GENERALIZATIONS

Following the box below are three groups of facts. Study each group. Then choose the statement in the box that is the best generalization for each group. Write the letter of the statement on the line.

> **a.** Computers have gradually become smaller, more efficient, and more available.
>
> **b.** The computer's influence is evident in business, medicine, and education.
>
> **c.** Many features of today's computers have resulted from discoveries made many years ago.

1. Facts:
- Computers are used to store employee payroll data, such as weekly salary, taxes, and benefits contributions.
- Computers are used to diagnose medical problems and to monitor patients' progress.
- Computer-assisted instruction is found in most schools.

Generalization: _____

2. Facts:
- The abacus was the first mechanical calculator.
- Babbage's Analytical Engine could be programmed to carry out different functions.
- Hollerith's punched cards and tabulating machine were used to compile information for the 1880 census.

Generalization: _____

3. Facts:
- Transistors reduced the size of the computer and increased its working speed.
- Integrated circuits and the microchip made communication possible over great distances, using telephone lines.
- The microprocessor led to the development of small home computers.

Generalization: _____

Reading-Writing Connection

On a separate sheet of paper, write a paragraph that explains how a computer can make learning more interesting for you.

Skill: Making Inferences

BACKGROUND INFORMATION

"What Is a Computer?" explains what computers can do and how they work. We are all living in the computer age. At home, computers help run our appliances and our cars. In schools and libraries, students use computers to research, write, and learn about many subjects. To make the most of these amazing machines, we should learn more about them.

SKILL FOCUS: Making Inferences

Writers don't always tell you everything in a text. Sometimes you have to make **inferences**, or figure out information that is not stated. To make an inference, you need to combine the details in a selection with what you already know.

Read the following conversation. Think of an inference you can make about where Dr. Dao lives.

> "I'd like to have a math conference with Dr. Dao at 9:00 A.M. tomorrow," Vance told Alicia. "Can you be on-line at his Web site then?"
>
> "9:00 A.M.!" Alicia replied. "Dr. Dao doesn't live here in New Jersey. It's three hours earlier where he lives."
>
> "Oh, I forgot about that," said Vance. "Okay, I'll e-mail him and see if he can do it at 9:00 A.M. his time."

The conversation tells you that Vance and Alicia live in New Jersey. It also tells you that Dr. Dao lives in a place where the time is three hours earlier. You may already know that the time on the West Coast of the United States is three hours earlier than the time in New Jersey. So you can infer that Dr. Dao lives somewhere on the West Coast.

▶ Use the details in the conversation to make an inference about who Dr. Dao is. Write your inference on the line.

_____

CONTEXT CLUES: Diagrams

Sometimes new science terms are explained in a paragraph and are also shown in a **diagram**. A diagram is a drawing or chart that helps explain a thing by showing all its parts and how it works. You can use the text and the diagram below to figure out the meaning of the term *Internet Service Provider (ISP)*.

> Your **Internet Service Provider** is your link to the Internet. Once you have logged on to it through your computer, it will send an electronic greeting through a telephone or cable network to the **server** where information about the Web site you are looking for is stored.

▶ To write the meaning of *server*, use the sample paragraph about the Internet and the diagram.

_____

_____

As you read the next selection, use context clues and the diagram on page 166 to help you understand the meanings of *arithmetic unit*, *input equipment*, and *output equipment*.

Components of the Internet

Your computer

Server

Internet service provider

Strategy Tip

Before you read "What Is a Computer?" preview labels in Figure 1 on page 166 and the boldfaced words in the selection.

What Is a Computer?

1. A computer is an electronic machine that can store and handle information and solve problems. You could think of a computer as a file cabinet, information organizer, and problem-solver all rolled into one.

2. Computers are sometimes called electronic brains because of the kinds of work they do. A computer can do many things the human brain can do. However, a computer cannot truly understand ideas. It cannot create things, or make them up. Unlike human beings, a computer has no imagination. The information that goes into a computer comes from people or from machines controlled by people. The problems computers work out also come from people. Even the methods for working out the problems come from people. Computers can do only what people program them to do.

3. A computer has certain advantages over the human brain. In some ways, a computer is much faster and more efficient than the human brain. A fast computer can solve millions of problems in a few seconds. Also computers do not make many mistakes. They can handle one dull problem after another without getting tired or bored. They are not distracted by noise or other interruptions.

4. The first computers could do only one kind of job. They could compute, or mathematically work out, number problems. Today's computers can do much, much more. They can store company records and create company payrolls. They can be used as teaching aids. They can help pilots fly. They can help weather forecasters predict weather. They can ring up a bill at the supermarket. They can help the grocer keep track of stock. They can deal with words, as well as numbers. If a number or word problem can be worked out in a series of fixed steps, a computer can do it.

TYPES OF COMPUTERS

5. Not all computers are the same. They do not all work in the same way. They are not all used for the same purposes.

6. A **personal computer**, or PC, is a small computer made to be used by one person at a time. A PC can do a few jobs at one time. People often use PCs at home, in school, or on the job. A PC can fit on a desk, small table, or countertop. Sometimes PCs are linked together in a network. This allows two or more people to use the same information at the same time. The term *personal computer*, or *PC*, has another meaning. It also can mean a type of computer that is not a Macintosh®. Macintosh computers were first made by Apple®. They operate differently from PCs, which IBM® made popular. Today, many different companies can make PCs and Macs.

7. A **mainframe** is a very large computer compared to a personal computer. It can be as big as a refrigerator. Mainframes are used by many people at the same time. They can store huge amounts of information. They can also do many jobs at the same time.

8. A **supercomputer** is a very fast mainframe computer. Supercomputers are used to do jobs at the fastest speed possible. In one second, they can do millions of math operations. They are often called "number crunchers." These large computers are very expensive. Governments, big businesses, and universities use mainframes and supercomputer.

COMPONENTS OF COMPUTERS

9. Each computer has three basic components, or parts. The basic components are made up of many smaller, complex parts. These basic mechanical parts of a computer are called its **hardware.**

Central Processing Unit (CPU)

10. The main component of any computer is its **central processing unit**, or CPU. It is in the CPU that information and instructions are stored and processed. The CPU has a memory, or storage, unit. This unit stores information and instructions. It holds information and instructions until they are needed. In some computers, the memory is a group of magnetic cores, or doughnut-shaped rings. In others, it is a magnetic tape, disk, or drum. Information appears on tapes and disks as magnetic spots. In the smallest computers, the memory, or even the whole CPU, may be on a tiny piece of equipment called a **chip**.

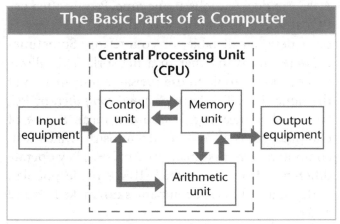

The Basic Parts of a Computer

FIGURE 1. **The three basic components of a digital computer are the CPU, the input equipment, and the output equipment.**

11. The CPU also has an <u>arithmetic unit</u>. This is the working part of the computer. It sorts information and computes—adds, subtracts, and so on.

12. The control unit of the CPU controls the work of the computer. It is the "captain" of the computer. First it gets instructions from the memory. Then it tells the memory what information to send to the arithmetic unit. Finally it tells the arithmetic unit how to process the information.

Input Equipment

13. **Input** means information that is fed into a computer. Before a computer can do any work, information and instructions must be put into it. Such information and instruction for a computer are part of its **software**. <u>Input equipment</u> is hardware that takes information and instruction from the outside world. Then it puts it into code for the computer to use. Special keyboards serve as input equipment on most home computers. Other input equipment includes a mouse or a disk drive.

Output Equipment

14. **Output** means information delivered from a computer according to coded instruction. Information can come out of a computer in many forms. It can show up on a display screen, or it can be presented on paper by a printer. It can also be the information sent from one computer to another.

15. Often input equipment and <u>output equipment</u> are attached to the CPU. However, input and output equipment can be far away from the CPU. Then they are connected by cables, wires, or remote-control equipment. Remote control is the ability to control the operation of a machine by means of radio waves.

16. The mechanical components of a computer are called hardware. The instructions and information that go into or come out of a computer are called software.

TYPES OF SOFTWARE

17. There are three main types of software. **System software** keeps track of things, such as where the CPU stores data. It controls the way the hardware works together with other software. **Applications software** lets you do a particular job with your input. Some jobs include writing a report, drawing a picture, and finding information on the Internet. **Utilities software** helps you keep a hard drive in order and a computer running smoothly. For example, it can help you find a virus. A **virus** is a program that stops your computer from working correctly. It can get into your computer accidentally.

1. How is input different from output?

   _____

   _____

2. Define the term *computer*.

   _____

   _____

3. Circle the letter next to each task a computer can do.

   a. organize   **c.** create

   b. solve problems   **d.** understand

4. Name three types of computers.

   _____

   _____

5. Name the three main components of a computer.

   _____

   _____

6. Define *hardware* and *software*.

   _____

   _____

7. What are the three main types of software?

   _____

   _____

8. Draw a line to match each term with its explanation.

   arithmetic unit   **a.** computer component that receives information and instructions

   input equipment   **b.** computer component that delivers information

   output equipment   **c.** computer component that sorts information and solves problems

CRITICAL THINKING

1. Name the kind of computer that would be used to figure out a government budget.

   _____

For items 2 and 3, circle the letter next to the correct answer.

2. In the future, computers will probably be

   a. larger and able to do more.

   b. the same size and able to do less.

   c. larger and able to do less.

   d. smaller and able to do more.

3. In the future, computers will probably replace workers who

   a. do large projects keeping track of things.

   b. solve problems that require inventing mathematical theories.

   c. create new ideas for designing things.

   d. try to understand how to prevent war.

Read each of the paragraphs as instructed. Put a ✔ next to each statement that can be inferred. Then write the details from the paragraph and what you already know that helped you make the inference.

Paragraph 2 (check two):

_____ **a.** A computer cannot store as much information as the human brain.

_____ **b.** A computer is like the human brain in some ways but not in others.

_____ **c.** The human brain can think, understand, create, and process information.

Details From Paragraph: _____

_____

What I Know: _____

_____

Paragraph 3 (check two):

_____ **a.** Some human beings never make mistakes.

_____ **b.** Human beings get tired and bored from handling dull problems.

_____ **c.** Human beings sometimes make mistakes when they handle dull problems.

Details From Paragraph: _____

_____

What I Know: _____

_____

Paragraphs 8 (check one):

_____ **a.** Many homes have mainframe computers.

_____ **b.** Supercomputers are useful for artists.

_____ **c.** Supercomputers can deliver information quickly if it is in the form of numbers.

Details From Paragraph: _____

_____

What I Know: _____

_____

Reading-Writing Connection

On a separate sheet of paper, write a brief explanation of what happens inside a computer from the time you type in information on the keyboard until the information comes out of the printer.

Skill: Using a Spreadsheet

BACKGROUND INFORMATION

The inventors of the first spreadsheet program, VisiCalc, wanted to use computers to make math easier to do. Software Arts, Inc. introduced VisiCalc in 1979. With this program, mathematical calculations that used to take hours could be done in minutes. VisiCalc had only 254 rows and 63 columns. Today's programs have thousands of rows and hundreds of columns. Even so, VisiCalc was a very important invention, because it helped make personal computers (PCs) more popular. Unlike other programs before it, VisiCalc was a program almost anyone could use.

SKILL FOCUS: Using a Spreadsheet

A **spreadsheet** is a table that displays data, or information, in **columns** and **rows**. A cell is where a column and a row meet. Each cell in a spreadsheet contains data. When you analyze, or try to understand, data in a spreadsheet, you may need to add, subtract, multiply, or divide some numbers. In other words, you must perform one or more **operations**. Below are the common symbols for operations in a spreadsheet.

Symbol	Operation	Result
+	addition	sum
—	subtraction	difference
*	multiplication	product
/	division	quotient
=	is equal to	equation

▌ Fill in the blanks in the sentences below with the correct words.

The first spreadsheet _____, was created in 1979.

It used only 254 _____ and 63 _____.

It helped make _____ more popular because almost anyone could use it.

WORD CLUES

When reading the selection, look for important words like *budget, formula,* and *function.* Look for other words around these words. They are context clues. They can help you understand the meaning of these important words. Knowing the important words will help you understand more about using spreadsheets for calculating.

Strategy Tip

As you read "Calculating with a Spreadsheet," remember that the symbols and letters in a spreadsheet have a specialized meaning. Although some words may have familiar meanings to you, you must learn their meanings as they apply to computers and spreadsheets.

Calculating with a Spreadsheet

What Is a Spreadsheet Formula?

A spreadsheet is a useful tool in many areas. Businesses, individuals, and other people who work with numbers often use spreadsheets. They help with making **budgets**, or plans for how money is used, and other complicated mathematical tasks. A spreadsheet can do math quickly and easily. First, however, you must tell it what to do by writing a spreadsheet **formula**. A formula is a math expression that shows a calculation. It is a way of telling the computer what operations to perform in what order. You write a formula using numbers, cell names, and math symbols.

With a formula, you can use a spreadsheet like a calculator. Every spreadsheet formula begins with an equal sign (=). Look at the examples below.

=1+4–3	Add 1 and 4; then subtract 3.
=9*5	Multiply 9 by 5.
=50/2	Divide 50 by 2.
=C3*2	Multiply the data in Cell C3 by 2.
=A3+A8	Add the data in Cells A3 and A8.
=B6–B5	Subtract the data in Cell B5 from Cell B6.

Suppose you wanted to plan how to spend your money. You could make a budget spreadsheet that shows what you spend. Then you could use formulas to find answers for your data. You could use formulas to find the average amount you spend for a month. These are ways to analyze data using a spreadsheet.

Math in a Spreadsheet

To use a spreadsheet like a calculator, you must enter a formula in the formula bar. First you must click in a cell to make it active. (This means that it is ready to perform some task.) Then you type an equal sign. You also type the numbers and operations you want to use, without typing spaces between them. Look at Screen 1.

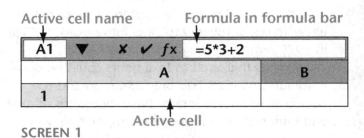

SCREEN 1

When you press the ✔ button, or the Enter (or Return) key, the formula will calculate an answer. The answer will appear in the active cell. If you click in the cell with the answer in it, the formula will appear in the formula bar. Look at Screen 2.

A1	▼	x ✔ fx	=5*3+2	
		A		B
1		17		

Answer in cell

SCREEN 2

Spreadsheet formulas follow the order of operations for doing arithmetic, as shown in Screen 2. Parentheses can be used in formulas to change that order. For example, typing =5*(3+2) would give an answer of 25 in the cell. If, however, you typed =5*3+2 without the parentheses, the answer in the cell would be 17.

If you use the correct formula, you can add, subtract, multiply, or divide several cells at once. A function, or command, helps you calculate using a series of steps. The SUM function, for example, allows you to add the contents of many cells at once. This is useful when you want to find a total of many numbers. The AVERAGE function helps you find the average of several numbers.

Suppose cell A1 has 5 and A2 has 8. Here is how you would add them. In the cell where you want the answer—say A3—you type =SUM(A1:A2). The number that will appear in Cell A3 is 13. If you change the number in either A1 or A2, the answer in A3 will automatically change too.

1. What is one advantage of using a spreadsheet to analyze data? _____
_____

2. What should you type to start a spreadsheet formula? _____

3. What symbols do you use in a formula? _____

4. What is one way to edit a formula? _____
_____

CRITICAL THINKING

1. How is a spreadsheet different from a calculator? _____
_____

2. What quotient would appear in the active cell if you typed =12/3 in the formula bar? _____
_____

3. What formula would you type to divide 6 by 3? _____
_____

4. Suppose the contents of cells A1 to A4 are 4, 17, 32, and 39, in that order. Write a formula to find the average of these numbers. _____

SKILL FOCUS: CALCULATING WITH SPREADSHEETS

Draw a line from the formula on the right to the correct answer on the left.

1. =5+4   a. 1
2. =5*4   b. 6
3. =12/(4–2)   c. 9
4. =12/4–2   d. 15
5. =16–4+3   e. 20

Reading-Writing Connection
On a separate sheet of paper, write one formula that equals 10 and one formula that equals 50.

MATHEMATICS

Skill: Using Reference Books

You use **reference books** to find all kinds of information about a subject that you are studying or want to know more about. You need to know the kind of information contained in different types of reference books so that you can select the one you need. By using the right reference books, you can locate the kind of information you need.

Dictionary

Suppose that some friends of yours are discussing a gibbon and you do not know what a gibbon is. You can find the word *gibbon* in a **dictionary**. You already know that a dictionary defines words. It also shows how words are spelled, pronounced, and divided into syllables, and it states what parts of speech they are. Because many people do not know what a gibbon looks like, some dictionaries include an illustration with the entry.

Below is a sample dictionary entry for the word *gibbon*.

gib•bon (gibʹən) *n.* a member of the *lesser ape* family, having very long arms and being found in southeastern Asia.

gibbon

Encyclopedia

After you learn what the word *gibbon* means, you may want to find out more about the animal. You may become curious about exactly what part of southeastern Asia it is from or if it can be found at a zoo. The next reference book that you would use is an **encyclopedia** because it contains articles on many different subjects. An encyclopedia would provide an explanation of a gibbon that is more detailed than a dictionary definition.

Here is an encyclopedia article about the gibbon.

Gibbon is the smallest of the apes. Scientists classify the several species (kinds) of gibbons in the lesser ape family. All other ape species—the bonobo, chimpanzee, gorilla, and orangutan—make up the *great ape* family. Gibbons live over a wider range than do the great apes. They inhabit forests in the Indian state of Assam, as well as in Indonesia, Malaysia, Myanmar, Thailand, and elsewhere in Southeast Asia. All species have long arms and legs but no tail. Most weigh from 10 to 20 pounds (5 to 9 kilograms) and stand 15 to 36 inches (38 to 91 centimeters) high. Adults typically range from black to light tan, with males often darker in color than females.

Gibbons live in the tops of trees and rarely come to the ground. They eat fruits and leaves. Gibbons use their arms to swing from branch to branch. They also walk on tree branches using only their legs. This way of walking resembles the way human beings walk on the ground. Gibbons live in family groups that usually consist of a male, a female, and one or two of their young. A gibbon family claims an area called a *territory* and uses loud calls and songs to warn other families to stay away.

Atlas

After you have read the encyclopedia article for *gibbon*, you may become curious about Assam, one of the places where the gibbon lives. You may want to look at a map to see the location of Assam in India. The best reference book to check is an atlas. An **atlas** contains different kinds of maps.

Almanac

Once you learn where Assam is, you may want some specific information about India, including its size and population. To locate this kind of information, you would use an almanac. An **almanac** is a book with the most up-to-date information on many different subjects. The information in an almanac is more current than information found in other references because it is published every year. An almanac contains weather reports, statistics, facts about the United States and other countries, current events, sports facts, and world records.

Area and Population by Country
Mid-2007 Estimates

Country	Area[1]	Population	Country	Area[1]	Population
Afghanistan	647,500	31,889,923	Hungary	93,030	9,956,108
Albania	28,748	3,600,523	Iceland	103,000	301,931
Algeria	2,381,740	33,333,216	India	3,287,590	1,129,866,154
Angola	1,246,700	12,263,596	Indonesia	1,919,440	234,693,997
Antigua and Barbuda	442.6	69,481	Iran	1,648,000	65,397,521
Argentina	2,766,890	40,301,927	Iraq	437,072	27,499,638

[1]Area figures are measured in square kilometers.

Complete each sentence by underlining the name of the correct reference book. More than one answer may be correct.

1. If you want to know how to spell the word *cantaloupe*, you should use the _____.
   atlas   dictionary   almanac

2. If you want to find out about the mountains of South America,

   you should use the _____ or the _____.
   dictionary   atlas   encyclopedia

3. If you want to know how many people were married in the United States

   in 2005, you should use the _____.
   atlas   encyclopedia   almanac

4. If you want to find out how to pronounce the word *kayak*, you should use the _____.
   encyclopedia   almanac   dictionary

5. If you want to learn which types of birds live in cold climates, you should use the _____.
   dictionary   encyclopedia   almanac

6. If you want to find out how many miles or kilometers it is from Quincy,

   Massachusetts, to Newport, Rhode Island, you should use the _____.
   atlas   dictionary   encyclopedia

7. If you want to see how to divide the word *molecule* into syllables, use the _____.
   atlas   dictionary   almanac

Skill: Reading a Job Application

When you apply for a job, an employer may ask you to fill out a job application. A **job application** is a written form that asks for information about your work experience, your education, and your interests.

Study the sample job application below.

CAL COMPUTER COMPANY

APPLICATION FOR EMPLOYMENT

(type or print in ink)

PERSONAL

Name	Last: LORENZ	First: SARAH	Middle/Maiden: ANN	Telephone: 555-7431
Address	Number: 1154	Street: 23rd Street	City: SANTA MONICA	State: CA	Zip: 90404	Social Security No.: 555-55-5557

EDUCATION

	Name and Location	Dates Attended From	To	Diploma Received
High School	SCOTTSDALE HIGH SCHOOL SCOTTSDALE, AZ	9/99	6/02	HIGH SCHOOL DIPLOMA
College	ROLLINS COLLEGE SCOTTSDALE, AZ	9/02	6/06	B.S.
Other	COMPUTER TRAINING INSTITUTE SANTA MONICA, CA	9/07	1/08	COMPUTER CERTIFICATE

Hobbies and Interests: SWIMMING, PLAYING THE PIANO, SPEAKING SPANISH

EMPLOYMENT RECORD (Start with last job)

Name and Location of Employer	Dates From	To	Job Title	Name of Supervisor
LINDSEY AND STERLING ACCOUNTANTS SANTA MONICA, CA	1/08	7/08	BOOKKEEPER	BERT GOLDBERG
DAILY NEWS SCOTTSDALE, AZ	7/06	8/07	WORD PROCESSOR	ROSA ALVAREZ

REFERENCES (Not former employers)

	Name	Address	Telephone
1.	MS. DIANE BARTON	80 WILSHIRE BLVD. LOS ANGELES, CA	555-4418
2.	DR. LOUIS GRAYSON	880 W. CALMELBACK SCOTTSDALE, AZ	602-555-3099

EMPLOYMENT DESIRED

Position: COMPUTER PROGRAMMER
Date you can start: 8/17/08
(Check one) Full-time ✓ Part Time _____

Today's Date: 8/10/08
Signature: *Sarah A. Lorenz*

Most job applications begin with a section for personal information. The first space is for your last, first, and middle names. Sometimes a married woman writes her maiden name, or her last name before she was married, in the space for the middle name. Spaces are provided for your address, telephone number, and Social Security number.

Most job applications have sections for your education or training. Certain jobs require a particular type of education or training.

Job applications also have a section for information about jobs that you have held in the past. This section may be labeled "Work Experience" or "Employment Record." Start with your most recent job and work backward in time. You will usually be asked to list your employer (the company for which you worked), the dates you worked for the employer, your job title (what you did for the company), and the name of your supervisor (the person who gave and monitored your work).

Applications often require you to provide references. References are people who know you well enough to give information about you and how you might perform at a job. Family members and friends should not be listed as references.

Possible references might include a teacher; a family doctor; or a pastor, priest, or rabbi. You should ask these people if you can use them as references before you do so.

Applications may ask for your interests and hobbies, such as playing tennis or speaking French.

A section labeled "Employment Desired" may provide a space for the name of the job that you want and the date that you can begin. You usually sign your name at the end of the application.

Print in ink or type your answers on the application. A neat application with complete answers will make a good impression on an employer. Correct grammar and spelling and clear expression will also make a good impression.

A. Circle the letter next to the phrase that correctly completes each sentence.

1. An employer is a
   a. person hired by another person or company.
   b. person or company that hires people.
   c. person who can give information about your education.
   d. person applying for a job.

2. A supervisor is a
   a. person who oversees your work.
   b. place where you have a job.
   c. family member who can give information about you.
   d. person applying for a job.

3. An example of a good reference to use on a job application might be
   a. an employer you did not get along with.
   b. your best friend.
   c. your English teacher.
   d. your mother.

4. An application may ask for the name of your supervisor at a previous job so that this person
   a. will be informed if you get another job.
   b. may be offered the job that you applied for.
   c. may recommend other applicants for the job.
   d. may be called to confirm information about you.

B. Use the information on the application on page 174 to answer each question.

1. Who filled out the application? _____

2. What job is she applying for? _____

3. What was her last job? _____

4. How long did she work at her last job? _____

5. How soon can she begin a new job? _____

CONTEXT CLUE WORDS

The following words are treated as context clue words in the lessons indicated. Each lesson provides instruction in a particular context clue type and includes an activity that requires you to use context clues to find word meanings. Context clue words appear in the literature, social studies, and science selections and are underlined or footnoted.

CONCEPT WORDS

In lessons that feature social studies, science, or mathematics selections, words that are unique to the content and whose meanings are important in the selection are treated as concept words. These words appear in boldface type and are often followed by a phonetic respelling and a definition.